POETRY AND CHILDHOOD

POETRY AND CHILDHOOD

*Edited by Morag Styles, Louise Joy
and David Whitley*

Trentham Books

Stoke on Trent, UK and Sterling, USA

Winner of the IPG DIVERSITY Award 2010

Trentham Books Limited
Westview House   22883 Quicksilver Drive
734 London Road   Sterling
Oakhill   VA 20166-2012
Stoke on Trent   USA
Staffordshire
England ST4 5NP

First published 2010

British Library Cataloguing-in-Publication Data
A catalogue record for this book is available from the British Library

ISBN: 978 1 85856 472 2

The editors would like to thank Victor Watson most sincerely for compiling the excellent index to this book.

Cover image: from an unattributed illustration in *A Treasury of Nursery Rhymes* edited by Michael Foss and published by PictureMac, Michael O'Mara Books, 1985, Macmillan children's Books, 1987. Every attempt has been made to trace the copyright holder of this book, which is long out of print.

Designed and typeset by Trentham Books Ltd and printed in Great Britain by CMP (UK) Ltd, Dorset

CONTENTS

Foreword

Andrew Motion

This collection of essays is an appreciation which is also a celebration. That's to say, it gives a large clear picture of the wealth and diversity of recent poetry for children – noticing trends and traditions, pointing out highlights – while at the same time allowing readers to enjoy the wealth of achievement that it describes. It leaves us in no doubt that the pleasure of poetry is inseparable from our sense of its importance, or that what might be appreciated in comparatively sophisticated terms is essentially a very primitive and fundamental thing.

This is why poetry matters so much in children's lives, and why every possible effort should be made to promote its appreciation, and encourage its creation. Through the mingled sense and non-sense of poetry, through the charge of its rhythms and the magnetism of its rhymes, through the various colourations and configurations of its language, it allows children to feel a profound sense of connection with their interior spaces, and also to make links with the wider world which lies around them. It is a representation of life which is also a kind of life in itself – a self-sufficient delight, which is simultaneously a way of looking forward and preparing to meet the future; a confirmation of the self, which nevertheless allows the growth of sympathy with others.

By helping to explain the paradoxes, and deepening our enjoyment of them, this book performs a vital function. It is a great pleasure to commend it.

Introduction:
Taking the Long View – the State of Children's Poetry Today

Morag Styles

Preamble

I have been reading and writing about children's poetry all my professional life so clearly I thought I knew what children's poetry was. Maybe so, but this volume begins with a section that asks fundamental questions about what constitutes children's poetry and why it has never been adequately theorised. Reading and rereading this volume has made me rethink some certainties and opened up new ground. Whatever children's poetry is, it gives rise to many debates and concerns and the contributors to this volume tread new ground as well as giving fresh life to some of the discussions surrounding children's poetry that have been around for a long time. Indeed, by editing a volume on poetry and childhood, rather than 'children's poetry', some novel ideas and juxtapositions have come into view.

What this introduction will not be doing is summarising each chapter and picking out salient themes, which tends to be repetitive and rather like unnecessary throat-clearing. We would, however, like to take this opportunity to thank all our contributors for their hard work, for keeping to deadlines, for putting up with a trio of editors and, most of all, for their wit, wisdom, knowledge and understanding; between them, and from many different angles, they have redefined the field of children's poetry. Without discarding important insights gleaned from poets and critics of the past, they have charted new territory in chapters that cross and interconnect different times, places, cultures, languages, forms and audiences, as well as negotiating the links between the oral and aural, reading and writing, and the traditional and modern in poetry for children.

The genesis of this volume was a large international conference on poetry and childhood organised by the Cambridge Faculty of Education and held at the British Library. The Call for Papers offered myriad possibilities; in the event, we accepted more than sixty speakers on a wide variety of topics. Most of them were willing to write for this volume and it was unfortunate that some excellent possibilities didn't fall within the shape of the book as we envisaged it. Furthermore, some topics that we would have liked to cover were not offered: for example, we received no proposals relating to Caribbean poetry and very few relating to gender. These topics and others of special importance to the editors and to the study of children's poetry don't appear in the book which, with one exception, is composed of papers given at the conference that have been rewritten for publication. Discussion of some of the great poets of the past for children, and a few of those who deserve to be better known, are included in this volume, but there are omissions, too. However, the haunting voices of William Blake, Edward Lear, Eleanor Farjeon and others who do not have space devoted to them are still there at the heart of this book as powerful influences on other poets and, indeed, our contributors.

Special thanks are due to Michael Rosen, co-organiser of the British Library exhibition, *Twinkle, twinkle little bat! 250 years of poetry for children*, which coincided with the conference. It is fitting that Rosen's uplifting opening lecture becomes the chapter opening the book. Lissa Paul, our keynote speaker, went so far beyond the call of duty that she came all the way from Canada to London to examine the exhibition before it opened to ensure that her talk was in tune with the spirit of the poetry on display. Her stimulating chapter closes the introductory section of the book and looks ahead to what is to follow. We are also grateful to Andrew Motion who, in his last few weeks as Poet Laureate, closed the conference and has written the Foreword.

What constitutes the poetry of childhood?

This is a book about poetry for children, but we have to take proper note of the word *childhood* in our title. Children's poetry could have limited itself to what is written for children, but then we would have had to leave out all those poems appropriated, begged, borrowed or stolen from the adult canon for the pleasure of children. Furthermore, by highlighting childhood we have the perfect opportunity to look at its different representations over the centuries. Following on from its initial phase as a vehicle for didacticism and explicit morality, children's poetry underwent a sea change during the Romantic era, where it began to enshrine a belief in the child's essential innocence and, therefore, *natural* access to *poetic truth*. This faith in childhood as revelatory and regenerative has, in turn, been transformed, but never quite obviated, by all the uncertainties about what childhood signifies in the modernist and post-modernist eras.

Despite such fundamental shifts in perspective, there are strong, resilient lines of continuity that run across the centuries. For example, the link between poetry, childhood and nature has been a rich source of inspiration in the work of many poets – from Bunyan's 'country rimes' to Stevenson's 'garden', Potter's and Milne's light verse, and Hughes' imaginatively stirring animal poems which, with their harder edged realism, engage profoundly with many of the ecological issues that so exercise us today. We devote a section of the book to exploring this connection in detail. Humour is another strand running all the way through this volume, be it in children's own rude rhymes, or brilliant nonsense created for them or fairy-tale poetry, or nursery rhymes honed over time, described by Graves as 'nearer to poetry than the greater part of *The Oxford Book of English Verse*' (quoted in Opie, 1951:2). There is also a clear historical component to our book, which considers verse from the seventeenth century to the present day, while casting a backward glance to poetry's more ancient roots as an oral form.

There are some surprising commonalities in what our varied contributors with very different content have to say about children's poetry. So many return to the same touchstone works of poetry or criticism: Blake's *Songs of Innocence and Experience*; Wordsworth's lyrics; TS Eliot's writing about the 'auditory imagination'; Ted Hughes' seminal *Poetry in the Making*; the influential critical work of Margaret Meek and Iona and Peter Opie; the oral tradition and nursery rhymes; even *Alice in Wonderland* casts its light through the pages of this book. Some key poets of childhood from the past – and their legacies for children's poetry – are interrogated and celebrated. Contemporary children's poetry is also explored, including the work of the current Poet Laureate, Carol Ann Duffy. We are privileged in having two fine poets as contributors – Michael Rosen and Philip Gross. Poetry as high art is considered alongside poetry as popular culture, and, although the volume inevitably has a British bias, poets from Australia, Brazil, Iceland, the USA and Canada are also given attention. Serendipitously, several of the chapters explore recurrent themes such as the centrality of linking poetry with musicality, the spoken voice and, of course, the emotions.

The state of children's poetry in the twenty-first century

Most of our contributors take delight in, and give serious attention to, prosody. However, it is a discouraging truth that technical discussion of poetry puts off not just some readers, but also those who should be inspiring the young – the teachers. Undoubtedly, the plethora of literacy initiatives forced on British schools in the last twenty years have been very hard on teachers, and it is understandable that they have had detrimental effects on the teaching of poetry. For example, a recent Ofsted report suggests that 'poetry was underdeveloped in many of the schools surveyed', is less well taught than other aspects of English, and is a 'weaker element of provision' in classrooms where other aspects of teaching are strong (Ofsted, 2007:3). The same few lightweight poems are 'studied across most schools' and pupils have 'limited experience of poems from other cultures and traditions'. Such evidence is backed up in a topical research study by UKLA (*Teachers as Readers: Phase I-2006-7*) in the form of a questionnaire carried out with over a thousand British teachers. Led by one of our contributors, Teresa Cremin, it showed weak subject knowledge in relation to poetry: 22 per cent of teachers could not name a single poet, 58 per cent named only two, one or no poets, and only 10 per cent named six (Cremin *et al*, 2008). This is a worrying trend, and we hope that this book offers a timely corrective, not just by drawing attention to a wide range of poets of the past and present, but also by showing how an understanding of the technical features of poetry can illuminate it and add to its satisfactions.

More encouragingly:

> Good quality writing has often been produced as a result of effective residencies by poets in school. These events provide a good opportunity for pupils to discover their own voices as writers. (Ofsted, 2007)

Our book celebrates poets as teachers of the young. A talented poet working with children in the classroom can, of course, have an inspirational effect on that class's attitudes to reading, writing and performing poetry. However, the poetry itself, or writing about poetry, as in the case of Ted Hughes, reaches many more pupils – with lasting benefits, as some of our contributors have demonstrated, especially when young writers are able 'to discover their own voices'. Confident, enthusiastic poetry teachers work their magic on a daily basis in the classroom. Even Ofsted agrees that: 'the best of [pupils' own poetry] demonstrate[s] a level of sophistication and self expression that is a direct result of effective and engaging teaching...' (*ibid*).

The relative neglect of children's poetry is regrettable for many reasons, not least for the fact that young children are so responsive to musical language; they are hard-wired to rhyme and rhythm, you might say. Regrettably, poetry is also the Cinderella of children's literature, receiving very little scholarly attention. It is usually poorly represented at academic conferences and is the subject of minority interest. In a new *Companion to Children's Literature* (2010) poetry is subsumed within a section on 'neglected aspects of children's literature'. In critical writing, poetry is thin on the ground in comparison to fiction and picturebooks. As a result, children's poetry remains radically under-theorised, as Peter Hunt's chapter attests.

Furthermore, with the output of single-poet collections for children dwindling, and the pathetic representation of children's poetry in most bookshops, it is no surprise that Chris Holifield of the Poetry Book Society and Antonia Byatt of the Arts Council of England used their seminars at the conference to investigate what could be done about the parlous state of children's poetry today. There are many fine poets from all over the world who write well for children and young adults, so the problem does *not* derive from a lack of quality material. In part, it springs from the apparent unwillingness of publishers to promote single-poet collections in an accountancy-driven era that is preoccupied with bestsellers and commercial success. Partly, it is explained by pressure on schools to use their budgets to buy mechanistic publications, rather than literature, further sidelining new poetry for children.

But it is not all bad news. There are also promising signs of renewal in poetry for children. Our conference was oversubscribed, with participants from many different parts of the world coming together to celebrate children's poetry. Two Poet Laureates took part, alongside other prominent poets for children, including Jackie Kay. As Children's Laureate (2007 to 2009), Michael Rosen was highly successful in revitalising children's poetry. His priority was to put the pleasure back into poetry, and he set out to promote new classics in practical ways, coming up with a range of lively ideas. These included setting up an interactive poetry You Tube site and getting up and running a Poetry Roadshow that involves a team of poets performing for children in small groups up and down the country. During his tenure as Poet Laureate (1999-2009), Andrew Motion created an online Poetry Archive – recordings of poets reading their own work – keeping their spoken voices alive for a wide audience and future generations. Philip Gross, another contributor best known for his poetry and fiction for young adult readers, won this year's TS Eliot Prize for an adult poetry collection. There was a big poetry splurge on British television in the autumn of 2009, entitled 'Let Poetry into your Life'. And with the new Poet

Laureate, dividing her writing time – like Ted Hughes before her – between child and adult audiences, children's poetry looks set to be put high on the agenda.

Writing a review of a poetry collection in *The Observer* newspaper (21.02.10), Kate Kellaway asks: 'What is poetry for?' We hope this book will go some way to answering that question. As well as making a contribution to the scholarship of children's poetry, we hope it will remind hard-pressed teachers how essential poetry is to the lives of their students – and of the need to learn how to love it for themselves, if they want to teach it well. We also hope to show parents and general readers how rich and rewarding poetry for children can be. One answer Kellaway offers is that the best poetry says something that lasts. It leaves a footprint, not in the sand to be washed away, but deep in the earth of what it means to be human. If this book achieves anything, let it be to remind ourselves to equate poetry with sensuality, passion, and pleasure, as well as the intellect, and to share with others the glorious sound of it – Heaney's 'round gift of the gab' – through performances. Such public sharing has a vital place alongside thoughtful private reading and reflection. It is no accident that we close the book with poems created at the conference by scholars, teachers, librarians and other enthusiasts, as they became a community of writers encouraged along by a gifted poet. Most of all, we hope that the delight in poetry integral to this book will by some means resonate with the young, our ultimate audience. To deny children poetry is to deny them powerful sustenance. As Vernon Scannell puts it in 'Poem on Bread', anyone:

> ...who needs no poetry or bread
> Is really in a devilish bad way.

Works Cited

Cremin, T, Bearne, E, Mottram, M, Goodwin, P (2008) Exploring teachers' knowledge of children's literature. *Cambridge Journal of Education* 38 (4) p449-464

Kellaway, K (2010) *The Observer* 21.02.10: p13

Ofsted (2007) *Poetry in Schools: a survey of practice 2006/7*. London: Ofsted

Opie, I, Opie, P (eds) (1951) *The Oxford Book of Nursery Rhymes*. Oxford: Oxford University Press

Rosen, M (ed) (2009) *A-Z: the best children's poetry from Agard to Zephaniah*. London: Puffin

Rudd, D (ed) (2010) *The Routledge Companion to Children's Literature*. London: Routledge

Scannell, V (1993) *Collected Poems, 1950-93*. London: Robson Books

1

Theory, Texts and Contexts: A Reading and Writing Memoir

Michael Rosen

Every artistic endeavour has a theory hovering around it. What I mean by this is that when human beings do things, we are not only capable of having ideas about what we're doing, but that the very *act of doing* and the product of *that doing* spring from a world of talk, ideas and theory. Whereas in the past, one major school of criticism tried to unpick author intention from analysis of texts, there is now a body of material where critics can engage with the stated intentions of authors through interviews and their writing.

Any piece of literature, group of texts, or a single author's *oeuvre* sits amongst many kinds of secondary texts and conversations, including those with fellow writers. This context has an impact on when, how, why, where and what a writer writes. But texts aren't just produced in a world made up of texts. They are part of a real world going through its convulsions, struggles, moments of calm and the like. No matter how hard writers might try to keep that world out, the truth remains that they have to feed, clothe and house themselves and they experience a range of desires. These needs have to be met and different societies cater for them in different ways. There is, therefore, a complex web of intertexts surrounding any work of literature and these interact with the complex real world.

Usually, there's a division of labour. The writer writes primary texts or *literature*; the critic writes secondary texts or *criticism*. But there are no real lines of demarcation. There is nothing to stop a writer being a critic. And, to go further along this line, there's no law to stop a writer being the kind of critic who is concerned with analysing what's inside the bath of ideas surrounding their own texts and material contexts.

In my own case, much of my writing for children has come from my personal and cultural history, including 'My Brother' and 'Harrybo's Grandad':

My brother is making a protest about bread.
'Why do we always have wholemeal bread?
You can't spread butter on wholemeal bread
You try and spread the butter on
and it just makes a hole right through the middle.'

He marches out of the room and shouts
Across the landing and down the passage.
'It's always the same in this place.
Nothing works.
The volume knob's broken on the radio you know.
It's been broken for months and months you know.'

He stamps back into the kitchen
Stares at the loaf of bread and says:
'Wholemeal bread – look at it, look at it.
You put the butter on
And it all rolls up.
You put the butter on
And it all rolls up.'

Once my friend Harrybo
came to school crying.

We said:
What's the matter?
What's the matter?
And he said
his grandad had died.

So we didn't know what to say.

Then I said:
How did he die?
And he said:
He was standing on St Pancras Station
waiting for the train
and he just fell over and died.

Then he started crying again.

He was a nice man
Harrybo's grandad.
He had a shed with tins full of screws in it.

Mind you,
my gran was nice too
she gave me and my brother
a red shoe horn each.

Maybe Harrybo's grandad gave
Harrybo a red shoe horn.

Dave said:
My hamster died as well.
So everyone said:
Shhhh.
And Dave said:
I was only saying.
And I said:
My gran gave me a red shoe horn.
Rodge said:
I got a pair of trainers for Christmas.
And Harrybo said:
You can get ones without laces.
And we all said:
Yeah, that's right, Harrybo, you can.
Any other day,
we'd've said:
Of course you can, we know that, you fool.
But that day
we said:
Yeah, that's right, Harrybo, yeah, you can.

I was brought up in a home environment where both my parents were on a journey transforming themselves. They came from immigrant families who had arrived very poor, in my father's case almost destitute, into the East End of London in very overcrowded, difficult conditions. When I joined them, they had had two children – one had died, the other was four – and my parents had professionalised themselves by becoming teachers. We were living in North West London in a rented flat over a shop in a place that had once been a village but was now embedded within a suburbia that followed the building of the Metropolitan Line.

Though this time is often depicted as rather static, there were serious changes going on – changes which my parents' lives mirrored. A whole layer of the urban working class had done just what my parents had done: left the old traditional areas of what we now call the inner city, and started to live in the suburbs or in new satellite towns and, in so doing, they started to acquire non-manual skills.

A lot of what I have written focuses on describing the world I found myself in and exploring odd fragments of what remained of the past they came from – my parents and the language they brought with them, as you will see in the poem that follows, 'Don't Tell Your Mother':

When my mum goes to evening classes
my dad says,
'Don't tell your mother – let's have *matzo brei*[1].
She always says:
'Don't give the boys that greasy stuff.
It's bad for them.'
So, don't tell her, all right?'

So he breaks up the *matzos*
puts them into water to soften them up.
Then he fries them till they're glazed and crisp.
'It tastes best like this,
fried in *hinner shmaltz*[2]
skimmed off the top of the chicken soup,'
he says,
'but olive oil will do.'

Then he beats up three eggs
and pours it over the frying *matzos*
till it's all cooked.

It tastes brilliant.
We love it.
Then we wash everything up
absolutely everything
and we go to bed.

Next day,
Mum says to us,
'What did your father cook you last night?'
'Oh you know … stuff …
… egg on toast, I think.'

Another change we were all part of was the world of education, which itself is always interleaved and folded into the wider world. I didn't know at the time that my brother and I were part of what was, in effect, an experiment: the mass education of everyone beyond the age of thirteen in new types of schools. Primary schools came under the umbrella of the state – except for the private sector – then everyone went to a secondary school – single-sex, mixed, church, non-denominational, local authority ... and, most famous of all, selective grammar schools. Eighty per cent of children failed the selection exam at eleven and Technical schools and Secondary Modern schools served or failed the majority. All this required a great new positioning for people in this country. In families where no one had ever received an education beyond the age of thirteen, all children were now staying on in some kind of school till they were fifteen, some choosing to stay at school till sixteen, some till eighteen and beyond to various kinds of college and university education.

But this wasn't some kind of smooth roll-out. It was riven with division, conflict, snobbery and tension. The last years of primary school, in my memory, were wracked with anxiety, horse-trading and fiddles. The curriculum was obsessed with getting the children up to the level required of the infamous 11+ exam, which I mock in 'The Homework Book':

> Miss Williams said that from now on
> we would have homework
> and that we were to bring
> a homework exercise book to school.

> This was serious stuff:
> all about passing The Exam,
> The Exam called 'The Eleven Plus'.
> Everyone was worried about
> The Eleven Plus.
> Would I pass?
> Would I fail?
> Everyone was worried.
> Teachers, parents, us.
> I couldn't get to sleep.
> Mum brought me hot milk.

> On Mondays
> Miss Williams went through
> the homework in our homework books.
> While she was talking, I got bored.

I drew a picture in my homework book
of a man with a big beard
right in the middle of my maths homework.
He was carrying a bag.
He put things he picked up off the pavement
into his bag.
I called him Trev the Tramp.

Miss Williams went on going through
the homework with the whole class.
This was really important.
We had to listen or we wouldn't pass
The Eleven Plus.
Everyone was listening.
Everyone was concentrating
so that they could pass
The Eleven Plus.

I bent down behind the boy
sitting in front of me.
I looked across to my friend Harrybo
and held up my picture of Trev the Tramp.
I pointed at Trev the Tramp.
I whispered, 'Trev the Tramp.'
Miss Williams saw me
holding up the homework book.

She was on to it in a flash.
'What's that, boy? What is it!'
I quickly shut the homework book.
'Nothing, Miss Williams.'
She rushed over.
(She was brilliant at rushing over.)
She grabbed the homework book.
She flicked through the pages.
She found the picture of Trev the Tramp.
Right there in the middle of 23 x 12.

'This is it, isn't it?' she said.
'In your homework book!
I'll tell you what's going to happen
now, boy,' she said.

6

'You're going to take your homework book
home to your parents along with a
letter from me.'
She pointed at herself when she said, 'me'.
'My goodness, you're in trouble, boy.
Serious trouble.'

For the rest of the day,
I was very quiet. I put my feet down
on the ground carefully and I made
sure I didn't bump into anything.
At going-home time, she handed me
A big white envelope.
'The letter to your parents is in there,
along with the homework book.'

But when I got home,
I couldn't face giving it to my Mum.
I couldn't face giving it to my Dad.
I nipped upstairs and slipped it
under my bed.
All evening I was thinking
about the big white envelope
with the letter from Miss Williams,
The homework book and the
picture of Trev the Tramp.
I didn't want to give it to them
I didn't want to see their faces
as they read the letter and looked at
Trev the Tramp.

What I did was put the big white envelope
on their bed when I went to bed.

In the morning, my Dad said,
'Oh dear, you poor old thing,
you must have been so worried
about that letter, eh? I'll write one back.
I'll say some things in the letter
that will make sure you won't have
to worry about this stuff anymore.
And I'll get you a new homework book.'

At school my friends said,
'Did you get in trouble?
Did you get the whacks?
What happened?'
And I said,
'My Dad said I wasn't to worry.'
They didn't believe me.

And I don't know what my Dad wrote,
but Miss Williams never said
anything about it ever again,
the Head never said anything about it again.
My Dad was a teacher
and maybe he wrote in some kind of
special teacher language,
that meant Miss Williams wouldn't
ever say anything again.
Some kind of teacher code ...
That's what must have done it.

The grammar school had parallel anxieties about status, form and hierarchy. This was where I learned how to read, where I found my level and place in society, where I acquired the kinds of knowledge that society at that point thought was suitable for a boy who was going to pass the exam at 11. Because this is part of the way the middle class of my era defined itself, many of these processes have been naturalised. That is to say, the processes I went through have acquired a sense of being *natural*, right, appropriate, usual, legitimate, normal, correct – not just for then, but for all time.

However, I lived in a very particular bath of ideas in this new experimental and changing world. The years of my parents' teenage and young married life together had been infused with major political events arising out of what were their own particular real-life situations. Not only was it a time of poverty for them, it was also a time when one of the solutions being offered to society was to imprison, exile, persecute or even exterminate them. So, along with action against that poverty – through rent strikes and industrial strikes – they were participants in actions against those people locally, nationally and inter-nationally who wanted to impose the new world order which would involve their extermination. At the time, they thought that the way to fight was to join the Communist Party and though they would leave it in 1957, this was the formation and memory they brought with them into the suburbs, into our flat above the shop, and into their new profession – teaching.

From the perspective of the early twenty-first century, I can look back on my younger self and see that for me writing poems wasn't just a literary practice. It was an educational one too. Schools are where children learn about the kind of behaviour reading involves. Are books things that you get questioned about? Or things you read to yourself? Are books things that sit on shelves that you never read, because you only read worksheets? Do you hear books read to you? Are you expected to just read silently to yourself? Is it a private or a social behavioural act?

In my case, I can see clearly that it was an acutely *educational* practice.

My parents were teachers but they were also theoreticians. In the period covered by the time I started thinking about whether I could write, my parents were deeply involved in various kinds of educational work. My father had moved from teaching in a suburban grammar school, where he was black-listed and prevented from becoming a head of department, to one of the new comprehensive schools, situated off the Old Kent Road. From there, he moved to Borough Road Training College where he started teaching on a variety of courses for trainee teachers, until he became a lecturer at the University of London Institute of Education in the heart of Bloomsbury.

My mother, meanwhile, was teaching in a primary school in Croxley Green and began a life-changing course – a diploma in primary education – with the eminent Christian Schiller, doyenne of progressive education. My mother became a deputy head and then started to train teachers at Goldsmiths College. During this time, they were also involved, separately or together, in presenting poetry programmes for BBC Schools Radio, helping first James Britton and then Geoffrey Summerfield in producing groundbreaking anthologies for schools – the *Oxford Junior Poetry Collection* with Britton and *Voices* and *Junior Voices* with Summerfield. My father had prepared many documents, papers, essays and talks on a variety of topics based around the secondary English curriculum, including a policy document for the comprehensive school mentioned above:

> Whatever language the pupils possess, it is this which must be built on rather than driven underground. However narrow the experience of our pupils may be (and it is often wider than we think), it is this experience alone which has given their language meaning. The starting point for English work must be the ability to handle effectively their own experience. Oral work, written work and the discussion of literature must create an atmosphere in which the pupils become confident of the full acceptability of the material of their own experience. Only in this way can they advance to the next stage. (Harold Rosen, 1958, unpublished quotation from *Walworth School Syllabus*)

Later, engaged in his PhD – done mostly at the kitchen table, we would claim – my father critiqued a crude mechanistic system of classifying children's sentences that had taken off in the USA. Then, together my parents wrote a book called *The Language of Primary Schoolchildren* which was discussed over teatimes, during holidays and the like as it was being assembled and written. These are the opening words:

> Language is for living with. Children's language emerges from the lives they lead and we cannot hope to make sense of it without understanding their lives. (1973:21)

My parents, of course, mothered and fathered my brother and me in their own idiosyncratic ways and with all the baggage they brought with them from the East End into the suburbs. They were also educationists who mothered and fathered with their knowledge and ideas. Education is very octopus-like. Its tentacles reach out into real life, up into theory, back into anecdotes about classrooms, about individual children, along with stories about colleagues, struggles with authorities, off into the resources that can be brought into the classroom. All these different kinds of conversations took place around my brother and me. Now, in my head, I can see both parents crawling along the floor, looking at Summerfield's handwritten notes and copies of the poems he had found for *Voices*; going for a walk in a bit of suburban woodland with my mother while she gathered up what she called 'bits' – holly berries or beech masts – which she would take back to her class; my father reading out why he thought that this or that statement by this or that American professor talking about T-units was nonsense; my mother reading out poems that the children she taught had written; my father reading out a talk that my mother would type for him, the pair of them working out a bit of linguistic theory, and so on. It was going on around us all the time. As I happened to be a child who enjoyed listening to these conversations, then it was in me as well.

I think my parents left the Communist Party in order that their lives could accommodate the kinds of ideas that they were developing around the teaching of literature and language to school-age children. At the time, the Communist Party's education policy-makers had a very reductive idea about the education of working-class children which followed a determinist model: if the ruling class deprived the working class of its true deserts it also deprived it of language and culture. My parents were developing a counter-theory that if you wanted children to get hold of education, you had to start with the languages and cultures of the children in front of you. The starting point for children should come from the language-base of the child itself. Here they are in the preamble to a long transcript of three children discussing 'Old Florist' by Theodore Roethke:

> We can hear their talk developing and absorbing the poem as they surround it with their experience of language and of life and their readiness to project *outwards* from it into their own imaginings in order to penetrate *inwards* to its meaning for them. Collaboration it is, but at the same time they demonstrate how active a process reading has to be for the individual reader; every story and poem has to be placed in the reader's world, made part of his patterning of life; every story and poem must be actively worked upon so that its design can be added to a larger design. (1970:104)

[Reference is made in a footnote to the then unpublished study which became the seminal *Language and Learning*, 1970, edited by their friend and colleague, James Britton.]

Part of this approach also involved the championing of particular kinds of literature that embraced the everyday, which worked with and not against contemporary vernaculars. This was not about excluding other kinds of literature, but was meant to spread the net more widely than was traditionally the case. My mother, for example, was very fond of WB Yeats, who doesn't fit this pattern of writing at all, and yet she was always on the hunt for poems about objects around the house to slip into her radio programmes. Sometimes she enlisted my help in finding suitable poems from her collection of anthologies. This was a direct trigger for me to start writing and one of my poems was included in a schools radio programme. It's not hard to see that this is both filial and theoretical. The poem that follows was written to my mother but it was also something that fitted a particular educational philosophy that was being developed at that time, which valued children's own experiences and encouraged them to write poems themselves. This theory was developing the idea that children could be writing readers and reading writers – and in a poem like 'Stop!' I was writing to that theory:

Every few weeks someone looks at me and says:
my you've grown
And then every few weeks someone says:
they've grown too long

and silver scissors come out of the drawer
and chip at my toes and run through my hair.

Now I don't like this one little bit.
I won't grow if I'm going to be chopped.

What's me is mine and I want to keep it
so either me or the scissors or my nails had better stop.

My first book of poems, *Mind Your Own Business*, appeared in 1974 when I was 28. My mother was now at Trent Park Teacher Training College – which became part of Middlesex University – running the kind of Diploma Course that Christian Schiller had inspired, while my father was at the Institute of Education, falling with a mix of delight and cynicism on poststructuralist theories of narratology, reader-response, interpretation and language which, in due course, he and his colleagues would teach higher degree students.

As for me, I was taken into a place called 'Children's Literature', a network of libraries, schools, colleges, book clubs, book shops and magazines. You are embraced and then pushed in front of an audience.

For some writers and illustrators this is not a happy experience. For me, it was at first curious, embarrassing and awkward, but soon became the most important thing I found that I could have done. I had written the poems in what could be called a mixture of cool and warm contexts. The cool context was the passing of books between adults or reading poems yourself. The warm contexts were the broadcasts and readings on disc and tape that my parents played to us in our front room: Robert Graves, Dylan Thomas, Richard Burton reading Dylan Thomas, poets reading their own poems on the BBC Radio's Third Programme, actors reading the poems my mother had chosen for her schools radio broadcasts. The hot moments for literature related to theatre: Shakespeare, Pinter, Osborne, Wesker, Shaw, Arden, Brecht; my acting class at Questors Theatre; sketches in revues at university; the two plays I had written myself. With my poetry collection in my hand, standing in front of a class or a whole school of children, my first inclination was to go warm: to read the poems as if it was a schools radio broadcast, to perform them. Suddenly, a world that had been building up behind the dam burst out: the mix of theories about working with everyday experience and writing readers and reading writers, the kinds of performance methods I had learnt at Questors or, for that matter, watching my parents tell stories about their day at work, all came together in this act of *performance*.

But where was I at this moment? Was I in that northwest London primary school in 1955? Was I even with the offspring of children who had been to that kind of school? Not very often. Mostly, I found myself in and amongst the children who had themselves recently arrived in this country or who were the children of arrivants.

At this point, I see that another mechanism came into play – feedback. The problem with the word is that it doesn't indicate just how complicated it is. If you write something and perform it, or work with it in a classroom, you discover all sorts of things about the poem, about the child, about yourself. Next time you write anything approximating to that field or structure of writing, you cannot escape the sensations and understandings that you experienced on the occasion you read the poem to an audience. In one sense, you now write with that sensibility added in to everything else you are. Then, in turn you take the next piece of writing out into performance in front of an audience and, in turn that goes through the same process. You and the writing are changing all the while, often in ways that you're hardly aware of yourself. An inflection, a phrasing, a topic you've chosen to write about, such as 'The Rhythm of Life' :

Hand on the bridge
feel the rhythm of the train.

Hand on the window
feel the rhythm of the rain.

Hand on your throat
feel the rhythm of your talk.

Hand on your leg
feel the rhythm of your walk.

Hand in the sea
feel the rhythm of the tide.

Hand on your heart
feel the rhythm inside.

Hand on the rhythm
feel the rhythm of the rhyme.

Hand on your life
feel the rhythm of time
hand on your life
feel the rhythm of time
hand on your life
feel the rhythm of time.

But something else was going on. Education has always been of particular interest to politicians. Throughout the whole period I've been publishing books, education has been a battleground for competing ideas. If people wanted me in the midst of their classrooms and schools, then coming from my kind of background, I could hardly stay aloof from these debates. Or put another way, these debates would themselves be part of what and how I write.

I think we have reached a key moment for literature in schools. At present, it's no exaggeration to say that for children between the ages of nine and fourteen, books are an optional extra. It's literacy without literature. Literature can be reduced to an extract on a worksheet where the questions asked are about facts, chronology and logic.

The education theory that has taken over the teaching of literature is logical positivism. That is to say, it is the notion that every process can be reduced to its component facts, chronology and logic. This is a lie. When we engage with reading or writing, we become involved in patterns of feeling. Our feelings about people, scenes and outcomes ebb and flow and change as the drama unfolds. This is how we grapple with the ethics inside ourselves and which we perceive as immanent in what we read. This is the stuff of reading and writing. The tyranny of the last fifteen years has been to exile feelings and leave them outside the classroom. And part of this has been the rise of many different kinds of selection processes, inside classrooms, inside schools, between schools: the regime of the SATs, the smiley faces chart, the quick and slow tables, and the non-selective schools that select. Children who come from homes with few books may well rarely encounter whole books as part of their education. In so doing, they are discriminated against, because it's through the reading of whole books that we most pleasurably and most easily access complex and abstract ideas. Only the other night while reading a Greek myth with my eight year old daughter, we discussed what the word *pity* meant.

Under this polity, poetry has become a bit of elastoplast that is slotted into the curriculum after tests at the end of term, as part of a ludicrous process of working through poetic forms because this is markable, testable knowledge. You can't mark what people feel. Once again, logical positivism wins out over humanism. Anthologies have been produced that fit the educational agenda, so that the idea of engaging with a poet has in many places been squeezed out. Teachers have to fight the pressure of SATs and Ofsted to develop humanistic approaches to literature. To be true to my beliefs about education, and be true to those who fought for educational ideals before us – in my case, the incredible luck to have such inspiring parents who exerted a powerful influence on who I am and what I do – the fight for what matters in everything to do with reading, writing and literature in schools goes on:

'The Two Poems'

Once there were two poems.
One day they went to school.
The first poem went into class
and the teacher had been given some questions to ask:
Ask the children what kind of poem it is?
Ask the children why it is an effective poem?
Ask the children to underline the adjectives in the poem.
Ask the children what kind of green is pea-green?
Ask the children to tell you where was the ring before it was bought.

The second poem went into class
but this teacher had left the list at home.
The poem sat down and one child said,
'You remind me of when my auntie died.'
Another child said,
'I like the way you say things
over and over again in a sing-song sort of a way.'
Another child said, 'I'm going to write a poem
about being in a crowd of people.'
And another child said,
'I'm going to find some more poems like you.'
Soon the room was full of poems.

That night,
when the poems got home,
the first poem said,
'Today I had a strange day.'
The second poem said,
'Today I made lots of friends.'

Notes

1 *Matzo brei* is the Yiddish name of a dish made of *matzos* and egg. *Matzo* is the word for un-leavened bread that tastes like water biscuits.

2 *Hinner shmaltz* are the Yiddish words for chicken fat.

Works Cited

Britton, J (ed) (1958) *The Oxford Book of Verse for Juniors*. Oxford: Oxford University Press

Rosen, C and H (1973) *The Language of Primary School Children*. Harmondsworth: Penguin

Rosen, M (1974) *Mind Your Own Business*. London: Andre Deutsch

Rosen, M (1977) *Wouldn't You Like to Know*. London: Andre Deutsch

Rosen, M (1988) *The Hypnotiser*. London: Andre Deutsch

Rosen, M (1996) *You Wait Till I'm Older Than You!* London: Viking Penguin

Rosen, M (2009) *Michael Rosen's A-Z, the Best Poetry from Agard to Zephaniah.* London: Puffin

Rosen, M (2010 *Michael Rosen's Big Book of Bad Things.* London: Puffin

Summerfield, G (ed) (1969) *Voices.* Harmondsworth: Penguin

Summerfield, G (ed) (1970) *Junior Voices: an anthology of poetry and pictures.* Harmondsworth: Penguin

Many of Michael Rosen's poetry collections are available in newer editions from Puffin Books.

2

Confronting the Snark: the Non-Theory of Children's Poetry

Peter Hunt

He had softly and silently vanished away –
For the Snark was a boojum, you see. (Lewis Carroll)

Poems for children. This will kill you and the children. (Dylan Thomas)

t is an uncomfortable – possibly blasphemous – thought that very many people fundamentally do not believe that children's poetry exists: it is, like children's literature, an oxymoron. The logic is simple. There is a common, basic assumption that poetry – at least, post-romantic poetry – although essentially indefinable, is static, thoughtful, sophisticated, skilled, philosophical – and concerned with sex and death and interiority. The general concept of children is that they are NOT any of those things. Therefore, children's poetry cannot exist. QED.

Of course, it would be idle to deny that something that is not prose is produced and marketed in large quantities for children – but is it *poetry*? As Roy Fuller intoned: 'those who write poetry for children perforce enter the field of light verse' (quoted by Scannell, 1995:95). JRR Tolkien famously remarked that fairy-tales 'have been relegated to the 'nursery', as shabby or old-fashioned furniture is relegated to the play-room, primarily because the adults do not want it ... It is not the choice of children that decides this' (Tolkien, 1964:34); with poetry it is rhyme and metre, narrative, and doggerel that find themselves labelled *for children*. As Brian Morse observed: 'Much [poetry] is produced for children nowadays ... on the assumption that they need constant thrills ... But once you've had the quick laugh, where do you go from there?' (Morse, 1992:3)

At its worst, this kind of writing gives non-prose a bad name: it is, as Jan Mark observed, 'the look-kids-I'm-on-your-side rib-nudging which in the hands of some writers is beginning to look like child molesting' (Chambers, 2009:183). At its best – or, at least, at its most well-meaning – *children's poetry* is regarded as no more than an instrument of acculturisation, a step on the way to *real* poetry, to a certain kind of appreciation of a certain kind of text – a kind of text both owned and defined by a certain kind of adult. Even Jan Mark occasionally slipped into this way of thinking, as when she described a book of poetry 'for adults' as 'a book for those who have ARRIVED rather than those who are still on the way' (Chambers, 2009:274). And so, until children 'arrive', they are to be given apprentice work, something that is the same thing as poetry except simpler, suitable for less skilled hands, less experienced eyes – the intellectual equivalent of the 'children's food' described in Mick Gowar's famous 'Dinner Party Blues' (Gowar, 1981:61). But the analogy doesn't really hold, because poetry is not a form but an essence, and that is, so the reasoning goes, not accessible to children, by definition.

In short, when it comes to deciding what poetry is, adults are better judges, and a child's opinion does not count; after all, 'It is necessary to read a great many poems and read them attentively in order to develop a discriminating taste' (Hill, 1983:200). In fact, children can neither write nor, by implication, understand poetry. Vernon Scannell, whose credentials as an advocate for poetry in schools were impeccable, nevertheless observed of poetry by children:

> I can't think that a child of under, say, fourteen could write a poem that could truly be called a poem ... I can cite alleged poems by children which contain absolutely none of the qualities I've mentioned: craftsmanship, form, thought, apprehension of reality. (Chambers, 2009:100)

This is so adultist that Neil Philip, who quoted it in his article on the *Signal* Poetry Award in 1985, could not quite bring himself to agree:

> But children can – and, with astonishing frequency do – make things out of language which, *if you can't strictly call them poems*, have more poetic intensity than most of what is written for them. (Chambers, 2009:100, *my italics*)

The implications of that statement need rather a lot of unpacking, but one reaction might be that the propriatorial attitude to the very word *poem* betrays a certain confusion in the minds of even the best critics. In the face of this, it is important to theorise: we are, perhaps, hunting a Snark, but if the Snark turns out to be a boojum, then maybe a lot of assumptions, difficulties and contradictions that surround children's poetry may vanish away.

Definitions of children's poetry are rarely helpful: poetry may exploit the indeterminacies of language, but that is not a particularly fruitful mode to use when trying to describe it. Morag Styles, in her Introduction to the only full-length English-language study of the subject, makes 'no attempt to provide a definition of poetry ... as no two poets or teachers or critics seem able to agree on even a working definition' (Styles, 1998:xxv). Others have been less circumspect: Iona and Peter Opie in *The Oxford Book of Children's Verse*: 'Naturally, the more pure the poetry, the more difficult it can be to say for whom the poet is writing' (1973:ix); Neil Philip in *The New Oxford Book of Children's Verse*: 'There is in the best children's poetry a sense of the world being seen as for the first time, and of language being plucked from the air to describe it' (1996:xxv); or Pie Corbett in *The Works. Every Kind of Poem You Will Ever Need for the Literacy Hour*: 'poetry is a serious game' (Cookson, 2000:xxiv). As Peter Hollindale has concluded: 'Where four or five dozen [anthologies] were gathered together, they announced a corporate uncertainty on the fairly fundamental question of what a children's poem actually is' (Chambers, 2009:367).

We might use Dr Johnson's approach: when Boswell asked him, 'Then, Sir, what is poetry?' Johnson replied: 'Why sir, it is much easier to say what it is not. We all *know* what light is; but it is not easy to *tell* what it is' (*Life*, 11 April 1776). It is not, as Jan Mark, perhaps a little intemperately, observed, the fashionably over-designed:

> To look at some of the book production that has socked us in the eye recently, you would think that publishers knew no children, had no children, had never been children; this must be so. Why else would they so bitterly despise the little bastards and toss jazzy garbage in their general direction. Where? Oh, over there somewhere. Market Research has the coordinates. Araminta Bourne-Wytless is in charge of design. She'll tell you. (Chambers, 2009:293)

Nor is it what John Rowe Townsend called *urchin verse* – the motives for producing which are not, incidentally, necessarily careless or malign – merely misguided. As Robert Bridges noted:

> There has been with regard to poetry a pestilent notion that the young should be gradually led up to excellence through lower degrees of it ... and this has been carried so far that writers, who else make no poetical pretence, have good-naturedly composed poems for the young, and in a technique often as inept as their sentiment. (Danby, 1983:18)

But neither is children's poetry necessarily produced by the revered poets. John Wain, selecting Ted Hughes as the first winner of the *Signal* Award, conceded:

> None of this is exactly poetry for children; have we, as selectors, simply yielded to the temptation to pick the book that seems to us to contain the best poems, as poems, and devil take the hindmost classroom teacher? (Chambers, 2009: 27)

Or, he might have written, the classroom occupants.

As a term, *children's poetry* offers the same problem as *children's literature* – it consists of two complex terms and a possessive. *Children* denotes a broad and highly variable construct, often bearing little relation to reality – although its use is often unavoidable. By the possessive, do we mean belonging to, written by, written for, adopted by, of childhood ... and so on. As AA Milne said of the poems in *When We Were Very Young*: 'They are a curious collection; some *for* children, some *about* children, some by, with or from children' (Thwaite, 1992:53). *Poetry* is equally problematic; the judgement that something is *poetry* or *good poetry* is nothing to do with what is on the page – it is nothing to do with form: it is a cultural value-judgement, exactly equivalent to the decision as to what literature is. As Sir Philip Sidney wrote in his *An Apology for Poetry* (1595), 'it is not Rhyming and Versing that maketh a poet' (1962:11). Poetry does not even require words. Equally, you cannot call *yourself* a poet, although many do, any more than you can claim to write literature; you produce text: the dominant critical culture decides its status. Thus the term *poem*, like the term *literature*, is more confusing than useful when used in the context of children-and-texts, precisely because it sets up false comparisons, and leads directly to the devaluing of texts that connect most appropriately with childhood, however defined.

The problem is not so much that adults – because of the power imbalance between adults and children – feel that they can presume to know what a child does or should make of a text. It is that lurking behind even the most well-intentioned and empathetic approaches to children and poems is the idea of absolute values in literature and art. These values may not be definable – hence the adoption of a canon as a substitute for individual appreciation or thought – and they lead to the *why*-Beowulf-*rather-than*-Harry-Potter-*won-the-Whitbread* syndrome. This is not relativism: the real relativists are the followers, consciously or unconsciously, of critics such as FR Leavis, who in 1930 produced one of the most extreme statements of a relativist creed, which has dogged literature and poetry – and children's literature and children's poetry especially – ever since:

> In any period it is upon a very small minority that the discerning appreciation of art and literature depends: it is (apart from cases of the simple and familiar) only a few who are capable of unprompted, first-hand judgement. They are still a small minority, though a larger one, who are capable of endorsing such first-hand judgement by genuine personal response. (Leavis, 1930:3)

And the rest of us, especially children ... well ... We can but aspire. Common sense and democracy may perhaps have nibbled away at the canon of literature, but the attitudes behind it are still a formidable presence.

If we are to have something that can genuinely be called *children's poetry*, we require a seismic shift in thinking: a quantum leap, perhaps. We should, simply, make the possessive come into its own, and, as adults, relinquish the power over what there is to read and what is supposed to be read and valued, however illusory this may be: we have the power to say what is available to children to read, but not how they shall read it.

We need to confront unconsidered, received wisdom, such as WH Auden's dictum from the 'Introduction' to *A Choice of de la Mare's Verse* (1963), which is frequently quoted with approval by writers on children's poetry: 'while there are some good poems that are only for adults, because they presuppose adult experience in their readers, there are no good poems which are only for children' (Styles and Powling, 1996:5). This is almost as arrogantly demeaning to and dismissive of the primary audience as CS Lewis's also widely-quoted, and equally pernicious dictum: 'I am almost inclined to set it up as a canon that a children's story which is enjoyed only by children is a bad children's story' (1966:24). Both these attitudes keep power and judgement firmly with the adults and insidiously disparage the children.

But there are good signs that such a shift from adult power to child power is not impossible, one of which is that children's poetry as now produced can easily be seen as repressive. Neil Philip, for example, points out that 'From the moment they can talk till the moment we finally convince them that what they have to say is not important, children are producing poetry the whole time'; Margaret Meek concurs: 'Children are natural poets, singing before they speak, metaphor-making before they prose their way to school' (Chambers, 2009: 86, 43). If there is an air of resignation in these comments, it is because of the mismatch between what poetry is so frequently declared to be – innovative, mind-expanding, fresh, new, individual – and what the adult literary establishment purports to admire, and imposes upon children. Children should be given the chance, as Alan Tucker put it, to 'build word castles and throw words around, more mess but more energy, light, and colour. Clearing up comes later' (Tucker, 2003:228).

Another good sign is that at least some children's literature criticism is ahead of the game. Perry Nodelman describes the difference he found on moving, in his university, from English Literature to Children's Literature. The children's literature critics:

> all made judgements of excellence in terms of the effects of books on their audience – and that astonished me, for in the ivory tower of literary study I had hitherto inhabited, one certainly did not judge books by how they affected audiences; in fact, one often judged audiences by the extent to which they were affected by books, so that, for instance, anyone who wasn't overwhelmed by Shakespeare was simply assumed to be an intransigent dummy. (Nodelman, 1985:4)

This shift in attitude was presaged by the poet John Drinkwater in his review of AA Milne's *When We Were Very Young* in *The Sunday Times* (23 November 1924). Drinkwater distinguished between 'the good Mr Milne' who writes verses for his son like 'The King's Breakfast', and the 'bad Mr Milne' who says, 'If you are going to have a book of poetry, you must put some poetry into it' and who then produces 'Twinkletoes' or 'Water-lilies', with their pseudo-romantic 'fairy' images. Drinkwater quotes from Milne's 'child-centred' poems and concludes: 'It is all great larks, but I wonder whether the Sterner Critics will realise that [they are] also a very wholesome contribution to serious literature' (Thwaite, 1992:66).

I think that we need to establish, to evangelise, two basic ideas. The first is that, in opposition to Auden and CS Lewis, and, perhaps, much of the literary establishment, genuine *children's* literature and *children's* poetry is precisely that which has *NO* appeal to adults (see Rudd, 2000). Charles Causley once, in cautionary mood, observed that 'almost the whole of children's poetry – verse, that is, written specifically for a child audience – has faded away' (Mole, 2002:84) and we can forcefully argue that its evanescence does not make it lesser. The second basic idea is that children's poetry should not be seen as a bridge or a ladder to anything – except, perhaps, as part of an openness of mind to language and its possibilities. As Margaret Meek put it: 'Part of the puzzle and the fun of poetry for the young is that it works contrary to what they are learning to do to be good at reading' (Chambers, 2009:91).

The fact that genuine, liberated *children's poetry* might not look much like anything that bears that label now, and that it is likely to be unpredictable in form and anarchic in content may frighten both the poetical and educational establishments. But, in the end, *children's poetry* is no more than a respectful negotiation of the Tom Tiddler's Ground between the writers – people with experience and certain acquired ways of seeing the world and expressing it – and child readers – people with less experience and, probably, radically different, or undisciplined, ways of seeing the world and expressing it.

This Snark, theorising about children's poetry, *is* a boojum, because if we face its implications then we should be left with children freely interacting with words, and all the rest of the paraphernalia, such as the conferences about children's poetry at which no children are present, will softly and silently vanish away.

Works Cited

Carroll, L (1967) *The Annotated Snark*. Harmondsworth: Penguin

Chambers, N (ed) (2009) *Poetry for Children. The Signal Award 1979-2001*. South Woodchester: The Thimble Press

Cookson, P (ed) (2000) *The Works. Every Kind of Poem You Will Ever Need for the Literacy Hour*. London: Macmillan

Danby, J (1983) The difficult poem. *Signal* 40 p18-25

Gowar, M (1981) *Swings and Roundabouts*. London: Collins

Hill, HM (1983) How to tell a sheep from a goat – and why it matters. In R Bator (ed) *Signposts to Criticism of Children's Literature*. Chicago: ALA

Leavis, FR (1930) *Mass Civilization and Minority Culture*. Cambridge: The Minority Press

Lewis, CS (1966) *Of Other Worlds*. London: Geoffrey Bles

Mole, J (2002) Tune, Argument, Colour, Truth, *Signal* 98 p79-90

Morse, B (1992) *Poetry Books for Children*. South Woodchester: The Thimble Press

Nodelman, P (ed) (1985) *Touchstones: Reflections on the Best in Children's Literature. Volume 1*. West Lafayette, In: Children's Literature Association

Opie, I and Opie, P (eds) (1973) *The Oxford Book of Children's Verse*. Oxford: Oxford University Press

Philip, N (ed) (1996) *The New Oxford Book of Children's Verse*. Oxford: Oxford University Press

Rudd, D (2000) *Enid Blyton and the Mystery of Children's Literature*. Basingstoke, Macmillan

Sidney, P (1962) An Apology for Poetry, In DJ Enright and E de Chickera (eds) *English Critical Texts*. London: Oxford University Press

Styles, M (1998) *From the Garden to the Street: Three Hundred Years of Poetry for Children*. London: Cassell

Styles, M and Powling, C (eds) (1996) *A Guide to Poetry 0-13*. Reading: Books for Keeps and the Reading and Language Information Centre

Thomas, D (1968) *A Prospect of the Sea*. London: Dent

Thwaite, A (1992) *The Brilliant Career of Winnie-the-Pooh*. London: Methuen

Tolkien, JRR (1964) *Tree and Leaf*. London: Allen and Unwin

Tucker, A (2003) The Mouse and the Doormat, *Signal* 100 p227-46

3

What Is Children's Poetry?
Children's Views of Children's Poetry

Stephen Miles

'A child is a mental depiction, made only by adults who forget what it was like'
(Jack aged 12)

'**W**hat is children's poetry?' is a question that can be asked in many ways, as the other chapters in this section demonstrate. It is a question that adults ask, and look to other adults to answer. Almost all the discussions about what does and does not constitute children's poetry, the writing and anthologising, the criticism and analysis, are conducted by adults. I decided that it might be enlightening to investigate this question from the perspectives of children themselves. Could they appreciate the validity of asking: 'What is children's poetry?'

I had two days in school to carry out the research with a group of 30 pupils – 20 twelve year olds and ten fourteen year olds selected by their teachers as 'more able' in English. These young people were close enough to childhood to consider what constitutes *children's* poetry, yet old enough to tackle the historical and cultural challenge of some of the texts I wanted them to scrutinise. The venue for the research was the school library, a somewhat more relaxed and democratic environment than a classroom.

Our first session established a baseline by exploring what poetry meant to the young people involved. Subsequent sessions introduced them chronologically to examples from the canon, posing questions about the nature of children's poetry throughout. The first poems we examined were published between 1480 and 1715, and included works by Bunyan, Watts and Foxton, emphasising the didactic and religious purposes of those authors. The next session was based on typical material from the second half of the eighteenth to the middle of the nineteenth century. The aim was to see if the pupils could perceive any changes in tone, subject matter, implied reader, purpose or context in the poems they were studying. Although not contemporary from a child's perspective, Stevenson's *A Child's Garden of Verses* marks, for me, the starting point of modern children's poetry, so this formed the basis of our third session. The final session was a plenary.

After a brief introduction, the discussions were self-regulated by the children. Four to six young people from mixed age-groups interrogated the poems I provided – about fifteen per session – and their deliberations were taped. They also made some annotations and recorded a few overall thoughts in writing. All the quotations that follow are directly from the pupils involved.

The initial discussion of poetry in general was uncontroversial. One girl characterised poetry tellingly as 'a way of expressing beliefs, opinions, thoughts and desires in verse'. Some felt that analysis and criticism were essential when tackling 'difficult' poems but ran the risk of destroying the 'primary thoughts and emotions of the poem' or the 'impression it paints in your mind' and making it 'boring' by 'repetition'. None of the pupils agreed with my suggestion that poetry might be more special than other kinds of writing; nor did they feel that school-approved poetry was intrinsically better than song lyrics or popular verse. Their unanimous belief was that it was not the genre but the individual work that mattered.

Isaac Watts, of course, defended poetry for children vigorously, and as a taster for the material to come, we discussed his declaration that:

> What is learnt in Verse is longer retained in Memory, and sooner recollected ... There is something so amusing and entertaining in Rhymes and Metre, that will incline Children to make this part of their Business a Diversion ... This will be a constant Furniture, for the Minds of Children, that they may have something to think about when alone. (1715:144-6)

Because poetry was perceived as often originating in strong feeling, pupils agreed on the whole that it had something to say, that it 'taught' you something. However, they added, 'We think that poets write poems for personal reasons and not to be taught in classrooms.' They also uniformly agreed, 'What is the point in a poem unless it is to be enjoyed?' They also posed a question that became a common refrain throughout the two days: why 'children'? What in Watts' argument, they demanded, only applied to children?

26

Nothing seemed to rankle with this group more than the suggestion that any literature or learning was for children only.

This took us neatly to our exploration of early exponents of children's verse and questions such as: 'What view of children and of childhood do the poets seem to have?' and 'What tone do the poets adopt?' 'Symon's Lesson of Wisdom for all Manner of Children' (c1500) provoked a strong reaction:

Child, climb not over house nor wall
For no fruit nor birds nor ball.
Child, over men's houses no stones fling
Nor at glass windows no stones sling ...
Child, keep thy book, cap and gloves
And all things that thee behoves.

They're basically saying that children are inferior ... just stupid little creatures to be disciplined.

Believe in God and do well in your schoolwork and you'll do well. It's quite scary. Be thankful!

Basically, they just don't like children.

As adults, we make concessions for the moral and religious sentiments that produced these texts. The young people made allowances too, but were firm on the impossibility of a poet who didn't trust children being able to write enjoyable poems.

They're teaching children how to be good. They think children are naturally bad, and need help.

They're not really for children. They're for the adults who'll sit and read them to children.

It was agreed, however, that these poems contained some elements of children's experience. I asked the pupils, therefore, to see if they could deduce from the texts what children typically got up to in the period, which was, of course, what adults frequently didn't want them to do!

So far I've got, little boys used to catch snakes, play with whipping tops, lie through their teeth ...

Brothers and sisters used to fight ... .They were renowned for quarrelling with their siblings. They were renowned for having poor table manners.

They were like Dennis the Menace characters.

This activity helped us to appreciate that children's lives were represented in the poems they had read, but also to realise this in itself wasn't enough to make it *good* children's poetry. Subject matter alone could not be the touchstone of what constituted successful children's verse, when the didactic motivation or manner of the authors alienated the implied audience.

After this, we moved on to the early nineteenth century, featuring poems from a range of authors including Sara Coleridge, Charles and Mary Lamb and the Taylor sisters. Ann Taylor's 'To a Little Girl That Has Told a Lie' (1804) concludes:

> Yes, GOD has made your duty clear,
> By every blush, by every fear;
> And conscience, like an angel kind,
> Keeps watch to bring it to your mind:
> Its friendly warnings ever heed,
> And neither tell a lie nor need.

Although the poems in this selection were often still didactic and/or religious, the pupils definitely preferred them and noticed a small, inconsistent, yet significant change in mood in terms of their constructions of childhood. Several children wondered perceptively whether it was as a result of the authors being less concerned with hammering home the moral that they were more able to put effort into making the poems entertaining. The response to Sara Coleridge's 'Mama's Advice to Herbert' was perhaps typical. 'When you see the title, you think 'uurgh,' but it's nice.' Twenty-first century children have a very different view of their place in the scheme of things and their relationship to adults. But some responses were still surprisingly positive.

> It seems to me they're more giving advice than actually telling. And I think they're a lot more for children.

The word 'advice' was seen as significant: advice offered a choice, whereas Bunyan and Watts simply ordered. It also implied a more respectful author, and therefore one who could be respected, in turn.

> They're still getting across their opinions and beliefs, but a bit more gently and a bit more realistically.

'Gently' and 'realistically': these two words embrace the key feelings expressed by the pupils. They didn't want rules in matters of thought and morality, even though they recognised the need for adult intervention and guidance. They wanted gentle and realistic parental or quasi-parental support. The milder blend of advice and child-centred activity in the setting of family life which many of these poems implied was therefore more attractive to them than the former offerings:

> I think they're sort of discovering them [child readers] on a new level. It's like they're looking at them more equally, from their own height, not looking down on them. They're discovering their own opinions and maybe taking into account their feelings and things like that.

The Romanticism which was transforming the best poetry for adults can barely be seen reflected in the poems we studied in this session, but the Taylors' Preface to *Original Poems for Infant Minds* (1804) suggests that the decline of Puritanism had enabled a more child-centred approach to emerge and that a study of children's 'capacities, habits, and wants' had informed the poets' work. The Taylors were hardly disciples of Rousseau, but they did claim to have a 'hearty affection for that interesting little race, the race of children' (1804: Preface). Instead of towering over little children, wagging a warning finger, adults were just beginning to crouch down and say to themselves, *I wonder what the world looks like from down here?*

With that new position in mind, how would pupils respond to Stevenson? The next session introduced the children to a selection of poems from *A Child's Garden of Verses*, and asked them to consider the voice of the author, the implicit view of childhood, and the moral dimension of the poems. Given that brief, would the pupils recognise for themselves the fresh emphasis on play, the celebration of imagination, or the credible use of a more child-centred voice?

> Here is Mount Clear, Mount Rusty-Nail,
>   Mount Eagle and Mount High; –
> The mice that in these mountains dwell,
>   No happier are than I!
>
> O what a joy to clamber there,
>   O what a place for play,
> With the sweet, the dim, the dusty air,
>   The happy hills of hay!

'The Hayloft' is a good example of a poem that pupils appreciated and was the favourite of many:

> It makes us think of summer days and memories.
>
> It's from the kid's point of view.

The last verse ends the poem on a happy note. With 'joy' and 'play' and 'sweet' and 'happy.'

They use their imagination to create their own toys out of rusty nails and stuff.

Discussion of this poem also took us back to the ideas we had had at the beginning about what childhood was. 'I think you are a child,' said one, 'if you think in your heart that you are'. The same pupil characterised herself as 'a child on a journey to becoming an adult,' and said that 'the features of a good poem are ones that make you think and that provoke feelings and memories,' citing 'The Hayloft' and 'Summer Sun' as examples of this in action.

The few poems in my selection from Stevenson that were more didactic and less child-centred were fittingly castigated, particularly 'Whole Duty of Children', which one group confidently and rather cheekily scribbled right through in their copy, writing 'red herring' – complete with fish drawing – next to it. 'Good and Bad Children' was dismissed simply with 'Don't like it!': it was considered 'absurd' to expect children to 'play in the grass but not get dirty' or for 'babies not to cry'. But even these poems were seen as preferable to the earlier texts, as they discussed 'rewards about behaviour, not threats,' and showed a child's perspective: the poem is 'not about how adults think, but [is] still written by them.'

There was criticism too of the apparent privilege that Stevenson's child appeared to enjoy. 'The fact that he has a nurse demonstrates that he is rich.' But even in such poems, Stevenson still compared well with his predecessors, since 'these poems are focused on cheering the children up and keeping them happy, rather than talking about them being bad and the consequences.'

'Picture-books in Winter', for example, 'takes into account what kids like'. It's 'from the kid's point of view', has 'a lively beginning' and 'a good use of rhyme,' celebrates 'the joys of childhood', and provides a kind of moral at the end that says, in effect, 'enjoy your childhood':

> How am I to sing your praise,
> Happy chimney-corner days,
> Sitting safe in nursery nooks,
> Reading picture story-books?

When Stevenson admitted in a letter to a reviewer that his own childhood was 'in reality a very painful experience' but averred that it was 'of its pleasures that our common poems should be formed', he was striking the happy chord that resonated in my pupils in this session (quoted in Rollin, 2002:74). To them, Stevenson 'sounds as if he enjoyed' childhood, rather than coming across as distrustful of it: his memories are 'sentimental,' of 'unforgotten times,' and are always 'celebrating.' But again and again, it is the sense that Stevenson's verse speaks from a child-high view of the world that was re-iterated as the winning characteristic of his verse. It 'uses the right language for kids ... looking back on childhood but not looking down.'

The fact that in 'My Kingdom' he 'loves to be little and hates to be big' shows what side he is on, so to speak. The key words were 'imagination,' 'play,' 'curious,' and 'reality'. 'Reality' meant 'what kids actually do – in everyday life,' like making sandcastles and playing on swings and hurting their knees. Signi-ficantly, despite Stevenson's positive depiction of childhood, 'reality' also meant that childhood was *not* to be idealised. Children are 'not all happy to be children all the time'; and despite his statement above, it was *because* Stevenson depicted an 'imperfect childhood, but not a bad one', that he won them over.

In setting up this small project, what I had really wanted to know was whether young people could tackle the question, 'What is children's poetry?' The answer was emphatically 'Yes'. As one pupil aptly put it:

> Children's poetry is defined as things which they think the children will under-stand and relate to and enjoy. [But] it depends on their definition of 'children' a lot, because the tone and attitude of their poems all comes down to how they see the children.

The pupils concluded that poetry from a child's point of view tended to be more successful in its appeal to them than other kinds, but while children's verse might be expected to cover certain areas of experience, no topic or sub-ject matter was in itself 'for children' or 'not for children'. It was neither the form nor the content that ultimately mattered to them, but the *intent*: what really mattered was that the poet respected them as children.

Although certain language use could perhaps exclude younger readers, 'diffi-culty' was not otherwise of particular relevance to pupils' judgement of a poem's success for children. 'Simply to know who you are writing for should be enough to know what you should write about,' one pupil confidently asserted. Another girl wrote that the best outcome for her was a practical one: 'I have a clear idea now of what to look for in a children's poem, which gives me a head-start in writing my own. You just need to know who you are writing for and what they are interested in'.

Ultimately, the answer to the question: 'What is Children's Poetry?' hinges on the constructions of childhood employed by both the authors and the readers, and since my research found these to be almost as varied as the pupils I engaged with, there can perhaps never be a definitive answer. 'What is a child?' one pupil repeated disarmingly. 'This is a CRAP question, because who can define a child? I think that even a thirty-year-old can still be a child at heart. He has just grown bigger.'

> We stop being a child at no definite age. Everyone is still partly a child.

> I am not an adult, but I am no longer a child. I remember being a child.

Children's poetry has to be enjoyed and appreciated by children to be classed as successful in its ambition, but that does not mean that adults are excluded from the fun, as one of the pupils reminded me:

> Parts of us are young and playful and like five year olds, but other bits are much more grown up, so we need poems for the different parts of us.

That we all 'need poems for the different parts of us' was what these two days taught me most of all. And that, together, with a renewed respect for the judgement, acuity, wit, and curiosity of young people, is what I hope others might take away from this chapter.

Works Cited

Rollin, L (2002) A Child's Garden: Toward a Neurological Aesthetic of Children's Literature, *Children's Literature Association Quarterly*, Volume 27, Number 2

Stevenson, RL (1885) *A Child's Garden of Verses*. London: Longman and Green

Taylor, A and J (1804) *Original Poems for Infant Minds*. London: Darton

Watts, I (1715) *Preface to Divine Songs Attempted in Easy Language for the Use of Children*. http://www.gutenberg.org/etext/13439, accessed January 2010.

4

Ted Hughes and the 'Old Age of Childhood'

Lissa Paul

A standard trope about the enduring appeal of children's literature is that it is prophetic for children looking forward and nostalgic for adults looking back. Childhood, however, isn't like that: prophecy and nostalgia switch places. Parents project charmed childhoods for their children – as do the spell-casting, gift-bestowing good fairies in *Sleeping Beauty* – while grown-up children reflect on what they believe to be their messed-up childhoods, and so tell tales for psychotherapists. The irony is that the childhoods parents imagine for their children are unlikely to be the ones their children remember. Philip Larkin's too-frequently quoted observation from 'This Be the Verse' crystallises the hard-line view that 'They fuck you up your mum and dad/They may not mean to but they do' (1974:30).

In the fall of 2008, *The Times* asked sixteen authors, including former Children's Laureates, Anne Fine and Michael Morpurgo, to respond to Larkin's 'cynical view of families'. Roger McGough even wrote a rebuttal to Larkin in verse. But it was a remark by Frieda Hughes, born in 1960, author, artist and daughter of Ted Hughes and Sylvia Plath that caused me to freeze. Frieda says she was just 'nine-and-a-half' when she made a conscious decision not to have any children of her own ('Was Larkin Right?' *The Times*, 2008:1-3). Although her comment has the feel of a painfully overexposed photograph, it instantly brought to mind a letter Ted Hughes had written to his brother Gerald in Australia fifty years earlier, around Christmas 1958 – so well before Frieda had even been conceived. Hughes was writing from Boston, where he and Plath had been living and working. They were on the cusp of turning themselves into full-time professional writers: 'When we have children', Hughes writes, 'I want them to be rooted in a life with meaning, where one thing is connected with another, where the seasons, birth and death are real...' Hughes was just twenty-eight. The letter, now in the Hughes archive at Emory University in Atlanta, continues with optimistic projections of a future as a professional author and as a parent: 'You make your own life', says Hughes with the conviction of a young man with a bright future ahead of him, 'and you make your children's with it.'

Hughes' vision of a childhood 'rooted in a life with meaning' seems to speak equally to his sense of what children's poetry could be like. So when I stumbled on a phrase Hughes had apparently cut from a draft of his poem, 'Green Wolf', while working in the manuscript archive at the British Library, I felt I'd found an encrypted message for unlocking my own narrative about children's poetry. 'Plucks me out of the old age of childhood', the fragment begins, 'Because the star and man's book and women's blood are/one' (BL Additional Manuscript 53784). The phrase 'old age of childhood' seemed to implode with inherent contradictions, while it simultaneously held culture – 'man's book' – genetic transmission – 'women's blood' – and cosmic time – 'the star' – suspended, weightless, in perfect tension. That's when Hughes became my guide, as I navigated my keynote talk for the conference (on which this chapter is based). There he was, at every turn, commenting, offering a needed observation or critique, providing exactly the right lens for articulating what the 'old age of childhood' might mean. One of Hughes' poems, 'That Morning', became the perfect imaginative expression of the phrase, and an antidote to Larkin's view. The narrator and a companion stand in an Alaskan river, in 'pollen light', and in 'a mauve light of drifted lupins', watching two gold bears eating pierced salmon off their talons. Although the men are not named, Nicholas Hughes, Ted's son, who was a marine biologist working in Alaska, often fished there with his father. At the end of the poem, Hughes pulls back, as in a long shot at the end of a film, and directs the reader's gaze at the two men standing 'waist-deep in wild salmon swaying massed/As from the hand of God'. It is Ted Hughes I hear narrating the voiceover:

> So we found the end of our journey.
>
> So we stood, alive in the river of light
> Among the creatures of light, creatures of light. (2003:664)

Behind and beneath the golden 'pollen light', the 'mauve light of drifted lupins' and 'the creatures of light', standing in 'the river of light', there is an unspoken allusion to Wordsworth's 'celestial light' from his famous poem about childhood, 'Intimations of Immortality': 'meadow, grove and stream/ Apprarell'd in celestial light,/the glory and freshness of a dream' (1969:460). Wordsworth's nostalgic view of childhood innocence, the sadness of its loss and the assertion that it needs to be protected and sheltered, has come to define what we know as the Romantic view of childhood; it's the default position. Hughes alters it by having father and son stand together at the 'end of the journey', 'alive in the river of light' where they are forever 'among the creatures of light'. The poem moves beyond the chronological limits and petty concerns of an individual human lifetime, and reaches instead towards the riot of exuberant, renewable life. The same pattern also occurs in *What is the Truth?* (1984), a collection of animal poems framed by a prose narrative in the manner of traditional Buddhist Jataka tales. The book ends with an inclusive celebration of life. 'I am each of these things', says the God character in reference to being, or playing, all the animals in the poems: 'And each of these things is Me. It is. It is. That is the Truth' (p121). Hughes describes *What is the Truth?* as being 'about animals for the infantile'. 'Every bard speaks for a Tribe', he says, and 'mine is the universal infantile, a mighty people' (BL manuscript, Hughes to Baskin, 1983). And as I looked back into the kaleidoscope of assembled fragments of poems and comments I'd collected, 'the old age of childhood' made sudden, perfect sense.

I've taken to heart Ted Hughes' affectionate embrace of the potential audience for children's verse as a 'universal infantile', though truths about poetry and childhood are as multiple and varied and as unstable as the truths about the animals in *What is the Truth?* Children's verse is made up of sacred and profane truths; it is intimate and domestic as well as nationalistic and stirring. Historically, children's poetry moves from Rationalism to Romanticism, as FJ Harvey Darton has it in *Children's Books in England*, and from the garden to the street as Morag Styles (1998) has it in the memorable title of her book. Verse for children is didactic and it is emotional, rural and pastoral, urban and urchin, high art and popular, standard English and dialect. It is addressed to children, and it is voiced by children. It can be, as Richard Flynn fears, 'goofy, sentimental or recycled from days of yore' (2009:76), or it can bed the ear, as Seamus Heaney says in *Preoccupations*. It promotes particular ideological agendas – and resists them. There is pragmatic instructive poetry and poetry that insists on children who are at one with the natural world. There is poetry that carries cultural codes of literary language, makes proverbial wisdom memorable, and instills national pride or faith in the divine. There is poetry transmitted from adults to children, and there is poetry transmitted from child to child. Adult to child poetry often revels in the wonder and magic of children and communicates love for those children. Child to child poetry tends to hold adults up as objects of ridicule or scorn. All are truths about poetry, but in arguing for any one truth, others are forgotten. So instead of arguing for any particular truth, I'm arguing for truth held in body memory, in the genetically coded memories in a strand of DNA – and in the memory of the library. As this chapter is a celebration of the *Poetry and Childhood* exhibition in London at the British Library (2009), it is fitting that so many truths about childhood and poetry live inside its walls.

The British Library's slogan, 'The World's Knowledge', is a rhythmically uplifting phrase – metrically an antispast (an iamb followed by a trochee) – which has, to adapt Hughes' words, 'root[ed] itself directly in the nerves of [my] ear'. The fact that I remember and respond to the slogan testifies to its aptness. Hughes appreciated the value of memorable lines. In his introduction to *By Heart: 101 Poems to Remember*, he writes about submitting an entry to an advertising slogan contest for Heinz beans in 1959, and losing to the winner- Beanz Meanz Heinz – which he then praises for its commercial catchiness (1997:xiv). For poets, memorable verse, marked or unmarked as being for children, is tossed from hand to hand, line to line, heart to heart, breath to breath, and from generation to generation: the very embodiment of 'the old age of childhood'. It is a 'singing school' to use WB Yeats' phrase from 'Sailing to Byzantium' (first published in 1928):

> An aged man is but a paltry thing,
> A tattered coat upon a stick, unless
> Soul clap its hands and sing, and louder sing
> For every tatter in its mortal dress,
> Nor is there singing school but studying
> Monuments of its own magnificence. (1996:193)

As Yeats suggests, poets communicate in songs that are 'Of what is past, or passing, or to come'. With that in mind, here is one small example of the process, via 'The Ceremonial Band' by the British poet, James Reeves:

> The Old King of Dorchester,
> He had a little Orchestra,
> And never did you hear such a ceremonial band.
> > 'Tootle-too', said the flute.
> > 'Deed-a-reedle', said the fiddle.
> For the fiddle and the flutes
> Are the finest in the land. (1973:68)

The poem lends itself to being performed in a choral setting, with groups of children playing and singing the parts of the instruments. But attend a little more closely to the flute, and the sound of one poet speaking to another across generations becomes audible. 'Tootle-too said the flute', subtly echoes the same voice in William Blake's 'Spring' from *Songs of Experience* (1789):

Sound the flute!
Now it's mute.
Bird's delight
Day and night.

'Said the flute' in 'Ceremonial Band' is a tribute to Blake's 'Sound the flute!', and an example of the endurance of the 'old age of childhood'. Reeves picks up an amphimacer, rhythmically marked as a weak beat dropped between two strong ones. The metrical link between Blake and Reeves is just one small example of how a poetic trait moves from generation to generation. Let me offer another, this time through a maternal line, but one that speaks to the 'star and man's book and women's blood' of the Hughes fragment.

The title of the British Library exhibition which inspired this essay, 'Twinkle Twinkle Little Bat', itself demonstrates a reproductive link between generations of poets. The line is, after all, Lewis Carroll's naughty child of Jane Taylor's 'The Star', from *Rhymes for the Nursery* (1806), the volume Jane published with her sister Ann as a sequel to their hugely successful *Original Poems for Infant Minds*, published two years earlier. Even though *Original Poems* announces its kinship with the early Romantic preference for originality over mimesis, both Taylor volumes are keyed to what is best described as *maternal* verse. A curious twenty-first century coincidence suggests that the Taylor sisters might even be contenders as founding mothers of children's verse.

A few months prior to the British Library exhibition, Michael Joseph, Rare Books Librarian at Rutgers University, also mounted an exhibition on the history of children's poetry, 'My Infant Head', which is a line from Ann Taylor's 'My Mother', the hit single from *Original Poems for Infant Minds*. Though the phrase 'my infant head' has long since passed its best-before date in popular culture, it had a very good run – at least sixty years according to Darton.

The fact that two rare book libraries on opposite sides of the Atlantic simultaneously decided to mount exhibitions on children's poetry in the same 2008-2009 academic year, each keyed, albeit glancingly, to a two-hundred year old poem by a Taylor sister, seems a marvellous coincidence. What's also interesting is that though the Taylor sisters, along with Lucy Aikin and her 1801 *Poetry for Children*, are generally mentioned at the dawn of published poetry for children, they are not given first-mother status in the same way as, say, Isaac Watts and John Bunyan are given first-father status. The twenty-first century British and American exhibitions were both lovingly curated to construct distinct maternal lines in the chronology of children's verse.

Styles literally 'open[ed] up' the nursery door of women's poetry for children, first in her 1990 *Signal* essay, 'Lost from the Nursery', then later in *Opening the Nursery Door*. In a discussion of Christina Rossetti's *Sing-Song*, Styles observes that 'the mother's eyes are always on the baby' in the verse (1998:148). In conversation, just prior to the opening of the British Library exhibition, Styles commented again on the lovingly held gaze between mother and child in Rossetti's work but this time with reference to the delicate pencil and red crayon drawings in the bound handwritten and illustrated original of *Sing-Song*.

In *Sing-Song* (1872), there is frequently an entwined double address, something flickering between mother and child. Is Rossetti as author taking the position of a mother writing about her child? Or is Rossetti remembering herself as child and projecting the mother? Syntactically, the following lines appear to be spoken by a mother to her child:

> You are my one, and I have not another,
> Sleep soft, my darling, my trouble and treasure
> Sleep warm and soft in the arms of your mother,
> Dreaming of pretty things, dreaming of pleasure.

The feeling conveyed is both of the child 'warm and soft', who is 'Dreaming of pretty things', and of the mother holding the child and projecting the warmth and peacefulness she wishes for her child. It probably doesn't matter whether Rossetti casts herself as mother, child, or both, as the symbiotic mother/child relationship is the tender thing, exemplifying, as Nancy Chodorow says, the 'reproduction of mothering' (2007:27). Rossetti also constructs what feminist critic Sara Ruddick (1989) calls 'maternal thinking': something which pragmatically mediates between intimate, protected domestic space and the scrum of open public space; between cerebral life and the practical world of work and money.

The idea that children's verse could move between domestic prattle and commercial poetry arose in the late eighteenth century, though the transition phase – from handmade, home-made verses to mass-produced purchased ones – is difficult to trace. One extant missing link is however available in Jane Johnson's private nursery library of reading games, cards and verses that she made for her own children in the mid-eighteenth century. Her domestic instructional playthings anticipate the public, published teaching materials of Anna Barbauld, Lucy Aikin, Ann and Jane Taylor and Sara Coleridge a few decades later.

In an illustrated card from set 21, number 19 of Jane Johnson's Nursery Library (Lilly Library, University of Indiana), Johnson portrays a working girl:

> This girl to get money does dance on a rope
> She will sure have good luck if her neck is not broke
> Quite hard is her fortune, her fate most unkind
> If no way for a living but this she can find.

The well-observed vignette is at once a prediction and a reflection, a caution and a clarification on the delicate balance between life and livelihood, even though Johnson's own children were of a class that would have made it unlikely for them to even imagine tightrope-walker as a career choice. So the image itself stands as metaphor not lesson, as an aspect of maternal thinking exemplified by mothers attending to the 'preservation, growth and acceptability' of their children 'in a particular social world' (Ruddick, 1989:17).

Although Jane's materials for teaching children to be literate belong to the handmade, homemade sphere of maternal teaching, Anna Barbauld, just a generation or so later, provides the perfect model for graceful accommodation of both public commercial educational materials and private domestic education. Mothers in the newly forming middle classes could take her commercial lessons and adapt them as lessons with their own children. Maternal pragmatism is evident in Barbauld's 1781 *Hymns in Prose* – distinctly poetic in tone, imagery and rhythm. In the Preface she explains that the hymns are 'to impress devotional feelings as early as possible on the infant mind', and to do so:

> by connecting religion with a variety of sensible objects, with all that he sees, hears, all that affects his young mind with wonder or delight; and thus by deep, strong, and permanent associations to lay the best foundation for practical devotion in future life. (1820:v).

To my ear, Barbauld's lines echo forward a couple of centuries into Hughes' words in *Poetry in the Making*, where he writes about connecting the inner world of emotion with the outer world of experience, about keeping 'your eyes, your ears, your nose, your taste, your touch, your whole being on the thing you are turning into words' (1994:13). Another of the featured texts in the British Library exhibition, *Pretty Lessons* (1834), by Samuel Taylor Coleridge's daughter Sara, provides a further example. Her son Herbert is glimpsed doing ordinary things children do, such as pouting when he is supposed to be going out for a walk, or refusing to go to sleep. He is good and bad, loving and recalcitrant, laughing, playing, fighting, resisting, and learning; all the while negotiating intimately with his mother as she prepares him to live his life.

The British Library copy of *Pretty Lessons* is also interesting in that besides Sara's Herbert, another child reader is there. A boy named Arthur owned that particular copy and he passed it on to his younger brother, Herbert. The inscription reads 'to Herbert Baron from his affectionate brother Arthur'. In the endearing manner of such inscriptions, Arthur couldn't get the whole word on the line, so 'affectionate' is divided into 'affection' on one line with 'ate' on the next. Herbert revels in the pleasure of owning a book about himself, so re-inscribes himself first on the contents page, then writes 'Herbert Baron' on the dedication page, then again on the first poem; the multiple re-inscriptions creating additional layers of intersection between text and reader.

Before leaving Herbert and Sara Coleridge, this is a good place to break briefly from the long view of childhood and children's verse and its genetically-coded similarities across generations, and shift briefly to the shorter view measured in chronological time. For the nineteenth-century British child, the colonial empire was his to command. So Sara Coleridge writes confidently in 'Good Things Come from Distant Places':

> Tea is brought from China
> Rice from Carolina
> India and Italy
> Countries far beyond the sea
>
> Coffee comes from Mocha
> Wholesome Tapioca
> Is from the West Indies brought
> Where the Humming Birds are caught. (1834)

That world was a gigantic colonial cookie jar filled with sugar and spice and everything nice, from which the colonisers, like greedy children, grabbed and gobbled everything in sight. The turn to the twenty-first century finds the colonised reclaiming both goods and words, as in Pamela Mordecai's 'Lament of an Arawak Child' from *A Caribbean Dozen*:

40

Once I played with the hummingbirds
and sang songs to the sea
I told my secrets to the waves
and they told theirs to me

Now there are no more hummingbirds
the sea's songs are all sad
for strange men came and took this land
and plundered all we had. (1994:70)

Although the two centuries separating Coleridge from Mordecai reveal a change from exploiter of resources to guardian, the intersection between the private domestic world and the public commercial world remains constant.

Despite shifts in implicit ideological and cultural assumptions from generation to generation, mediating between what poets write and what children read remains a delicate minefield of conflicting interests. In the Hughes archive at Emory, there is a series of notes in which Hughes tries repeatedly to negotiate between parents who want to 'protect children from the harsh and ugly traits of life', authors who want to communicate, and publishers who want something that will entice parents to purchase. 'The writer who writes poems for children has ... a feeling that something will trigger the response in some of them somewhere' (Emory 122, 7 undated). There is no way to guarantee the nature of a reader's response. In a December 1984 letter to Leonard Baskin, Hughes describes a 'gloomy rat-faced teacher' who accused him of 'reading horrible sadistic, ugly poems to children'. Hughes says that he 'just stared at her and thought how sick she looked', but that's as far, he says, as he got in self-defence.

A carefully preserved draft of *Nessie the Mannerless Monster* (1963) (BL archive) speaks to the conflicted interests of writer and publisher. The *Teacher's World* dustjacket blurb in the published version focuses on its 'lolloping verse', but the manuscript drafts tell a darker story, one that seems to prefigure the characters of the Iron Man and the Space-Bat-Angel-Dragon, creatures blatantly monstrous but rendered invisible by their impossibility. One lost line is about Nessie as a 'rejected monster, a monster without protection' (BL manuscript 53784).

The Nessie in the draft seems closer to the Nessie Hughes discusses in a 1961 *New Statesman* review of a documentary book about Loch Ness monster sightings. 'Call a thing monster', says Hughes, 'and it disappears, submerging into a dream world among angels and black gods, a region where the simplest objects shed their reliable attributes and turn into supernaturally-endowed subjects not to be classified or even believed. Brain-warpers to be laughed out' (1961:112). Various incarnations of Nessie's descendents survive in Hughes' *The Iron Man* and in many of his other verses for children.

'Every new child,' says Hughes optimistically in *Winter Pollen*, 'is nature's chance to correct culture's error' (1976/1994:149). Ted Hughes remained faithful to the regenerative power of universal infantile. 'Let those infant feet pound through the universe,' he says at the end of one of his uncollected poems (2003:276). Infant eyes could also be counted on to re-new the world, as could infant ears and infant voices, as in 'Full Moon and Little Frieda' where Hughes immortalises his young daughter. It's dusk, the cows are coming home and the moon is rising. Little Frieda 'listening./A spider's web, tense for the dew's touch,' experiences the power of language to renew:

> 'Moon!' you cry suddenly, 'Moon! Moon!'
> The moon has stepped back like an artist gazing amazed at a work
> That points at him amazed. (2003:183)

But where are those childhoods resurrected? They're in, as Joseph T Thomas (2007) says, 'poetry's playground' of children's games. In *Children's Games in Street and Playground*, Iona and Peter Opie define 'death and-resurrection' games (1970:248), which do seem to ensure the constant renewal of childhood and children's verse. *Dusty Bluebells* is the title – taken from a playground game – of a BBC documentary, shot during the volatile 1970s in Northern Ireland. Against the harsh grayness of the working-class landscape and the visible presence of armed soldiers, the children play and sing resurrection songs, such as 'Wallflower, wallflower, growing up so high/All the little children are all going to die' and 'Poor Toby is Dead and he lies in his grave/lies in his grave, lies in his grave'. Or move to the racially segregated American South in the 1930s, when folklorist John Lomax collected what he called 'Negro' children singing a haunting version of 'Little Sally Walker, sitting in a saucer/Rise Sally, rise' (Opie, 1970:169). And if you know where to look, it is possible to see twenty-first-century children cheerfully re-creating other childhoods-and correcting culture's error. In 2009 I clicked on YouTube and found young American teenagers dressing up and filming themselves singing and dancing an upbeat variant on 'Little Sally Walker'. In their version the child who is *it* is 'walking down the street' inside a ring of other children. She stops in front of one of the children in the ring, performs a little dance move and sings:

Hey girl, hey girl
Do your thing and switch
Hey girl, hey girl
Do your thing and switch.

The selected child mimics the move and the two switch places. The dancer is born again. A new childhood springs up, testifying against repression, against death, against the limitations of chronological childhood. Who knew YouTube would turn out to be both an anthropologist's playground and poetry's playground, where every new child, is, indeed, correcting culture's error?

Acknowledgements

Lissa Paul gratefully acknowledges permission from Carol Hughes, literary executor of the Ted Hughes Estate, for the use of manuscript material from: the Ted Hughes Archive in the Manuscript Collection of the British Library; and the Ted Hughes Papers from the Manuscript, Archives, and Rare Book Library of Emory University. Pamela Mordecai is also gratefully acknowledged for permission to use lines from her poem, 'Lament of an Arawak Child'. With thanks to Claas Kazzer for helpful suggestions.

Works Cited

Arzipe, E, Styles, M and Brice Heath, S (2006) *Reading Lessons from the Eighteenth Century: Mothers, Children and Texts.* Lichfield, Staffordshire: Pied Piper

Barbauld, A (1820) *Hymns in Prose for Children.* London: Joseph Johnson

Chodorow, N (2007) Early Psychological Development: Psychoanalysis and the Sociology of Gender. In A O'Reilly (ed) *Maternal Theory: Essential Readings.* Toronto: Demeter Press

Coleridge, S (1834) *Pretty Lessons in Verse for Good Children.* London: John W Parker

Dinsdale, T. Review of Loch Ness Monster. *The New Statesman* (2 June 1961)

Erdman, D (ed) (1965) *The Poetry and Prose of William Blake.* New York: Doubleday

Finnerean, R (ed) (1996) *The Collected Poems of WB Yeats.* New York: Scribner

Flynn, R (2010) The Fear of Poetry. In M O Grenby and Andrea Immel (eds) *Cambridge Companion to Children's Literature.* Cambridge: Cambridge University Press

Hammond, D (Director) (1971) *Dusty Bluebells.* BBC Northern Ireland

Harvey Darton, FJ (1982) *Children's Books in England: Five Centuries of Social Life.* B Alderson (ed) Cambridge: Cambridge University Press

Hutchinson, T (ed) (1969) *The Poetical Works of William Wordsworth.* Oxford: Oxford University Press

Heaney, S (1980) *Preoccupations.* London: Faber

Hilton, M, Styles, M, Watson, V (eds) (1997) *Opening the Nursery Door: Reading, Writing and Childhood 1600-1900.* London: Routledge

Hughes, T (2003) *Collected Poems.* P Keegan (ed) New York: Farrar, Straus and Giroux

Hughes, T (ed) (1997) *By Heart: 101 Poems to Remember.* London: Faber

Hughes, T (1994) *Winter Pollen: Occasional Prose.* W Scammell (ed) London: Faber

Hughes, T (1984) *What is the Truth?: A Farmyard Fable for the Young.* London: Faber

Hughes, T (1967) *Poetry in the Making*. London: Faber

Hughes, T (1964) *Nessie the Mannerless Monster*. London: Faber

Hughes, T (1961) 'Five Ton Phantom' Review of Loch New Monster by Tim Dinsdale. *New Stateseman*. 2 June 1961: 112.

Hughes, T *Letter to Leonard Baskin*. 1983. British Library Manuscripts

Hughes, T *Letter to Gerald Hughes*. Christmas 1958. Hughes archive, Emory University, Atlanta, Georgia. Box 854, Letters to Gerald Hughes. Box, 2, folder 1. And undated manuscripts. 'Writing for Children is a Curious Occupation'. Box 122 folders 6 and 7.

Hughes, T *British Library Additional Manuscript 53784*, fragment of 'Green Wolf' and manuscript drafts of Nessie the Mannerless Monster.

Johnson, J (Jane Johnson Manuscript Library) Lilly Library, Indiana University Library, Bloomington Indiana

Larkin, P (1974) *High Windows*. London: Faber

Little Sally Walker, Sitting in a Saucer. Library of Congress. Folklife Center. John Lomax recording of 'Negro' Children singing 'Little Sally Walker; 1934. AFS88a2

Little Sally Walker. Game. Identified as Dance Team 18 March 2008. http://www.youtube.com/watch?v=PAY03o4ba18

Mordecai, P (1994) *A Caribbean Dozen: Poems from Caribbean Poets*. Boston: Candlewick

Opie, I, Opie, P (1970) *Children's Games in Street and Playground*. Oxford: Oxford University Press

Reeves, J (1973) *Complete Poems for Children*. London: Heinemann

Rossetti, C (2005) Sing-Song: A Nursery Rhyme Book. In *Norton Anthology of Children's Literature*. New York: Norton

Ruddick, S (1989) *Maternal Thinking: Toward a Politics of Peace*. New York: Ballantyne

Styles, M (1998) *From the Garden to the Street: 300 years of Poetry for Children*. London: Cassell

Styles, M (1990) Lost from the Nursery: Women Writing Poetry for Children 1800-1850. *Signal* 63 p177-205

Taylor, A, Taylor, J (1804) *Original Poems for Infant Minds*. London: Darton and Harvey

Taylor, A, Taylor, J (1806) *Rhymes for the Nursery*. London: Darton and Harvey

Thomas, J T (2007) *Poetry's Playground: The Culture of Contemporary American Children's Poetry*. Detroit: Wayne State University Press

'Was Larkin right to blame the mums and dads?' *The Times* 2 [London]: 10 October 2008

5

'Childish Toys' for 'Boys with Beards': John Bunyan's *A Book for Boys and Girls*

Pat Pinsent

John Bunyan's *A Book for Boys and Girls or Country Rhimes for Children* (1686), also known as *Divine Emblems*, is widely acknowledged to be historically significant as one of the earliest books of poetry explicitly addressed to young readers. Yet relatively seldom does it seem to have been valued as a work in its own right. Instead it is judged to lack intrinsic poetic qualities, though its critics sometimes admit that it was appreciated in its own period. Graham Midgley, for instance, cites a number of negative judgments, of which perhaps the strongest is GH Leonard's indictment of its 'astonishing doggerel, clumsy phrases and harsh inversion,' despite its occasional 'exquisite lines' (1980:xxvi). General literary reference books, such as *The Cambridge Guide to Literature in English*, often omit any reference to Bunyan's poetry. Their counterparts concerning children's literature tend to be some- what patronising: Humphrey Carpenter and Mari Prichard state: 'Although his verse now seems strained, it was fresh and original for its time' (1984:70), while Michael Lockwood claims that 'The rhyme and metre, as well as the comparisons, are sometimes rather forced' (in Watson, 2001:176). My inten- tion in this chapter is to suggest that Bunyan's poetry has qualities beyond its undoubted historical significance, qualities which relate to the serious wit which Bunyan has in common with many of his seventeenth-century pre- decessors.

The first edition of Bunyan's book consists of 74 poems varying between four lines and three pages. Material specifically addressed to children includes items frequently found in hornbooks, such as 'An help to Chil-dren [*sic*] to learn and read Eng-lish,' and 'To learn Children to know Figures, and Numeral Letters,' plus simplified versions of the commandments and the Lord's Prayer. Although Seth Lerer describes the collection as 'a blend of primer exercise and folk poems' (2008:93), to regard it as appealing only to children and those with little education would be a mistake. The initial poem, 'To the Reader' (from which I draw my title), together with some of the later items, such as the extensive and allusive 'Of the Spouse of Christ' (LVIII), seem to be addressed to a more sophisticated audience.

Some of Bunyan's themes are indeed homely and natural: they include such subjects as the swallow, the sinner and the spider, the mole, the cuckoo, the frog, the cackling of a hen, a stinking breath, fly-blown meat, and 'Of physick' – which he says works by vomit, urine, sweat or stool. However, to regard the subject matter as 'low' is to disregard the fact that during the latter half of the seventeenth century there had been a change in standards of poetic decorum from those which existed earlier in the period, a change which minor writers such as Bunyan were slow to embrace. Work like his gains from being seen in the context of literature which preceded it by a few years rather than of exactly contemporary poetry. For instance, John Donne's 'The Flea,' in which the insect is used to illustrate the relationship between two lovers, serves as a better parallel to Bunyan's work than does the more decorous imagery of John Dryden. Other examples of what in the latter half of the century came to be seen as unsuitable for poetry are to be found in the very popular collection of *Emblems* (1635) by one of Bunyan's predecessors, Francis Quarles; for instance, Emblem IV, 14, 'I sat down under his shadow,' compares a sheep far from the shepherd and beleaguered by flies with the situation of a wandering soul.

By the time that Bunyan's book was published, taste was changing; metaphysical poetry was no longer produced by fashionable writers. This gentrifying process became more marked a few years later, so that it is no surprise to find that the children's poet with whom Bunyan is generally paired, Isaac Watts (*Divine Songs*, 1715), seems to have imbibed the Augustan belief in decorum with nearly as much commitment as his great contemporary, Alexander Pope. In fact, the new standards prevalent at the beginning of the eighteenth century seem in the 1701 edition of Bunyan's book (subtitled *Temporal Things Spiritualised*), thirteen years after the author's death, to have motivated the omission of the more down-to-earth verses. Only 49 of the original 74 emblems appear, those omitted including, as anticipated, verses about stinking breath, flyblows and 'physick', together with some of the pedagogical material. In the 1701 edition there are also a number of textual alterations which, in his Introduction to the facsimile of the 1686 edition, John Brown describes as 'tam[ing] down' and 'weaken[ing]' Bunyan's words (1890: xv).

I like to describe poetry as a serious language game, played by the poet with self-imposed rules, which may relate to form – such as the use of iambic pentameters or the complex rhyme scheme of the sonnet – or to language and imagery. I would suggest that nowhere is the idea of poetry being a game more evident than in poets who in one way or another exploited the emblem tradition. One way of playing this game is to link stanza form and meaning, a fusion which may be made explicit in the actual shape of the poem, as in George Herbert's 'The Altar' and 'Easter Wings', as well as in the extravagances of some of Herbert's imitators such as Mildmay Fane's *Otia Sacra*, 1648. More often, this is done in less explicit ways, as in Herbert's 'The Deniall'. Bunyan lacked the poetic ability to play with metre and rhyme like his greater predecessors, but he seems to have delighted in his self-imposed task of matching everyday objects, familiar to all, with far-fetched moral meanings – an enjoyment perhaps allied to his indulgence in Sunday sport before his conversion.

Bunyan's similes have a good deal in common with the 'metaphysical conceit' defined by Helen Gardner as 'a comparison whose ingenuity is more striking than its justness' (1957:19). Bunyan's work provides many instances of this, for example in 'Upon a Ring of Bells' (pxxix):

> These Bells are like the Powers of my Soul;
> Their Clappers to the Passions of my mind.
> The Ropes by which my Bells are made to tole,
> Are Promises (I by experience find.)
> My body is the Steeple, where they hang.

This extended comparison between the human body and the bell-tower of a church is as notable for the yoking together of 'heterogeneous ideas' as are any of the poems castigated by Dr Johnson in his 1779 'Life of Cowley' (1964: 14). Readers may be reminded that in Bunyan's youth he was apparently an enthusiastic bell-ringer (Brown, 1890:xxiii).

As well as repenting his indulgence in Sunday sport, Bunyan also expressed contrition for his early reading of chivalric romances, and Margaret Spufford (in Hilton, 1997:58) suggests that his writing for children may well have been among the earliest deliberately to attempt to substitute wholesome texts for the 'fanciful histories' he and others had delighted in. Midgley suggests that

Bunyan was influenced by the religious ballads which circulated during the seventeenth century (1980:xxx); like their authors, Bunyan was wise enough to realise that instruction would have little effect unless it was accompanied by some qualities which would make people *want* to read it, while the elaborate games of his comparisons resemble the kind of riddles perennially popular with the young. The early editions of the book relied on the poems to create the images, though the text was accompanied by woodcuts in later editions. In originally being published without illustrations, the book differs from its most popular predecessor, Francis Quarles' *Emblems Divine and Moral* (1635), which has pictures attached to every poem but makes no claim to be addressed specifically to the young.

Rosemary Freeman's classic work, *English Emblem Books* (1970), sees Bunyan as representing the 'end of the tradition' of which Quarles, Wither and Herbert were the most significant English Protestant exponents. Bunyan would un-doubtedly have known the work of these writers, all of whom implicitly envisage an adult audience. As Freeman observes:

> The value of the emblem convention was for him not so much imaginative as practical: the people whom he wished to instruct had read Quarles and had amused themselves with Wither's Lottery [a device for choosing poems]: to the methods of Quarles and Wither then would he turn. Men of letters already despised such devices, but Bunyan's purpose was not 'literary' ... nor were the tastes of his readers cultured or informed. (p207-208)

Like other poets in this tradition, Bunyan generally 'make[s] his poem a meditation on one of the innumerable hieroglyphs [i.e. emblems] in nature [or] art' (Summers in Keast, 1962:216), and it is in this context of 'meditation' that some of his poems can be most profitably read. As Martz observes, 'What Miss Freeman says (p173) of the English Catholic emblem-books will hold also for Wither and Quarles [and, I would suggest, for Bunyan]: 'Their main purpose is the practice of meditation, and to this purpose the emblems are no more than contributory factors' (1962:61). Christopher Hill notes, 'Not the image, but the Word and the Book of Nature are the message' (1988:268), while Matthew Grenby observes that in the Protestant tradition it was impor-tant that the pictures should be taken from the natural world and from ordinary life (2008:34). Other, earlier, Puritan writers also made use of the emblem format, sometimes with far-fetched but everyday comparisons: the anonymous 'BV' in Thomas Jenner's *The Soules Solace* (1626) compares Christ's freeing men [sic] to the water from a pail covering the floor (Pinsent, 1965:86).

Francis Quarles is probably the exponent of the emblem tradition within religious verse who was most popular in his own period – even more than George Herbert. Several of Quarles' emblems resemble Bunyan's in their use of homely comparisons, which would be familiar to children, and the illustrations provided in the earlier poet's collection are often of childlike figures with wings. One of the most interesting parallels, which also highlights their differences, is between Bunyan's 'Upon the Bee' (pix) and Quarles' Emblem I,3; the latter is preceded by a picture of a small figure, watched by an angel, rifling what appears to be a globe-shaped hive, and beset by flying insects. The first two of the seven stanzas of the poem immediately underneath the picture are:

> Alas! fond child,
> How are thy thoughts beguil'd
> To hope for honey from a nest of wasps?
> Thou may'st as well
> Go seek for ease in hell,
> Or sprightly nectar from the mouths of asps.
>
> The world's a hive,
> From whence thou canst derive
> No good, but what thy soul's vexation brings:
> But case thou meet
> Some petty-petty-sweet,
> Each drop is guarded with a thousand stings.

The poet goes on to warn his youthful implied reader that the delights of earth are fleeting and accompanied by pain. The relatively elaborate stanza form is typical of the variety to be found in Quarles' *Emblems*.

Bunyan, however, takes an entirely different and probably to us unexpected perspective:

> The Bee goes out and Honey home doth bring;
> And some who seek that Honey find a sting.
> Now wouldst thou have the Honey and be free
> From stinging; in the first place kill the Bee.
> *Comparison*
> This Bee an Emblem truly is of sin
> Whose Sweet unto a many death hath been.
> Now would'st have Sweet from sin, and yet not dye,
> Do thou it in the first place mortifie.

In this short complete poem, Bunyan's directness, supported by his consistent use of the iambic pentameter, is appealing. His message comes over more concisely than that of Quarles, but it is perhaps more surprising, and even provocative. So much is the bee traditionally associated with the virtue of hard work that it is a little surprising to find it figuring sin – we might be happier to recognise the wasp in this guise.

What is particularly notable is the contrasted use of the bee or wasp and the honey images in the two poets. For Quarles, the sting of the wasp is real, but not the honey, and the comparison between the hive and the world is quite explicit in both picture and poem; no good is to be found within the world. The moral therefore is the necessity of looking towards the next world for happiness. This may well reflect the troublous state of England in the 1630s; Quarles as an Anglican with Puritan tendencies may have felt particularly threatened by the more extreme positions favoured by Laudian Anglicanism on the one hand and the rise of sectarian Puritanism – which would later espouse the Parliamentarian side in the Civil War – on the other. For Bunyan, however, both the sting and the honey are there, the sweetness being manufactured by the bee, which he uses as an emblem of Satan. The mood, however, is fairly optimistic: if the child gets rid of concupiscence, positive aspects of life will be there to be enjoyed.

The fact that in this poem Bunyan uses the bee as an image of Satan again recalls the metaphysical conceit; just as Donne is prepared to image the love relationship between the poet and his mistress by a flea or a compass, objects surprising to later readers, Bunyan feels free to shift his signifiers, here and elsewhere. He is by no means consistent in maintaining a fixed frame of reference. This is apparent in his use of birds: in emblem 23 a lark signifies Satan, in emblem 31 a bird represents sinners, and in emblem 43 fowls flying in the air stand for those people who are to be saved. I think the disquiet some readers, probably then as well as now, might feel about this kind of shift in referent is because humans seem instinctively to look for symbolism, whereas the metaphysical conceit, frequently linking things intrinsically unlike, does not demand resemblance in the same way as does the symbol – white lilies symbolising purity, for instance.

Possibly on the model of George Herbert's 'The Flowre' in *The Temple* (1633), and like George Wither, whose *A Collection of Emblemes Divine and Moral* (1635) includes 'Time is a fading flower' and 'The Marigold', Bunyan makes use of flower images to convey complex concepts. His ingenious verse 'Of the Rose-Bush' (XXXIII), after deploring the fact that plucking the rose will mean that 'Ten to one but the Bush will have my Blood' goes on to make this 'Comparison':

> This Rose God's Son is, with his ruddy Looks,
> But what's the *Bush?* Whose pricks, like Tenterhooks,
> Do scratch and claw the finest Ladies hands,
> Or rent her Cloths, if she too near it stands.
> This *Bush* an Emblem is of *Adam's* race
> Of which Christ came, when he his Father's Grace
> Commended to us in his crimson Blood,
> While he in Sinners stead and Nature stood.
> Thus *Adam's Race* did bear this dainty Rose,
> And doth the same to *Adam's* Race expose:
> But those of *Adam's* Race which at it catch,
> *Adam's* Race will them prick and claw and catch.

The comparison between the human race and a rosebush, with Christ as the sole flower of that race, is certainly one which is more ingenious than convincing, while the association between the colour of the rose and the 'crimson blood' of Christ might seem tasteless to a subsequent period. The final imaging of the hostility experienced by those who adhere to Christ, by the thorns of the rose bush, is an unusual way of castigating the secular world. Yet this very ingenuity can be part of the poem's appeal; as Gardner says of Donne's poetry: 'It makes demands upon the reader and challenges him [*sic*] to make it out' (1957:17).

Thus, in spite of its title, not all of the poems in Bunyan's book suggest that his audience was restricted to those of tender years. The initial address 'To the Reader' certainly does not imply that the poet is speaking only to young children; its style and complexity, as well as its subject matter, would deter all but the most enthusiastic and competent of such readers. It is apparent that he is using the words 'Boys and Girls' to accord with the childish behaviour he sees those of adult years pursuing:

> Their antick Tricks, fantastick Modes, and way,
> Shew they like very Boys, and Girls, do play
> With all the frantick Fopp'ries of this Age;
> And that in open view, as on a Stage;
> Our Bearded men, do act like Beardless Boys;
> Our Women please themselves with childish Toys. ('To the Reader')

To achieve his objective of instructing such people, he casts aside his own beard, symbol of maturity, and on the model of St Paul who did not hesitate to play the fool in order to gain 'those that were Fools indeed,' entices his readers 'To mount their Thoughts from what are childish Toys' (p47) to Heaven. As Styles observes, 'he is severe with adults who act like children' (1998:9). After a lengthy address to these 'artificial Babes', he turns his attention to those who are truly babes in years, for whom he starts the book by the aids to literacy I have indicated above.

Seth Lerer suggests that 'the experience of reading the sequence of *Country Rhimes* may be akin to the experience of Christian's journey throughout *Pilgrim's Progress*: we are always coming upon cryptic messages, strange emblems, and representations of ideal and vicious behavior that we need to interpret' (2008:93). Thus, what Michael Davies claims about the process of reading Bunyan's prose narratives seems to me equally valid of his poems:

> This demands a reading of 'things unseen' via the light of the Spirit, not of the mind. It is this need to read the self in terms of an unworldly faith that Bunyan's narratives always, and often quite forcefully, encourage in the reader ... They demand a response from the reader in absolute terms ... insisting upon a serious consideration of whether one's faith is saving or damning. (2002:6-7)

Such a process, while its beginnings can certainly be glimpsed in the young child, demands the kind of maturity that Bunyan sought to instill into his adult readers, so that they might outgrow their preoccupation with 'childish toys.'

Bunyan's place in the canon of English Literature, and of Children's Literature, is secured by *Pilgrim's Progress* rather than by his emblem book, but I would still contend that his poetry is well worth attention for its own sake. Freeman claims that 'In both parts of *The Pilgrim's Progress* there is much that can be related in general terms to the emblem convention. It was part of Bunyan's design to make use of emblems in the course of the story and he introduces them in groups from time to time' (1970:216). Without the qualities that are displayed throughout Bunyan's *Book for Boys and Girls*, I suspect that one of the major and most influential works of English prose would never have achieved the popularity that it has sustained throughout so many centuries.

Works Cited

Bunyan, J (1890) *A Book for Boys and Girls; or Country Rhymes for Children*. London: Elliot Stock

Davies, M (2002) *Graceful Reading: Theology and Narrative in the Works of John Bunyan*. Oxford: University Press

Freeman, R (1970) *English Emblem Books*. London: Chatto and Windus

Gardner, H (1957) *The Metaphysical Poets*. Harmondsworth: Penguin

Grenby, M (2008) *Children's Literature*. Edinburgh: University Press

Hill, C (1988) *A Turbulent, Seditious, and Factious People: John Bunyan and his Church*. Oxford: Clarendon Press

Hilton, M, Styles, M and Watson,V (eds) (1997) *Opening the Nursery Door: Reading, Writing and Childhood 1600-1900*. London and New York: Routledge

Johnson, S (1964) *Lives of the Poets*. London: Oxford University Press

Keast, WR (1962) *Seventeenth-Century English Poetry*. New York: Oxford University Press

Lerer, S (2008) *Children's Literature: A Reader's History from Aesop to Harry Potter*. Chicago and London: University of Chicago Press

Martz, L (1962) *The Poetry of Meditation*. New Haven: Yale University Press

Midgley, G (ed) (1980) *John Bunyan: The Poems (vol 6) The Miscellaneous Works of John Bunyan*. Oxford: Clarendon Press

Ousby I (ed) (1988) *The Cambridge Guide to Literature in English*. Cambridge: Cambridge University Press

Pinsent, P (1965) The Theme of Christ in Minor Religious Verse of the Seventeenth Century. University of London, unpublished MA thesis

Quarles, F (1818) *Emblemes*. London: Chiswick Press

Styles, M (1998) *From the Garden to the Street: An Introduction to 300 Years of Poetry for Children*. London: Cassell

Watson V (ed) (2001) *The Cambridge Guide to Children's Books in English*. Cambridge: Cambridge University Press www.poemhunter.com/poem/the-marigold/ accessed on 20/3/2009 www.scribd.com/doc/12822052/scriptural-poems-by-John-Bunyan, accessed 18/3/09

6

'Those first affections': Wordsworth and Mournful Adolescence

Louise Joy

n 1815, Wordsworth organised his complete short works into a single edition, ordered, he suggested, in such a way as to map out a chronology of human development from infancy to maturity. At the beginning of the collection is a group of poems called *Poems Referring to the Period of Child-hood. Poems Referring to the Period of Old Age* stands near its close (Words-worth, 1940-49). However, there are no groups of poems that explicitly address the periods of life in between these two poles. Instead, there are groups of poems organised around subjects such as the affections; fancy; the imagina-tion; sentiment and reflection, as well as others relating to places Wordsworth had visited. Early readers were contemptuous of this taxonomy on the basis that it failed to fulfil the task it sets itself. Ever since, scholars and editors have tended to disregard Wordsworth's stated organisation of his poems, despite the fact that the poet himself adhered to it for the rest of his life. Most editions of his complete works favour a chronological order instead of the thematic order that Wordsworth devised.

However, while it is true that there are no classes of poems directly named after the phases of life in between childhood and adulthood, suppose we take Wordsworth at his word, and use the taxonomy as a tool for understanding Wordsworth's theory of human affective development? This would mean that we could take the section that follows the poems on childhood, that is, *The Poems founded on the Affections*, to relate to adolescence; and the poems founded on fancy, those founded on imagination, and those founded on sentiment and reflection, to relate to variegated stages of adulthood. If we take Wordsworth's taxonomy at face value, and accept that the poems founded on the affections are poems that address adolescence, we can infer that Wordsworth takes this category of emotions called *the affections* to be somehow emblematic of this stage of life. What, then, does Wordsworth's emblematic use of the affections propose about adolescence, and how might it help us to think about the ways in which poetry might negotiate this phase of life poised between childhood and adulthood?

In the eighteenth century, what today we might call emotions or feelings tended to be more differentiated than our current vocabulary allows. Feelings tended to be divided into *passions* and *affections* – passions if they were strong, unruly and accompanied by physical disturbance, and affections if they were calmer, regulated by reason, and purely mental rather than physical. Such usages of the term were common in the period, and numerous social commentators, with theological, moral, political and even aesthetic interests in mind, sought to promote the affections as preferable types of emotions to the passions. Wordsworth, following this trend, is also drawn to the category of the affections as posing an appealing union between thought and feeling. He refers to the affections repeatedly in his works, and the term acquires a very particular meaning in his hands. This meaning is illustrated by a letter Wordsworth printed in Numbers 17 and 20 of Samuel Taylor Coleridge's *The Friend*. He writes:

> There never perhaps existed a school-boy who, having when he retired to rest carelessly blown out his candle, and having chanced to notice as he lay upon his bed in the ensuing darkness the sullen light which had survived the extinguished flame, did not, at some time or other, watch that light as if his mind were bound to it by a spell ... It protracts its existence so long, clinging to the power which supports it, that the observer, who had lain down in his bed so easy-minded, becomes sad and melancholy: his sympathies are touched – it is to him an intimation and an image of departing human life ... This is nature teaching seriously and sweetly through the affections. (Wordsworth, 1974:16-17)

The knowledge towards which the schoolboy is 'seriously and sweetly' steered is the realisation that human life, like the flame of a candle, ultimately expires. The affections make palatable the fact of human mortality by enabling the child to pre-empt, or even to rehearse, the deaths of his loved ones. At this point in his development, the boy's recognition of mortality extends only to the deaths of others, specifically to the deaths of those on whom he relies for nurture and sustenance: his parents, siblings and servants. It is not until he advances to adulthood, when according to Wordsworth he is able to engage 'thought' on the matter, that he can rebound this realisation on himself and confront the inevitability of his own death. The affections thus cultivate awareness and acceptance, but do not stimulate further reflection. Indeed, the pupil does not seek to interrogate or account for what he has learned; he merely acknowledges the shift that has occurred, adjusting without resistance to his altered world.

By defending the importance of the affections as a conduit for learning during adolescence, Wordsworth pays tribute to the species of understanding he believes them to facilitate: a state of comprehension arrested at the threshold between sensation and reflection. He conceives the affections as transitional or intermediary emotions – emotions in suspension – poised on the brink of a lapse either back into childish sensations or forwards into adult reflections. Pertinently, within the scene of learning Wordsworth conjures in the letter, the affections deliver their seminal lesson through an appeal to the sense of sight. This casts the schoolboy in the role of observer; he is witness to, and crucially not a participant in, the activity that takes place before him. Indeed, his help-lessness as a mere spectator – his inability to do anything to avert the extinc-tion of the flame – is inscribed within the knowledge he acquires. From the first, the child's sense of the mortality of others is inflected with an experience of aloneness, of disconnection from the event at hand. It records his power-lessness to intervene. On watching the expiring flame, the boy presages that when those close to him decease, he will once again be a helpless bystander, unable to contribute anything to the scene but his 'sad and melancholy' affections. Yet, as disinterested onlooker, the boy is confounded by the flame's refusal to give in to what he perceives to be its inescapable fate. Through the accumulation of language that emphasises the persistence of this struggle – 'recovers', 'continues', 'protracts', 'hang upon' – Wordsworth represents the captivation of the schoolboy's mind in a state of perplexed wonderment at the flame's tenacious prolongation of the process. For Wordsworth, then, the affec-tions prepare us for the most brutal of life's eventualities whilst also protecting us from the despair that this might engender, by shielding us from the fact that such a fate ultimately lies in store for us too.

We might therefore expect that a group of Wordsworth poems entitled *Poems founded on the Affections* might share a common interest in the onset of an adolescent grasp of mortality. And indeed, when we turn to the poems, it is striking that, almost without exception, the poems in this cluster fix on a scene of loss. Included in this group of 38 poems is 'The Brothers', the 'Lucy poems', 'A Complaint of a Forsaken Indian Woman', 'Maternal Grief', 'The Idiot

Boy', and 'Michael.' The loss – or departure – on which the poems in this group are predicated tends already to have occurred prior to the poem's opening. Like the affections on which they are founded, and like the state of adolescence itself, the poems thus look in two directions at once: they extend forwards, enduring into the future beyond the loss that has occurred, and yet they also extend backwards, cleaving onto that which is no longer present. These are all poems, then, that perform an act of mourning: an attempt to come to terms with a loss. Indeed, if we can put it this way, they perform an act of mourning for the passing of belief in immortality, an attempt to come to terms with mortality. They represent the struggle of carrying the knowledge of, and carrying on in the knowledge of, death. But while, on the one hand, these poems are mournful, by pointing towards the endurance of the bereaved figures in the poems, and flagging up their stamina and capacity to go on, *The Poems founded on the Affections* commemorate the capacity of the adolescent psyche to sustain loss without defeat. These poems don't merely characterise adolescence as a time of mourning; they celebrate it as such.

Interestingly, in our own age, commentators studying adolescence from a clinical perspective have also observed a similarity between adolescence and bereavement, between what G Stanley Hall calls the *storm and stress* of adolescent behaviour and the process of adult mourning (Hall, 1904). The psychologist Ellen Noonan writes: 'the active and emotionally energetic process of mourning provides a model for the adolescent transition, since both are attempts to achieve a sense of personal continuity out of the confusion of drastic disruption' (Noonan, 1983:3). In grief, she suggests, people tend to withdraw, seeking time and space to concentrate on their loss and on the lost person. Mourning is characterised by 'flight into activity directed towards the future and retreat into broodiness about the past' (p4). We see precisely these patterns of withdrawal and broodiness in the adolescent, she observes; the adolescent attempts to 'convert childhood into a memory which is alive, if not palpable, inside us' (p5). Adolescents have to mourn aspects of their child-self, so that these may be internalised.

In the case of Wordsworth, the aspect of child-self that the poet seeks to internalise again and again in his poetry is the child's belief in immortality. We see this lament for the lost childish psyche throughout his work: in 'We are Seven', the 'Immortality Ode', *The Prelude*, in his prose *Essays on Epitaphs*. So intertwined is the concept of childhood with that of immortality for Wordsworth, that he appears to view childhood primarily in terms of the idiosyncratic comprehension of death with which it presents us. Children, at least as Wordsworth sees it, are unable, or refuse, to calculate that the immediate non-presence of an object derives from its non-existence. Or, as Michael Rutter puts it, they lack 'the ability to manipulate hypotheses or propositions in the absence of concrete or tangible referents' since 'children, unlike adults and unlike adolescents, are incapable of systematic and rational abstract thinking' (Rutter, 1979:3). While for twentieth-century and contemporary theorists, human ageing tends to be construed as a process of *development* – in Piaget's terms, a development from 'egocentrism' to 'the formal operations stage' (Piaget, 1953:386) – for Wordsworth, human ageing involves a decline. As has been well documented by Wordsworth scholars (see Peter de Bolla, 2001; David Whitley, 2009), Wordsworth takes adult consciousness to be an affliction. In Wordsworth's eyes, acquisition of the capacity to comprehend and be bound by reason takes the emerging adult ever further from the truth.

This is because, as the 'Immortality Ode' definitively records, Wordsworth believes that childish knowledge, since it accompanies us at birth and therefore comes with us from another world, is closer to 'glory' than any knowledge we acquire on earth. Adult thought, in fact, merely corrupts and distorts that which children instinctively recognise to be the case. Indebted to Plato's conception of otherworldliness as much as to Christian doctrines of the heavenly after-world and Rousseau's primitivism, Wordsworth claims the irrefutability of existence anterior to human birth and posterior to death – the two are collapsed into the same condition. For Wordsworth, the child's belief in immortality and the adult's belief in mortality are not alternative, conflicting theories about death; immortality, because it is the belief held by children, is a superior belief to any belief acquired or invented by the adult. The loss that adolescence entails for Wordsworth, therefore, is a substantial one. The passing of childhood does not merely mark the passing of a stage of life as any other; in losing our belief in immortality during adolescence, we lose the 'best part' of our 'nature' (Wordsworth, 1974:50).

How, then, do adolescents cope with this profound and irrecoverable loss? According to the psychologist David Elkind, adolescents resort to two main tactics in order to adjust to the transition between childhood and adulthood: the creation of an *imaginary audience* and the creation of a *personal fable* (Elkind, 1967). In explaining the first, Elkind suggests that, unlike the child, the adolescent can compute the thoughts of others, but he

> ... fails to differentiate between the objects toward which the thoughts of others are directed and those which are the focus of his own concern ... He assumes that other people are as obsessed with his behaviour and appearance as he is himself ... In a sense, then, the adolescent is continually constructing, or reacting to, an *imaginary audience*. (p1029-30)

In explaining the second coping tactic, Elkind goes on to write:

> Perhaps because he believes he is of importance to so many people (the imaginary audience) he comes to regard himself, and particularly his feelings, as something special and unique ... This belief in personal uniqueness becomes a conviction that he will not die, that death will happen to others but not to him. This complex of beliefs in the uniqueness of his feelings and of his immortality might be called a *personal fable*, a story which he tells himself and which is not true. (p1031)

In Wordsworth's *Poems founded on the Affections*, we see both of the coping strategies that Elkind outlines take centre-stage. For example, 'The Complaint of a Forsaken Indian Woman', a poem which falls towards the end of the group, narrates the anguish of a young, dying mother who has been abandoned by her nomadic tribe. With uncanny effect, the poem ventriloquises her final thoughts, giving voice to words which, by virtue of the circumstances, could never, in fact, be heard. The poem thus creates an imaginary audience for her grief, a grief that there is no one left to witness. As with the child watching the dying flame in Wordsworth's letter, the Indian woman too is compelled to confront mortality by the lesson of the natural world. But, though she turns to the fire in order to learn of the finality of death, initially, the realisation that she, like the flame, will also perish, eludes her. The capacity to conjure death as a hypothetical possibility when she is self-evidently a material reality at first escapes her:

My fire is dead: it knew no pain;
Yet it is dead, and I remain.

Addressing herself to her imaginary audience – the tribe, now long gone – she hallucinates about what might be, inventing a personal fable:

I'll follow you across the snow;
Ye travel heavily and slow;
In spite of all my weary pain
I'll look upon your tent again.

In her personal fable, the Indian woman is invincible, untouchable by physical and mental weakness – immortal; her fiction makes bearable the otherwise unpalatable, hopeless reality of the scenario. The poem depicts the woman suspended in a state of relentless self-reflexivity: the only object on which her thoughts can prey is herself. Disconnected from all others – to invoke that cliché of adolescence, no one else understands how she feels – she broods on the past and fantasises about the future. She vacillates awkwardly between a desire to cling onto that which has been lost – her childish belief in immortality – and recognition of the inevitable – her adult acknowledgement of mortality.

The *Poems founded on the Affections* testify to the care and insight with which Wordsworth theorised adolescence as a process of mourning: a process of withdrawal, broodiness, and isolation, in which we adjust to adult reality whilst also attempting to salvage the comforts of our childish outlook on the world. The poems testify too to the importance he accorded this phase of human development. Small wonder, some might say, that Wordsworth took adolescence so seriously, given the predominance with which adolescent egocentrism abounds in his works. After all, he dedicated his entire adult life to writing and re-writing an extensive personal fable – an epic poem proclaiming the uniqueness of his own poetic talents; and *The Prelude*, as its title recalls, was merely envisaged as the introduction to an even longer work elaborating on the theme of himself. We might bear in mind too that *The Prelude* is a sustained address to an imaginary friend, Coleridge, with whom Wordsworth had fallen out long before he completed much of the poem; and that the poem was never published in Wordsworth's own lifetime, so a public audience of any form was merely hypothetical.

Adolescent affections, then, Wordsworth's work suggests, are not merely available to us during the phase of development after childhood and before adulthood. Adolescence is a state of mind – a form of egocentrism – that might be re-inhabited at any point. More particularly, perhaps, adolescence is a state of mind that might be recuperated through poetry. Indeed, we might even go as far as to suggest that, for Wordsworth, adolescence is a state of mind that must be retrieved through poetry, if we are not to lose hold altogether of our childish fantasies, and the authentic realms of 'glory' to which these fantasies ultimately connect us.

Works Cited

De Bolla, P (2001) *Art Matters*. Cambridge, MA: Harvard University Press

Elkind, D (1967) Egocentrism in Adolescence. *Child Development* 28 p1025-34

Hall, GS (1904) *Adolescence: its Psychology and its Relations to Physiology, Anthropology, Sociology, Sex, Crime, Religion and Education*. New York: D Appleton and Company

Noonan, E (1983) *Counselling Young People*. London: Routledge

Piaget, J (1953) *The Child's Construction of Reality*. London: Routledge and Kegan Paul

Rutter, M (1979) *Changing Youth in a Changing Society*. London: The Nuffield Provincial Hospitals Trust

Whitley, D (2009) Hiding Places of Power: The Child as a Site of Resistance in William Wordsworth's Poetry. In Styles, M and Arizpe, E (eds) *Acts of Reading: Teachers, Texts and Childhood*. Stoke on Trent: Trentham

Wordsworth, W (1940-49) *The Poetical Works* (ed) de Selincourt, E and Darbishire, H. Oxford: Clarendon Press

Wordsworth, W (1974) *The Prose Works, Volume 2* (ed) Owen, WJB and Smyser, JW. Oxford: Clarendon Press

7

'The Land of Play' – Robert Louis Stevenson's
A Child's Garden of Verses

Shaun Holland

When at home alone I sit
And am very tired of it,
I have just to shut my eyes
To go sailing through the skies –
To go sailing far away
To the pleasant Land of Play. ('The Little Land')

Reading through the 101 small pages that make up Stevenson's *A Child's Garden of Verses* (1885, hereafter *A Child's Garden*) is to find oneself in the midst of a land of play. Play is not so much a theme of the collection as an overriding, all-consuming preoccupation. The child in the collection has an insatiable, inexhaustible appetite for play. Whilst much of that play is physical, Stevenson creates the sensation that good play is not so much a state of doing as a state of being. This notion of pure play creates a realm realised not primarily through action but through the capacity to imagine and invent on a vast scale. And the ease of the transition from *real* to imagined is startling – the child in the collection can, it seems, by closing his eyes, move effortlessly from the monotony of a limiting present to a limitless realm of make-believe, the simple, steady flow of rhyming couplets in 'The Little Land' mimicking the ease of this slippage.

Stevenson invests more in the imaginative creativity of the child than any other children's poet. He creates a unique poetic territory, in the form of the garden, for the child to realise his imagined play land. Thus, many of the poems in the collection depict the child in a state of 'making believe' (Stevenson, 1881:316). Henry James, one of Stevenson's first and most reliable commentators, notes Stevenson's capacity to capture the innocent wondering of childhood in his writing: 'He describes credulity with all the resources of experience, and represents a crude stage with infinite ripeness' (1887:119).

Yet, here is the rub and the paradox of any children's literature. For in writing as a child, the adult Stevenson is involved in the act of recreating the innocence of the child through the resources and ripeness of experience. Certainly, the childhood we find represented in *A Child's Garden* is comprised of Stevenson's remembered childhood. Yet, this process of reflection necessarily creates tensions and contradictions within the collection. Envisioned as an exploration of the pleasant Land of Play, in allowing the child's wondering centre-stage, the poems resist their mandate, creating instead a contrary and radical representation of childhood.

Stevenson deliberated over several titles for his collection of verses for children. Two alternatives, among others, were *New Songs of Innocence* and *Rimes of Innocence*. Interestingly, in his final choice of title it is the enclosed, constructed confines of the child's space that Stevenson elects to foreground. Yet Stevenson's alternatives, though not used, remain a nod of acknowledgement to Blake and a Romantic ideology of childhood still pervasive in Victorian England. Romanticism held heavy sway over many Victorian depictions of childhood, yet it also generated much debate about childhood. Educationalists such as Friedrich Froebel, philosophers such as Jean-Jacques Rousseau and writers such as Herbert Spencer, as Michael Rosen points out, had formally discussed the issue of play (Rosen, 1995). And Stevenson's was a voice in this debate. His three published essays about childhood – *Notes on the Movements of Young Children* (1874); *Child's Play* (1882); and *Memoirs of Himself* (1880) – are noteworthy in that they outline the influence that a Romantic sensibility of childhood held over him, whilst also charting a gradual move beyond this construct. Written in 1874, *Notes on the Movements of Young Children* depicts the child as a keen, intense receptor of life. The work is generated autobiographically and Stevenson remembers certain scenes from his childhood 'with a peculiar sparkle and sensuous excitement'. In the essay he shows his aptitude for recalling the particular perspective of the child, and the child's wonder of suddenly beholding new vistas:

> I had from the attic window, suddenly beholding, with delighted wonder, my ordinary playgrounds at my feet; and another outlook, when I climbed a hawthorn near my gate, and saw over the wall upon the snuff-mill garden, thick with flowers and bright with sunshine, a paradise not hitherto suspected. (p222)

Place this alongside the child's tree-climbing in 'Foreign Lands', and the influence of Stevenson's own childhood memories is salient:

> Up into the cherry-tree
> Who should climb but little me?
> I held the trunk with both my hands
> And looked abroad on foreign lands.
>
> I saw the next-door garden lie,
> Adorned with flowers before my eye,
> And many pleasant places more
> That I had never seen before.

Stevenson recalls the sudden jolt of surprise that a different perspective can give to the apparently familiar.

'Foreign Lands' evinces Stevenson drawing on memories of his childhood for the poems in *A Child's Garden*. Other commentators have noted Stevenson's ability to capture what it feels like to be a child (Darton, 1932; Rosen, 1995; Styles, 1998). Stevenson's ability to recall memories of childhood through the child's eye is hugely influential in determining the physicality and imaginative capacity of the child in *A Child's Garden*.

In *Child's Play*, Stevenson the essayist continues to be fascinated with childhood and the child's sensibility, yet, written seven years later, Stevenson is now theorising:

> Sensation does not count for so much in our first years as afterwards; something of the swaddling numbness of infancy clings about us; we see and touch and hear through a sort of golden mist. (1881:312)

This is, admittedly, shot through with Romantic diction. But, whilst childhood is again depicted as distinct from adulthood, and given a status and value in its own right, the child is not seen to possess the heightened sensibility that distinguishes the Romantic child and privileges the child's vision over the adult's. It is the very opposite. The child does not perceive the world as fully as the adult. The child is in a golden mist because, to quote further, 'he does not know enough of the world ... His experience is incomplete.' For Stevenson, this state of incompleteness explains the child's untiring ability to return to the Land of Play. Play becomes the perfect aesthetic. As he writes on observing children at play, 'Art for art' is their motto; and the doings of grown folk are only interesting as the raw material for play' (1881:316). The single-minded intensity of the child exploring haystacks, climbing trees, making shadows, building castles or making paper boats to sail downstream seems to be the very stuff of a white, middle-class childhood. The poems reflect back to child and adult what it is, or was, to be young, in a confirmatory and re-assuring way:

> What are you able to build with your blocks?
> Castles and palaces, temples and docks,
> Rain may keep raining, and others go roam,
> But I can be happy and building at home.
>
> Let the sofa be mountains, the carpet be sea,
> There I'll establish a city for me:
> A kirk and a mill and a palace beside,
> And a harbour as well where my vessels may ride. ('Block City')

This pure play is a game that seems both familiar and timeless. Intuitively, the poet empathises with and understands children's play. Indeed, on one level the collection reads as an illustrated guide to play. Take, for example, 'A Good Play'. Here, as the children create and provision the ship with everyday objects, we gain entry both to their domestic world and their imagined world, the children navigating with ease between the two:

> We took a saw and several nails,
> And water in the nursery pails;
> And Tom said, 'Let us also take
> An apple and a slice of cake';
> Which was enough for Tom and me
> To go a-sailing on, till tea.

The comma in the last line of the second verse perfectly weights these opposi-tions in ironic counterpoise: on the one hand the limitless horizon provided by the game and the imagination, 'To go a-sailing on' – on the other the com-forting limits imposed on such wild adventuring by domestic routine, 'To go a-sailing on, till tea.'

As the journey resumes, it is not without accident, but there is no wild rumpus at the end. As so often with Stevenson, it is the journey, not the destination that matters. Jean Webb suggests that Stevenson's emphasis on travel and adven-ture in *A Child's Garden* is 'essentially a British construct, derived from an imperialist/colonial adventuring sensibility' (Webb, 2002:364). The collection certainly conveys Stevenson's fascination with the remote and exotic. The imaginative journeying into the unknown is, however, essentially a child's con-struct: the possibility of a future and a future self that any journey implies is the central issue here.

It is a pleasant land of play that the child in the collection seeks – safe; secure; untroubled. Certainly, Stevenson set out to capture the pleasures of childhood in his verses. But does this leave the collection open to the charge of being little more than idle whimsy (Goldthwaite, 1996)? Stevenson's own childhood had been, as he wrote, 'full of fever, nightmare, insomnia, painful days and interminable nights' (Mehew, 1997:283). And so the act of returning to his childhood in the verses becomes a process of selection and preferencing. As he wrote of the ill-health that marred much of his childhood:

> But to what end should we renew these sorrows? The sufferings of life may be handled by the very greatest in their hours of insight; it is of its pleasures that our common poems should be formed; these are the experiences that we should seek to recall or to provoke. (Mehew, 1997:283)

'Provoke' tellingly hints at Stevenson's creative process – the poems in *A Child's Garden* may well originate from selected and selective memories, yet, once provoked, they often escape their author's intents. Indeed, Stevenson acknowledges in the collection's dedication to his childhood nurse, Alison Cunningham, it was not only the pleasures of that time that filled his thoughts as he reflected to write his verses:

> For your most comfortable hand
> That led me through the uneven land:
> For all the story-books you read,
> For all the pains you comforted,
> All you pitied, all you bore,
> In sad and happy days of yore. ('Dedication')

The contrasts are distinct. The reflecting, adult Stevenson, can posit childhood as a far-off realm – the use of the archaic 'yore' secures this. But whilst childhood is remembered as a time of comfort, enjoyment and security, it also holds pain and sadness. This is an uneven land and, in spite of his best efforts, it is this territory of contraries that the verses sometimes stray into. Whether dealing with duty and conformity, doubts or imagined threats, the collection gives a voice to the puzzles and perplexities of childhood. Further examples include the finality of leave-taking in 'Farewell to the Farm', the imagined threats of darkness and shadowy fears in 'North West Passage', or, again, 'Windy Nights', in which the storm takes on the form of horse and rider passing and re-passing the child's house late at night – it is a study in pure terror.

Fortunately, the child lies safe abed. It is the construct of the child's secure environment within the verses that allows both security and freedom for the child. However, one of the great appeals of the verses is the child's fascination with the terrain that lies beyond domestic boundaries. Stevenson creates the figure of the garden to contain and protect the child in the verses, poetry as an act of securing cherished memories, only to have the child do what many children like to do – stray and escape safe containment in favour of appealing dangers: breach the walls of the familiar to discover the foreign, the otherness of existence. Repeatedly, the poems depict the child itching to explore beyond the garden's walls. The excitement of 'The Swing' is not alone the rhythmic rush and fall through the air – it is the glimpse over the garden wall it provides:

> How do you like to go up in a swing,
> Up in the air so blue?
> Oh, I do think it the pleasantest thing
> Ever a child can do!
>
> Up in the air and over the wall,
> Till I can see so wide,
> Rivers and trees and cattle and all
> Over the countryside.

The rhyming pattern suggesting the steadily repeating motion of the swing, the enjambment in the second verse mimicking its stomach-turning rise and fall as with the end of the third line we fall back into the fourth – the subtle art of Stevenson as poet is typically at work here. But notice, even as the child is held by the pure momentum of the swing, it is the perspective over the boundary walls and beyond that attracts. The possibilities of perspective are similarly explored in 'Foreign Lands'. Here, the child's tree-climbing provides a panorama that slips into an imagined fairyland on the horizon:

> I saw the dimpling river pass
> And be the sky's blue looking-glass;
> The dusty roads go up and down
> With people tramping in to town.

All is new for the child who, suddenly beholding, is able to see beyond the limited perspective of the garden. The poem works like a filmic long shot, extending into the distance along road and river, the sky caught in the river's reflection with the clarity and wonder of the child's first seeing eye. Again, it is imaginative speculation, the childish *if*, that allows the poem to extend from the realised to the imagined.

It is in 'Keepsake Mill' that the themes of containment and escape, familiar and other, innocence and experience are most fully realised. In this poem, the child does not innocently stray from the garden, nor is the escape glimpsed or imaginative; it is determined and physical:

> Over the borders, a sin without pardon,
> Breaking the branches and crawling below,
> Out through the breach in the wall of the garden,
> Down by the banks of the river, we go.

The breach in the wall is an opening into a world that frightens even as it fascinates. It is an acknowledged sin to escape the garden, yet for the child that Stevenson creates, there is inevitability to the transgression. The child is drawn to the river and the mill-wheel even as he anticipates, as do we as readers, the dangers that the waters represent. The mill-wheel itself is signifier of all that is constant and unchanging for the child, in contrast to that which is finite. The poem shifts in time with subtle complexity, the child imagining the future and a future return to the mill-wheel:

> Home from the Indies, and home from the ocean,
> Heroes and soldiers we all shall come home;
> Still we shall find the old mill-wheel in motion,
> Turning and churning that river to foam.

> You with the bean that I gave when we quarrelled,
> I with the marble of Saturday last,
> Honoured and old and all gaily apparelled,
> Here we shall meet and remember the past.

As it moves from present to future, the poem voices anxieties about the passing of time and troubles the reader by reminding us of the ephemeral nature of childhood. Of course, the stance of the 'I' in *A Child's Garden* is both child and reflecting adult; innocence and experience; act and memory – a composite that resists a single, or simple meaning. The collection is both an attempt to understand the past through a return to it and a means of connecting past to future.

One key motif in establishing this continuum between past and future is Stevenson's use of the river in several of the poems in the collection. A site of possibilities, it is able to hold the child's image in its still surface. Constant and certain – it can be relied upon to be unchanging. Yet, the river moves through the child's domain and on to somewhere else – 'Where Go the Boats?' is the child's questioning response to this. This serves as an apt metaphor for the depiction of childhood that we find in Stevenson's collection. In the act of writing the poems, Stevenson secures childhood, just as the water can hold the child's reflection. But, as a falling leaf on the water's surface takes the reflection away, childhood is ultimately problematic in that it cannot be secured by the adult, for the very reason that the reflecting adult's childhood has passed. Stevenson, engaged as he was in a contemporary debate about childhood and child development, could not but invest the child in his poems with the qualities of childness he details in his essays: imaginative, playful, inquisitive, physical, restless, exuberant, reflective, wondering at the world – such a child could never be contained within an arcadia – indeed, who would wish it?

> When at home alone I sit
> And am very tired of it,
> I have just to shut my eyes
> To go sailing through the skies –
> To go sailing far away
> To the pleasant Land of Play. ('The Little Land')

Considered again, the imaginative leap captured in 'The Little Land' is not alone Stevenson's expression of the child's ability to slip into play. It also connotes his unique ability, as world-weary adult, to slip back into childhood memories and capture them with such perspicuity in verse. Sometimes confidingly, sometimes conspiratorially, sometimes quizzically, sometimes a shared whisper, sometimes an un-containable gasp of wonder, the enduring strength of *A Child's Garden* lies in Stevenson's capacity to give the remembered child's voice centre-stage.

Works Cited

Goldthwaite, J (1996) *The Natural History of Make-Believe.* Oxford: OUP

Harvey Darton, F J (1932) *Children's Books in England.* Cambridge: CUP

James, H (1957) Robert Louis Stevenson. In L Edel (ed) *The House of Fiction: Essays on the Novel by Henry James.* Glasgow: Hart-Davis

Mehew, E (ed) (1997) *Selected Letters of Robert Louis Stevenson.* New Haven: Yale

Rosen, M (1995) Robert Louis Stevenson and Children's Play: The Contexts of A Child's Garden of Verses. *Children's Literature in Education* 26 (1) p53-71

Stevenson, RL (1874) Notes on the Movements of Young Children. In *Memories and Portraits and other Essays and Reminiscences.* London: Heinemann

Stevenson, RL (1880) Memoirs of Himself. In *The Works of Robert Louis Stevenson, Other Essays and Reminiscences* (Vol. 25). London: Waverley Book Company

Stevenson, RL (1881) Child's Play. In *Virginibus Puerisque.* London: Collins

Stevenson, RL (1885) *A Child's Garden of Verses.* Harmondsworth: Penguin

Styles, M (1998) *From the Garden to the Street: Three Hundred Years of Poetry for Children.* London: Cassell

Webb, J (2002) Conceptualising Childhood: Robert Louis Stevenson's A Child's Garden of Verses. *Cambridge Journal of Education* 32 (3) p359-365

8

AA Milne's Poetic World of Childhood in
When We Were Very Young and
Now We Are Six

Jean Webb

The world created by AA Milne in *When We Were Very Young* (1924) and *Now We Are Six* (1927) is one which is popularly regarded with a sentimental fondness. Reviews from customers on the websites of on-line bookshops repeatedly recall the collections as being part of their childhood experience and essential for them to include in what they read to their children, one commenting on the poems as being 'both poignant and funny' (http://www.amazon.co.uk/product-reviews/0416152627 accessed April 3rd, 2009). There are several possible explanations for this attitude: that a tone of whimsicality which can be associated with AA Milne's work is appealing to contemporary adult readers as a respite and retreat from the cares and pressures of everyday life, and that the poems capture a particular essence of a construction of childhood which is very appealing to them. If one considers that these readers are enthusiastically identifying with Milne's created world *per se*, then that is somewhat perplexing, in that he was writing from a middle-class affluent background, of rural life in 1920s England and hearkening back to his own childhood in the 1880s. This suggests to me that the world which Milne creates within these collections of poems represents an idealised childhood, but one which also has a psychological veracity.

Close analysis of the poems indicates that the following aspects of experience are variously combined throughout the collections to construct this convincing world, which displays attractive characteristics and does not simplistically deliver a sentimental emotive fantasy of childhood. The poems variously include: the reality of the young child's life; commentary on social behaviour and the expectations of both the adult and the child; moral perspectives; play and fantasy. Furthermore, there is the inclusion of aspects of child development in terms of the child subject's relationship with the external world of reality and the internal development of the subject self. As one would expect of Milne's work, there are also humorous, ironic comments on the relationship between the child and the adult worlds.

The overarching perspective which underpins Milne's construction of childhood is that of Romanticism. Here there is a child who is depicted as moving from innocence to experience as the reader progresses through the poems. A close relationship with nature and the immediate environment are integral to the child's development. This child is initially depicted as being in a small, close world, which gradually opens up into the wide spaces of the imagined. In many ways, this is an idealised Romantic childhood, yet Milne also combines this with the uncertainties, questioning and fragmentation of Modernism. Across the two volumes there is a shift from the certainties of Romanticism to the uncertainties of Modernism, as it were, a slow disintegration of the idyllic image of the pastoral world of childhood. Milne begins *When We Were Very Young* with a short preface entitled 'Just Before We Begin', where he draws attention to his initial thoughts on composing the poems. He states:

> At one time (but I have changed my mind now) I thought I was going to write a little Note at the top of each of these poems, in the manner of Mr. William Wordsworth.

The implication here is that of Milne's strong leaning towards Romanticism, yet this is checked by the change of mind. Milne continues in his Preface by linking the generation of the poems to everyday experiences with his young son when they went to feed the swan:

> Christopher Robin ... has given him the name of 'Pooh' ... If you call him and he does not come ... you can pretend that you were just saying 'Pooh!'

The poems are thus related to the creative experience of language, the reality of everyday situations, the child's world and how language can effectively be used to produce a sense of duality. 'Pooh' is both a given name and an expression of a lack of interest, belying disappointment. In this playful manner, I think there is an indication, from the beginning of this collection, of the shift from Romanticism to the uncertainties of Modernism and the slippery use of language. Furthermore, Milne's prefatory note also discusses the uncertainty of the narrator of the individual poems:

74

> You may wonder sometimes who is supposed to be saying these verses ... If I had followed Mr. Wordsworth's plan, I could have explained this each time; as it is, you will have to decide for yourselves.

The reader is left to decide, to create the personae of the different narrators who are not always depicted in the illustrations. As a result, the reader becomes engaged in the process of creativity, peopling this world with figures which give substance to the narrative voices. Consequently Milne does not follow 'Mr. Wordsworth's plan', but acknowledges his influence whilst also making it clear that the plan of Mr. Wordsworth was not suitable for the contemporary world of AA Milne and his readers. The question therefore arises as to what was the nature of Milne's plan for writing *When We Were Very Young*. His own explanation of the generation of the poems is typically amusing and seemingly deceptive, implying that this was an unplanned collection:

> on the other side of the lawn was a child with whom I had lived for three years ... and here within me were unforgettable memories of my own childhood. (*ibid*)

He would write, as he says, for fun until he was 'tired of it'. However, close consideration of the subject matter and order of poems reveals a progression in the maturation of the child, combining reality and fantasy, the projection of Christopher Robin and the re-memory of Alan Alexander Milne.

When We Were Very Young begins with the poem 'Corner-Of-The-Street', the words in the title run together with hyphens, so that they become a single phrase, which produces a sense of solidity of place. The observing narrator emphasises the sense of location with the child at the centre:

> Down by the corner of the street,
> Where the three roads meet.

The narrator remarks upon the differing sounds made by the footwear of the passers-by. Squeaky leather shoes go 'Tweet, tweet, tweet', echoing a bird twittering, whilst Percy is recognisable by his wearing of slippers. No sound is given for them since they would be soft and silence any footfall. It does not matter that you do not know who Percy is because there is no need for the child character to rationalise and explain the world. The importance of the observation is that of location and sounds which are familiar to the child listener, enabling him/her to identify the wearers. One is also located in a realm of innocence and play, both in the child's actions themselves and also in the narrative tone. These are, after all, the words of an observer, whom one presumes to be adult, yet who is marking the otherwise inconsequential squeak of shoes in a playful manner and connecting this with the natural sound of birdsong. In this simple and short opening verse, Milne combines the embryonic components of his childhood world: that of reality, play, the child and childhood, nature and an observer.

'Buckingham Palace', the second poem in *When We Were Very Young*, situates the reader within a specific English location with the central image of Buckingham Palace. There are homely conversations about the soldiers:

> We saw a guard in a sentry-box.
> 'One of the sergeants looks after their socks,'
> > Says Alice.

Alice's comments are aligned with her knowledge of domesticity founded upon her knowledge of her own world. Milne captures a projection of the child's imagination into the lives of the soldiers and the inhabitants of the palace. Both logical and whimsical, the poem celebrates the child's fascination with the Royal Guard. It is also working with a model of childhood which takes a rationality – drawn from what the child knows – and applies that to other situations. In another way, the poem also both celebrates and deflates the grandeur and power of one of the central images of the state and disempowers this image by situating it within the child's frame of perception. Milne thus creates a subtle irony across the duality of adult and child readership.

The settings of the individual poems range from the grandness of the exterior of Buckingham Palace to the intimacy of the child's bedroom: from the external to the internal. In 'Brownie', Milne takes the idea that an unknown person lives behind the curtain in the bedroom. They cannot be seen but one is certain that they are there:

> Brownies never wait to say, 'How do you do?'
> ... (Nanny says they're tickly, too.)

The presence of imagined figures who are exotic and otherworldly, such as the Brownie fairy, is a normal part of the imaginative experience of most young children. Social mores are incorporated into this short account; the child has internalised the social niceties, references to which occur frequently in the poems. This is, after all, a middle-class English childhood. Nanny provides a sense of comfort, and intimates that she has also met these creatures from the supernatural world. An enclosed world of protection, old-world manners, curiosity and comfort is constructed around the child narrator. There are also opportunities for the less than comfortable aspects of childhood to be explored, for example, in the poem 'Independence', which follows 'Brownie':

> I never did, I never did, I never *did* like 'Now take care, dear!'
> I never did, I never did, I never *did* want 'Hold my hand.'

Milne captures the growth of independence in the defiant tone of voice of the child subject. Here the child is beginning to want to separate her or himself from the protective world of adulthood. There is a desire for adventurous activities, for stepping into danger, for challenging the safety given by adult authority. Nonetheless, the child feels that they cannot overturn such authority and the line given to the child voice, 'It's no good saying it. They don't understand,' marks that difference in power, opening up a sense of separation and lack of understanding between the generations. It strikes me that this is a condition which has, perhaps in contemporary times, been popularly consigned to adolescence, yet Milne attributes such feelings to and articulates them for the young child. Milne picks up this theme of the misunderstood child again in 'Rice Pudding'. Here the adults refuse to recognise that Mary Jane's temper tantrum is simply caused by dislike of this, in their perception, 'delicious' food. In 'Independence' the frustration is articulated, whereas in 'Rice Pudding' language is replaced by emotional outbursts. Screams and tears replace rational language, as though Milne is emphasising the child's words from 'Independence' which register the adult lack of understanding. The recognition, from the child, that 'It's no good saying it' has a certain resignation and poignancy. The sense of time expressed by the child is also one which belies the brevity of the young life, 'never' indicating an encompassing timelessness in which the child's experience has been engulfed by restriction and authority. For, although in 'Buckingham Palace' the authority of the State can be contained and re-shaped by the imagination, the adult figures have an authority within the immediacy of the child's life that remains unaltered – although it can be challenged, as Mary Jane does when she cries with 'all her might and main'.

How can the child, then, step outside this stultifying, protective adult barricade and find the desired challenge of adventure? Milne's answer is in the creation of imagined worlds and adventures, as in 'Nursery Chairs'. Here is adventurous fantasy play around the nursery furniture, the chairs variously becoming South America, a ship at sea, a cage for a lion and then, pragmatically, a chair for 'me'. Within the safe confines of the nursery, the child's imagination ventures into foreign exotic worlds of excitement. Here the child is in control and has a 'faithful' band' to whom he calls. He is in command, for if he does not wish to play with Indians, he can simply wave his hand 'And then they turn and go away – / They always understand.' In this fantasy world of the child's creation, the child is always understood. In the following poem,

'The Second Chair', the child further usurps adult power; he becomes a lion and frightens Nanny before returning to his child self to comfort her. The duality and fluidity of the self are realised through such imagination and play. As the child subject matures in the collection *Now We Are Six*, there is a greater emphasis on longer narrative poems such as 'King John's Christmas' and 'The Knight Whose Armour Didn't Squeak'. The imagined scenarios become more complex, and the figures represented extend the social world of the child, such as in 'The Charcoal Burner'. The poems in *Now We Are Six* also reflect the maturing mind, where the child is coming to terms with different concepts reflecting influences from outside the home, such as school, for example, and knowledge learnt at school, such as multiplication tables.

The way in which Milne combines elements of his world is sophisticated and subtle. From across the two collections, I have seemingly sorted examples of these elements into the discrete categories – reality, play, the self etc – outlined at the beginning of this discussion. However, these categories cross and inter-twine. In 'Us Two' from *Now We Are Six*, for example, Milne explores and demonstrates the need for extended social interaction which is of the child's own creation. To the child, Pooh is a living figure, a soul-mate who is always with him, and with whom he can ponder the daily events of his life:

> Wherever I am, there's always Pooh,
> There's always Pooh and Me.

Such reflections may derive from discussing the vagaries of arithmetic, as in 'What's twice eleven?' I said to Pooh, / ('Twice what?' said Pooh to Me'); or from pondering the need for a constant companion, an inner voice with whom to engage in private conversation – 'What would I do?' I said to Pooh, / 'If it wasn't for you,' and Pooh said 'True'. Pooh's responses are unemotional and matter of fact, yet indicative of the bond and synergy between him and Christopher Robin. Pooh is always a little more confused than the boy, yet there is a truth about his seemingly simple responses.

'Us Two' follows on, in terms of the inner world of the child, from 'Binker', which is a poem about an imaginary playmate who is 'the secret of my own' and 'the reason why I never feel alone'. Binker is a projection of the inner self, an alter-ego. In 'Us Two' there is a maturity about the conversation – the sophistication of the companionable, loving interchange is whimsical and poignant. There is an emphasis on the need for companionship, for reinforce-ment of ideas and conclusions: a psychological veracity. After all, who can argue with a close companion who confirms that your multiplication sum is right!

Milne's depiction of the complexity of the self moves the reader from Romanticism, which celebrates the close relationship with nature and the power of the imagination, towards the paradigm of Modernist thinking. Milne's collections also celebrate nature, particularly in *When We Were Very Young*, where 'Daffodowndilly' may well be a direct response to Wordsworth's 'Daffodils'. Milne personifies the daffodils of Wordsworth's poem. Whereas Wordsworth's daffodils 'flutter and dance in the breeze' (1802), Milne's daffodil 'turned to the south wind/And curtsied up and down.' The relationship between the child and the singular daffodil is more intimate and depicts the close observation in which young children engage, rather than the sweeping view of the adult coming upon a host of golden daffodils. As *Now We Are Six* draws to a close, the bright sunlight has gone and the child is 'In the Dark'. It is bedtime. He has done all that has been required: eaten; listened to the bedtime story; brushed his teeth; said prayers; been the subject of love and affection and been kissed. They have all said 'Goodnight' and now he is 'in the dark alone' where 'There's nobody here to see.' This world is self-contained – that is, it is the child's secret world. There are no recorded conversations with Pooh. Here there is autonomy for the child, for he can, as expressed in his own voice rather than through the adult as intermediary:

> Think whatever I like to think
>
> ...
>
> There's nobody here but me.

Time, place and action become fragmented and fused when the child imagines that he is talking to a rabbit, then the sun; he imagines that he is a hundred and then one. His mind races through various states of being, both physical and emotional. The significant factors in the final verse are that he is courageous enough to talk with a dragon – he is brave, and furthermore knows that tomorrow he will 'think a lot'. Here is the mind of a child exploring different states of being and also stating the rationality of his mind. It is a young mind, but at six, however, here is a nascent intellectual who has a host of tomorrows before him, whatever they may bring. Childhood is encapsulated in this reflective poem. Beneath the positive assertions, the voice is more fragmented; this is a brave child's voice, but a tired one. Perhaps Romanticism in its idealised form was also tiring by the 1920s, when the daffodils of Wordsworth had been overtaken by the poppies of Flanders Fields. Milne does leave the reader with a brave voice to face the future, and with a mind which is determined to think through matters. The child is becoming more independent and living in a more self-contained world, away from parental knowledge. There is, for me, poignancy and sadness, a sense of loss, or, maybe more precisely, a sense of losing. The saving factor is that the promise of the coming day brings hope symbolised by gentle laughter, which is always better shared, and is certainly one of the central components of Milne's poetry and prose to be enjoyed by both child and adult. Milne's gift to the reader is an insight into the worlds of childhood, and one hopes that the experiences and qualities he draws out and highlights are those which will always be important, irrespective of the era or social context.

Works Cited

Milne AA (2004) *Now We Are Six*. London: Egmont

Milne AA (2004) *When We Were Very Young*. London: Egmont

9

'The Penny Fiddle' and Poetic Truth

Michael Joseph

By the time Robert Graves published *The Penny Fiddle: Poems for Children* in 1960, he had already written and dedicated individual poems to two of the four children from his marriage to Beryl Pritchard. Each poem articulates one of Graves' mythopoeic convictions: 'To Lucia at Birth' asserts that woman is capable of transcending the terror of history, and 'To Juan at the Winter Solstice,' that every man's fate rests with The Goddess, and that the best of men, a poet like Graves himself, will surrender everything, even his life, for the fleeting privilege of becoming Her consort. *The Penny Fiddle*, dedicated to his son, Tomás, articulates a belief of equal personal and poetic significance, though it is not a single poem but a selection of poems, or what Graves calls 'an aggregate of instances from which the idea of poetry is deduced by every new poet' (Graves, 1948:471). This belief may be termed *poetic truth*, a concept that inhabits Graves' interviews and essays for forty years, beginning in the 1930s. In a conversation with Huw P Wheldon in 1959, a year before publishing *Penny Fiddle*, Graves, avoiding definition, only comments that poetic truth 'is a sort of supra-rational truth,' and that it 'comes very close to the natural faith of religion' (Wheldon, 1959:55). Adopting the terms of comparative religion, we can say that in the phrase poetic truth, truth implies the Classic Greek idea of *arête*, virtue or excellence, rather than propositional or historical truth; poetic truth equates to the sacred. According to Mircea Eliade, it is 'the experience of a reality and the source of an awareness of existing in the world' (Eliade, 1982:154).

The sequence of poems in *The Penny Fiddle* offers arguments for poetic truth while it attempts to engage young readers sensitive to poetry at the level of intuition and play. It is light-hearted, accessible in terms of topic, imagery, metre and diction to young readers, yet at the same time deeply aesthetically self-conscious as it offers proofs that poetry is not contingent, but transcends all barriers of gender, social class, and of course age, for those who are prepared to understand it. This qualifier stands against accusations that Graves is absolutist. He proffers no universal claims. His truth is not ontologically autonomous, but reified in the experience of poets and dependent on the receptivity of poets. In the preface of his *Collected Poems 1938-1945*, he asserts that he wrote poems for poets: 'to write them for anybody else would be wasteful' (Graves, 1945:3). By poets, he does not mean authors skilled in verse craft, but individuals born with a particular cast of mind – those able to grasp and abide by poetic truth.

By extension we might understand that the primary audience for *The Penny Fiddle* is therefore not all, but rather some, children: young poets. And we might describe the volume as a discourse about poetic pleasure within a meta-discourse of religio-poetic meaning, intended for an audience of poets – young and old alike. A significant underlying tenet of *The Penny Fiddle*, and one that resonates throughout Graves' writings and lectures on poetry during the fifties, is that discourse and meta-discourse are harmonious and continuous within poetry itself: pleasure is form – and form is governed by poetic truth – *arête*.

The origins of *The Penny Fiddle* reach back into Graves' post-war period. In the spring of 1918 he wrote some nursery verses, which he included in a typescript of forty-three poems called *The Patchwork Flag*. After abandoning the project on the advice of Siegfried Sassoon and Robbie Ross, he formed the idea of producing a volume solely of poems for children, which his wife, Nancy Nicholson, would illustrate. Soon he began shopping it around, without success, under the title *The Penny Fiddle* (Graves, 1999:349). The volume of poems he published in 1960 as *The Penny Fiddle: Poems for Children* is an elaboration on this earlier, identically titled project. However, the earlier manuscript has apparently perished and only inferential evidence remains for what it might have contained. While the degree to which Graves reconceived and restructured the earlier *Penny Fiddle* remains a matter of speculation, we can see at a glance that the *Penny Fiddle* in hand is unique and a work of its time. Seven of its twenty-three poems were composed after 1920, the most notable of which is the volume's concluding poem, 'Warning to Children,' whose markedly, indeed almost jarringly metaphysical character calls attention to the volume's intellectual pretensions. Six other poems, certain or very likely to have been in the original, have been extensively revised. In parti-

cular, the revision of the title poem, 'The Penny Fiddle,' attests to the importance as well as the disposition of the 1960 revival.

The theoretical significance of *The Penny Fiddle* can be seen more clearly
within the context of Graves' writings about poetry during this period, beginning approximately with the Clarke Lectures of 1954-1955. The lectures comprise a five-part historical précis of English poetry elaborating on one of the
themes of *The White Goddess* (1948) that poetry, as we have it, descends from
the ritualistic utterances of a Bronze Age faith in a triune Goddess – the ante-
cedent of The Muse. It is essentially a myth of a golden age replete with a subsequent fall. In the postlapsarian, secularised world of *belles lettres* there are
Muse poets, who, inspired by romantic love, spontaneously revive the original,
or true, system of belief, and then there are pretenders. The lectures culminate
in a remarkably aggressive essay titled 'These Be Your Gods, O Israel!', which
denounces as pretenders five of Graves' colleagues, the five most lauded
English poets of the day, Yeats, Auden, Pound, Eliot and Dylan Thomas. The
purpose of the Clarke Lectures is to re-contextualise contemporary poetry and
rescue it from the academic critics and reviewers who, to his way of thinking,
have bamboozled the public and dishonored the long poetic tradition of the
Muse (McGuinness, 1999:46-47).

Graves builds upon the connections between poetry and myth in a series of
subsequent lectures and essays that extends into the early 1960s, including
'Legitimate Criticism of Poetry' in *5 Pens in Hand* (1958), 'Case for Xanthrippe'
(1960), 'The Making and Marketing of Poetry' in *Food for Centaurs* (1960), and
Oxford Addresses on Poetry (1962). *Penny Fiddle: Poems for Children* makes
the case from a slightly different perspective, invoking the authority of childhood as it is troped in Romantic poetry – for example, Blake's *Songs of Innocence* – to support his arguments. That childhood is on his mind during this
period – a period in which he is helping to rear three young children – is
suggested by 'These Be Your Gods, O Israel!' which alludes to childhood in its
very first sentence: 'I was never one to stroll down the street with a catapult
and break windows just for the fun of hearing the tinkle of glass and seeing
furious faces peering out as I scuttle away' (Graves, 1959:112). Graves can
imagine the fun of being a bad boy, but, in truth, he behaved well, and a man
who behaved well as a boy can be trusted to behave himself as an adult.
Character trumps age.

By publishing 'poems for children' as a way of declaring that the character of
good poems also trumps age, and that 'poems [should also be] for children'
rather than restricted to what Patrick McGuinness calls 'the so-called discip-

line of literary studies, and the consequent cult of the contemporary poet' (McGuinness, 1999:47), Graves is reworking an idea he had introduced in 1927, in *The Less Familiar Nursery Rhymes*, when he observed that the older rhymes 'come nearer to poetry than the greater part of the *Oxford Book of English Verse*' (Graves, 1927:iii). That *The Penny Fiddle* claims three poems from the earlier volume, 'Henry and Mary,' 'Jock o' Binnorie' and 'What Did I Dream?', which appear there as *anonymous* nursery rhymes, might be seen to acknowledge their connection and perhaps to reassert his original claim, broadened to include poems for children.

We can immediately recognise Graves' seriousness of purpose in the revisions he made to *The Penny Fiddle*'s first, eponymous poem. The earlier version, published in the *Collins Children's Annual 1926* (Graves, 1926:12), quite likely introduced the 1920 manuscript and suggests a project of greater simplicity and transparency. The poem begins with a quatrain that remains unchanged in the later poem:

> Yesterday I bought a penny fiddle
> And put it to my chin to play,
> But I found that the strings were painted,
> So I threw my fiddle away.

However, the second quatrain ruminates on having wasted pennies on 'buns and plums' instead of saving them for a workable fiddle that could have played 'real music'. The penny fiddle cannot play real music, but only conjure up its spectre: 'But now the whisper comes.'

The speaker, a boy, we assume, doesn't stop with renouncing sweetmeats. For a real fiddle, he will sell his boots and walk abroad barefoot, paying no attention to the 'falling snow' , 'For what should a fiddler care?'

The later version excises all of this, removing the intellectual basis for a category of unplayable fiddles, or toy poetry that is not really poetry. Where the earlier poem contains a young, vaguely affluent male narrator who recounts a rite of passage, the revision marks him more clearly as male and affluent, and adds a second character clearly marked, in contrast, female and poor. The earlier poem emphasises the narrator's bold change of heart; the revision emphasises the fiddle. Instead of romanticising the masochistic sacrifices the boy envisions making for a better instrument, the later poem invests the detrital object with magical potency:

> A gipsy girl found my penny fiddle
> As it lay abandoned there;

When she asked me if she might keep it,
I told her I did not care.
Then she drew such music from the fiddle
With help of a farthing bow,
That I offered five shillings for the secret,
But, alas, she would not let it go.

Although the first stanza of the revision is identical to the original, one cannot resist wondering whether it meant something quite different to the older poet. By beginning the poem and volume, 'Yesterday,' Graves draws our attention to the act of revisiting an earlier work – discarded, like the fiddle. As well as signifying a personal investment in the narrative, 'Yesterday' signals that the volume itself is situated in a personal history, which we may choose to read as a private gesture to the volume's dedicatee, but which certainly suggests the plasticity of the past, its openness to revision and change, and, by analogy, the subordination of historical to poetic truth.

Besides the implied opposition of innocence and experience, 'The Penny Fiddle' constructs other oppositions: rich/poor; boy/girl; money/music; telling/asking; worth/worthlessness; literal/imaginary; real/unreal. It even suggests an opposition between the prosaic and the poetic, balancing the poem's bumpy first line of five trochees ('Yesterday, I bought a penny fiddle') with its final musical line of three reluctantly gliding anapaests: 'But, alas, she would not let it go.' A desire to contrast accords perfectly with the driving purpose of the volume: to model the distinctiveness of poems that manifest 'poetic truth.' This purpose is reified by yet another opposition, one between the present and the absent: the material poem stands in for the present, and the absent is signified by William Blake's 'Pretty Rose Tree,' the poem to which 'Penny Fiddle' alludes on multiple levels:

A flower was offered to me;
Such a flower as May never bore.
But I said I've a Pretty Rose-tree.
And I passed the sweet flower o'er.
Then I went to my lovely rose-tree
To tend her by day and by night
But my rose drew away in jealousy
And her thorns were my only delight.

There is an intimate phonological correspondence between the poems' narrative voices, in which we observe the same anapaestic trimeter, the same note of restrained whining, the pertinacious repetition of 'rose' and 'fiddle', and the anapaestic triplet that concludes each poem, regret snapping at its heels:

> And her thorns were my only delight
> But, alas, she would not let it go.

By metrically reincarnating 'Pretty Rose Tree,' Graves compels us to look more closely at the poem for other points of comparison, and we can see that he has restaged Blake's fiction. He has recast the female 'rose tree' as a magic-maker; and since 'magic is disreputable' (Graves, 1948: 3), he has constructed it as a symbol of tri-fold marginality – a young, female member of a homeless race – a 'gypsy girl.' Gypsy is a derogatory term that informs young readers that the male narrator's ill-regard for the girl is no less gross than his impatience with the fiddle. Mimetically invoking the lowly as a category of being, Graves draws upon an idea of transvaluation or the 'metaphorics of the valueless' (Turner, 2002:277), in which the transcendent is not disguised merely *as* but *is* the materially worthless. Graves does not suggest a way of reconciling the oppositions he has presented or negotiating between them, but rather points to a transcendent co-dependence. The humble gypsy is genuine – a truepenny – as is the fiddle; yet both must continue to be humble and low. Here, Graves brushes against what I think is a perception at the core of children's literature: the notional Child inhabits a space if not outside of history then at a tangent to it – an ontology one finds, of course, in Blake.

'Penny Fiddle' also enables us to read 'Pretty Rose Tree' through Graves' eyes. The rose tree is a symbol of the Muse, the incarnate source of inspiration. The narrator is her poet, a victim, according to Graves, of her implacability. While the narrator protests his innocence, his allusion to another 'sweet flower' both hides and reveals his indiscretion. How 'sweet,' if untasted? Therefore his misery merits no tears. However, Graves' readers will instantly recognise the narrator's poetic complaint that suffering at the hands of his muse forms his 'only delight.' This is the very fate of the poet-lover who treads the 'never altered circuit of his fate,' as Graves describes it in 'To Juan at the Winter Solstice'. Suffering on behalf of the Muse is a mode, or perhaps the lone mode, of inspiration, an idea we see Graves clumsily trying in the earlier 'Penny Fiddle'.

'The Penny Fiddle' recasts this fiction by transforming the rose tree into a social outcast of otherworldly vitality, and the 'sweet flower', paradoxically, desired and not desired, into an otherworldly fiddle, around which desire and repulsion rotate. The rueful narrator's sufferings, which overwrite the original narrator's eager anticipation of the sufferings of a materially deprived life, become a consequence of his own prejudices – against both cast-away fiddle and strange girl. However, it is crucial to note that these prejudices are inherited, which is to say, culturally constructed, and not inherent; he can change.

De-emphasising jealousy, Graves celebrates delight in creativity and transformation. Just as vague yearning for a simple tune has lured the young narrator into the ambiguous presence of magic, his disappointment has spurred him into song: the poem after all is the product of his suffering and remorse. Surely this is one of the most exceptional aspects of the re-written poem, and one of the easiest to overlook: the rude, materialistic prat is the poet!

The poem lures readers into feeling smugly superior to this callow narrator, but then demonstrates how imperfections, that is, meanness, dullness, bigotry, even suffering – perhaps especially suffering, since this is the point Graves would have made of the Blake poem – can be transmuted into poetry. The poem leaves open the question of whether the narrator realises the value of his own creation and connects his misery to the music of the poem. He may remain liminal, torn between desire and repulsion, trapped at the threshold of self-awareness; but readers can go further. 'The Penny Fiddle' provides us with a *coincidentia oppositorum*, a paradoxical co-dependence of opposites, thus a means of recognising the metaphor of the narrator's failings and of accepting that baseness – failure, pain – is a prerequisite of the creative process. And thus, by an act of apprehending the co-identification of the narrator's pain and the poem's value – appositely synthesised as meaning and music in the final line, 'but, alas, she would not let it go' – 'The Penny Fiddle' becomes about us and we can virtually complete the narrator's transformation.

In this process of creative hermeneutics, the reader's understanding recapitulates the changes inside the narrative, its poetic fusion. Understanding acts upon the poem, which signifies its own lowliness in its title, just as the narrator/poet has acted by force of inspiration upon the demonstration of his flaws and inadequacies, and the girl has magically acted upon the all-but-worthless penny fiddle.

Readers may differ in their speculations about whether the narrator will remain trapped at or will cross over the threshold of self-knowledge, but recognising the worth of the poem positions all readers to understand that understanding is transformative, and in this regard the poem objectifies our understanding of it. Graves means for our understanding to become an inseparable feature of the poem, and therefore a malleable part of its hermeneutic deposit and not a controlling force.

Each action might be thought of as an independent element of awareness that reifies value in the valueless and in the aggregate constellates poetic self-awareness, or a pattern of poetic truth. The girl realises the potential of the fiddle, her own deprecated potential. The boy apprehends the music, but not himself or the music of his own downcast utterance. Readers may comprehend both the disreputable magic of the children's poem and its relationship to the boy's loss, and, by analogy, how they are informed or reconstituted by understanding.

'The Penny Fiddle' therefore begins the volume of the same name by legitimating itself as a poem, and legitimating the circumstances of childhood, by demonstrating that although suffering may appear purposeless and incomprehensible, it grounds the poetic process, the process of making meaning. It instructs readers to disregard nothing – not their own clumsiness and frustration, not even an apparently trite, didactic, cast-off children's rhyme – because anything may be transvalued by poetic truth, regardless of gender, race or age. Poetic truth alone determines what has meaning and worth.

Acknowledgements
With thanks to Carcanet Press Ltd for permission to reprint material from 'The Penny Fiddle' in Robert Graves (2000), *Complete Poems in One Volume* (ed) B Graves and D Ward. Manchester: Carcanet.

Works Cited

Blake, W (1789) *Songs of Innocence: Shewing the Two Contrary States of the Human Soul.* William Blake

Eliade, M (1982) *Ordeal by Labyrinth: Conversations with Claude-Henri Rocquet* (trans) Derek Coltman. Chicago: Chicago University Press

Graves, R (1919) *The Treasure Box.* London: Chiswick Press

Graves, R (1926) 'The Penny Fiddle'. *Collins Children's Annual* 12

Graves, R (1927) *The Less Familiar Nursery Rhymes.* London: Benn

Graves, R (1945) *Collected Poems 1938-1945.* London: Cassell

Graves, R (1948) *The White Goddess.* London: Faber

Graves, R (1955) *The Crowning Privilege.* London: Cassell

Graves, R (1958) *5 Pens in Hand.* New York: Doubleday

Graves, R (1960) Case for Xanthrippe. *The Kenyon Review* 22(4) p597-605

Graves, R (1960) *Food for Centaurs.* New York: Doubleday

Graves, R (1960) *Penny Fiddle.* London: Cassell

Graves, R (1962) *Oxford Addresses on Poetry.* London: Cassell

Graves, R (1999) *Complete Poems: vol 3* (ed) B Graves and D Ward. Manchester: Carcanet

Hibberd, D (1990) The Patchwork Flag (1918): An Unrecorded Book by Robert Graves. *The Review of English Studies, New Series*, 41(164) p521-532

Wheldon, HP (1959) Robert Graves. In FL Kersnowski (ed) *Conversations with Robert Graves.* Mississippi: University of Mississippi Press

McGuinness, P (1999) Robert Graves, Modernism, and the 'Poetic Body'. In PJ Quinn (ed) *New Perspectives on Robert Graves.* London: Associated University Presses

Turner, HS (2002) *The Culture of Capital.* London; New York: Routledge

10

'A child, barefoot: alone':
Innocence in Charles Causley's Poetry

Debbie Pullinger

Despite producing six volumes of children's poetry as well as a *Collected Poems* and a *Selected Poems for Children*, Charles Causley claimed that he never wrote for children: 'When I write a poem I don't know whether it's for a child or an adult ... A children's poem must be one that works for the adult as well as the child' (Causley and Wilmer, 1994:68).

Nor is the boundary line clear. In his *Collected Poems 1951-2000* (2000), works originally published in books for children are silently slipped in amongst adult poems, whilst his *Collected* and *Selected* poems for children include works originally published in adult volumes. One of these, 'Nursery Rhyme of Innocence and Experience' (1996), by its explicit reference to William Blake's *Songs of Innocence and Experience* (1789), signals both Causley's Romantic lineage and one of his major interests. This theme of innocence and experience proceeds inevitably from his concern with childhood and with the loss of young life in war.

I suggest in this discussion that Causley's construction of childhood is indeed of Romantic descent, and explicitly so. But it is also distinctive in the way it portrays the child as simultaneously possessing childhood innocence and its associated qualities, and losing them. This construction emerges with clarity from the entire canon, but may also be inferred from the children's poems alone. Secondly, although the construction of childhood in the adult and children's poems is consistent, there are nevertheless marked differences in the way that construction is presented. Finally, from my reading of the canon, I concur with Michael Dana Gioia (1998) when he says that Causley's children's poetry explores all his major themes but exhibits the same formal and textual strategies found in his adult poetry. This not only supports Causley's own assertion, but also refutes any suggestion that children's poetry is inevitably watered down poetry. As I hope this brief examination of a very small selection will show, the children's poetry is full-strength Causley.

In Causley's adult poetry, the theme of childhood is an undercurrent that runs through his early war poems, his retellings of folktales, legends and Bible stories, and surfaces into full view in his recollections of teaching and his own childhood experiences. In 'Scenes from Childhood', for example, the first-person narrator recalls being a child in a specific time and place. With one or two exceptions, such as 'Tavistock Goose Fair' (1987), what we find amongst the children's poems is not so much solid images of real children, but something more like ghosts of childhood that drift in and out, as in 'Moor-hens' (1987):

> Living by Bates Pond, they
> (Each spring and summer day)
> Watched among reed and frond
> The moor-hens prank and play.

This first stanza contains a semantic surprise for the first-time reader. Coming fresh from the title, we tend to assume that the word 'they' at the end of the first line refers to the eponymous moor-hens. But arriving at the fourth line, we have to adjust our interpretation when it is revealed that 'they' are not moor-hens but watchers of moor-hens.

The next three stanzas describe how the (as yet) unidentified 'they' observe the moor-hens playing in the mud, very much in the way that children might, then listen to their '*kik! kik! kik!* of farewell/As they drifted south for the sun'. It ends:

> Whose are the children, and who
> Are the children who lived by the pond,
> Summer and spring year-long
> When the wild sun shone?
> Thirsty the stream, and dry;
> Ah, and the house is gone.

Ultimately the children are revealed as the subject of every sentence and of the poem itself, but by a kind of sleight of hand we are deflected from seeing this until the last. The poem's images, its title, even its placement in 'One by one', a section of animal poems, all focus our attention – just like the children who three times 'watched' – on the object, the moor-hens. It is as if the poem only notices the children when they have gone, as do we.

Only in the last line is a house mentioned for the first time – and by this point it, too, has already disappeared. Home, an acknowledged symbol of child-hood and adult protection in children's literature, has gone for good. Accord-ingly, the stream, a symbol frequently used by Causley for the course of life, is 'thirsty' and 'dry'. These two extra lines, falling after the natural end of the poem, read like an envoi that strengthens the abiding sense of loss. The poem's central idea is thus revealed through elements of poetic function as a loss of childhood that is noticed only after the fact. It feels like a very adult perspective. Dual address is of course a defining characteristic of children's literature, but the poem might also be seen as an example of its curious invitation to children, as noted by Nodelman, to share a nostalgia for that which they have not yet lost, to 'develop a double consciousness' (2008:46). In 'Moor-hens', that double consciousness seems almost inscribed into the lines: 'Whose are the children, and who/Are the children who lived by the pond'.

Childhood is here depicted as in unity with the natural world, very much in line with Romantic notions of innocence. The children are identified as wild creatures under the 'wild' sun, who 'lived by the pond', their affinity with nature given emphasis through the syntactically ambiguous line 'Watched among reed and frond' – which could refer equally to the children or the moor-hens. A similarly pastoral scene is conjured by 'Summer was always Sun' (1987). Here, the second and third stanzas:

Down from the moor the stream
Ran swift, ran clear.
The trees were leaved with song
For all to hear.

The seas, the skies were blue.
With stars the beach was sown.
Printing the endless shore,
A child: barefoot, alone.

It is an Arcadian world that speaks to the child in song, where the life-sym-bolising stream runs 'swift' and 'clear'. The truncated final lines in all but the third stanza have extra resonance, so that 'song/For all to hear' does indeed sing out – with distinct echoes of 'songs/that every child may joy to hear' from

Blake's 'Introduction' to *Songs of Innocence and Experience* (1789). The child is 'barefoot', signifying his natural condition, whilst the line, 'With stars the beach was sown' reveals him as a Romantic visionary. The child is also conspicuously alone; the images of stars on the beach and an 'endless' shore forge an association between the beach and the heavens which cast the child as a figure isolated not only on a beach but also in the vast expanse of the universe.

Again following the Romantic line, as well as Robert Louis Stevenson's seminal work, *A Child's Garden of Verses* (1885), Causley's conception of childhood is associated with play, and 'Come out to play' is the opening section in *Collected Poems for Children* (1987). The placing could be seen as announcing the poetry as a form of play with words, in the spirit of Lewis Carroll, and the section does include such ingenuously humorous poems as 'Mrs Malarkey' and 'Baloono'. So far, so unsurprising. It opens, however, with a poem that clearly foreshadows sexual experience ('Freddie Phipps') and ends with a rather bleak portrait of Causley's grandmother who 'Sees with unsparing eye the thread/Of broken words within my hand' ('Photograph'). The plaything is broken; from the outset, 'innocent' play appears contaminated. Other poems in the section paint the darker picture with unmistakable clarity. In 'Why?', the adult narrator addresses 'Susanna', a young girl who appears unduly anxious about bonfire-night rituals. The adult's words, 'Nobody's going to die', acquire a hollow, ironic tone – the truth being, of course, that all human beings eventually die. Unlike the kindly but seemingly oblivious adult, the child is able to see beyond the gaiety of the ritual to its sombre significance.

The children in these poems are naturally alive to the world of feeling and imagination, having easy access to the transcendent and an intuitive understanding of spiritual truths. Like Wordsworth, Causley depicts lunatics, poets and children alike as visionaries. And like Wordsworth, his picture of childhood is characterised by duality. But whereas Wordsworth sees destruction entering through neglect of the child, for Causley the very gift which affords children their life-enhancing vision also allows them to perceive the reality of suffering and death. Writing about Causley's poetry, Neil Philip observes that 'the innocence of childhood ... carries the seeds of its own destruction' (1982: 142), and nowhere is this more evident than in 'By St Thomas Water' (1996). Beneath the surface of the simple narrative is poetry of considerable complexity, replete with Biblical imagery and ecclesiastical language, and echoing the story of Adam and Eve in the Garden of Eden:

> By St Thomas Water
> Where the river is thin
> We looked for a jam-jar
> To catch the quick fish in.
> Through St Thomas Churchyard
> Jessie and I ran
> The day we took the jam-pot
> Off the dead man.

In their prelapsarian state, the children enjoy playing in the natural world. The word *quick* in line four has two meanings, and both are possible: the fish are both *fast* and *alive*. But *quick* is also aligned with the word *dead* at the end of the second quatrain, thus conjuring the phrase from the Apostle's Creed in *The Book of Common Prayer*: 'From thence he shall come to judge the quick and the dead'. This single, semantically ambiguous word is therefore highly active within the stanza: it produces an evocative image of young children trying to catch fish in a stream, it shows the children in metaphoric pursuit of life, and it quietly signals that one of the underlying themes of the poem is nothing less than life and death.

In the third stanza, the children enact a ritual that will enable them to 'hear a dead man/Speaking underground'. Their dancing round the grave reveals their 'innocence' in relation to death; like all children who have yet to assume adult inhibitions about the subject, they are fascinated by it. But even as they play, the sky darkens, they stop to listen, and the narrator recalls:

> I heard a voice as clear as blood
> Strong as the heart.
> But what words were spoken
> I can never say,
> I shut my fingers round my head,
> Drove them away.

Imagination and innocent play have opened up a new and shocking perspective on the world. And then the children notice the inscription on the tombstone:

> Jessie traced the letters
> Black as coffin-lead.
> '*He is not dead but sleeping,*'
> Slowly she said.

The children's fate is sealed by words. The idea that language is instrumental in the loss of innocence again reflects Romantic ideas about early childhood; similarly, the idea that children's integration into symbolic systems deprives them of access to imaginary language is a Lacanian notion that recurs through children's literature (Nikolajeva, 2000).

Taken literally, as a child might read it, the inscription raises the alarming possibility that the person beneath the stone is still living – and thus a potential witness to the sacrilegious act. This, then, is not only sin, but also guilt and shame; a parallel to Adam and Eve's fear of discovery by God. And beneath the literal surface lurks *the* question about life: what happens after death? The inscription that pronounces on the children ironically speaks the language of full-blown adult inhibition and euphemism, the language of the world which the children will enter. Here, almost between stanzas, the children are caught in the moment of transition – a moment for which, significantly, they themselves have no words:

> I looked at Jessie,
> Jessie looked at me,
> And our eyes in wonder
> Grew as wide as the sea.
> Past the green and bending stones
> We fled hand in hand,
> Silent through the tongues of grass
> To the river strand.

This recalls the fall in the book of Genesis: 'and the eyes of them both were opened' – the moment in which humankind becomes conscious not only of the impact of sin but also of self, and of self in relation to the other. In the children's 'flight from Eden', the gravestones, symbols of death, are 'green and bending', as if, like plants, they are somehow alive; the grass meanwhile, in contrast to the wordless children, becomes an agent of speech. Chattering children are silent; inanimate objects spring to life and mute forms speak. The picture is of a world in upheaval – a fallen world. The children return to the water, which is no longer a stream, signifying youth, but a river, signifying maturity. That the children's newly acquired knowledge of death is not merely general but personal is indicated by the lines 'In case they opened up their eyes,/Called us from below'. They realise that death could call *them*.

The 'fall' follows an act of theft – not of fruit, but at least a jar that contained it – and is also a consequence of the children's innocent engagement with life, as embodied in their play. Moreover, Causley chose to place the work not only in *Collected Poems for Children* but in the section 'Come out to play' – a move perhaps reminiscent of Blake's ironic use of children's poetry in *Songs of Innocence and Experience* in order to challenge the reader's assumptions about the values normally embodied in that form. Whilst I am not suggesting that Causley has any kind of comparable political purpose, this poem and its presentation could nevertheless be seen to represent a similarly challenging view for a twentieth-century society that would prefer children to be 'set aside as a safely isolated group, in a cultural reservation called Innocence' (Watson, 1996:12).

To see the full effect of the fall, we have to go to Causley's adult poems that draw on his experience of teaching in school. 'Conducting a Children's Choir' (1968) expresses his ambivalence:

> They hold before their faces masks of flowers.
> Their summer eyes anticipate the snow.
> In skin as yet untouched by ticking showers
> There lies the simple statement of the crow.

These images could appear quite bleak were it not for the fact that, as Philip observes, 'the central question Causley asks is: is it possible to battle through from an innocence which is unknowing to an innocence which is all-knowing?' (1982:142). This too is a Romantic line of enquiry that can be traced back to Blake, who saw the possibility of innocence and experience being reconciled into a higher form of innocence, and to Wordsworth, who was concerned with the way in which the adult could reclaim the child's instinctive and spiritual knowledge. He believed that this, the poet's task, could be achieved by delving into the memory to find 'spots of time', particular moments of 'renovating virtue' (*The Prelude*, 1805). 'By St Thomas Water' indicates that this interest was also Causley's. The moment described has all the hallmarks of a 'spot in time', and its special meaning is clearly signalled by the words '*The day we* took the jam-pot'. Even more significantly, the final stanza shows us the adult narrator's process of reflection:

> Many a day has faltered
> Into many a year
> Since the dead awoke and spoke
> And we would not hear.
> Waiting in the cold grass
> Under a crinkled bough,
> Quiet stone, cautious stone,
> What do you tell me now?

Dana Gioia (1998:33) suggests that the narrator 'spends the rest of his life wondering what the dead man tried to tell him'. But the question is, 'What do you tell me *now*?' (italics mine). A more fitting interpretation, I would therefore suggest, is that 'now' does not refer to all the years that followed, but specifically to this time of reflection. Through the process of recollection, the adult is seeking to reclaim the ability he had as a child to hear things beyond the physical world, and to heed them. From his perspective of age and experience, the narrator knows that knowledge of mortality is, paradoxically, the key to life. But death, symbolised by the stone, is 'quiet' and 'cautious', and the grass is now 'cold'. This, the narrator seems to be saying, is the irony of innocence and experience. As a child, he *could* hear the voice of the dead, but *would* not hear it; as an adult he would hear it, but cannot.

Causley's poetry presents a complex picture of childhood both lost and ever-present, of innocence as a precarious visionary state that is the cause of its own destruction, and of the quest for reclamation and integration. But what place have these things in poetry that, if not written for children, is at least selected and published for them? I think the answer is that the task of reclamation and integration begins in childhood, where the journey from innocence to experience is already underway. Just as seeds of destruction are sown in childhood, so are seeds of redemption. And growth is slow. As Charles Causley says:

> If, say, 80 per cent of a poem comes across, let us be satisfied. The remainder, with luck, will unfold during the rest of our lives. (1966:92)

Acknowledgements

With thanks to Charles Causley and to Macmillan for permission to quote from 'Moorhens', 'Summer was Always Sun' and 'By St Thomas Water' from *I Had a Little Cat*, and from 'Conducting a Children's Choir' from *Charles Causley: Collected Poems 1951-2000*.

Works Cited

Blake, W (1789) *Songs of Innocence and Experience: Shewing the two Contrary States of the Human Soul.* William Blake

Causley, C (1968) *Underneath the Water.* London: Macmillan

Causley, C (1987) *Jack the Treacle Eater.* London: Macmillan

Causley, C (1996) *Collected Poems for Children.* London: Macmillan

Causley, C (2000) *Charles Causley Collected Poems 1951-2000.* London: Macmillan

Causley, C and Wilmer, C (1994) Charles Causley. In C Wilmer (ed) *Poets Talking.* Manchester: Carcanet

Causley, C (1966) Poetry and the Younger Child. In T Blackburn (ed) *Presenting Poetry: A Handbook for English Teachers.* London: Methuen

Dana Gioia, M (1998) The Most Unfashionable Poet Alive: Charles Causley. *The Dark Horse*, 5-6 (Summer 1997 and Spring 1998)

Nodelman, P (2008) *The Hidden Adult.* Baltimore: Johns Hopkins University Press

Nikolajeva, M (2000) Tamed Imagination: A Re-Reading of Heidi. In *Children's Literature Association Quarterly*, 25(2) 68-75

Philip, N (1982) Magic in the Poetry of Charles Causley. *Signal*, 39, 139-151

Stevenson, RL (1885) *A Child's Garden of Verses.* London: Longman and Green

Watson, V (1996) Innocent Children and Unstable Literature. In M Styles, E Bearne and V Watson (eds) *Voices Off: Texts, Contexts and Readers* (pp 1-15). London: Cassell

Wordsworth, W (1805) *The Prelude.* London

11

'Not Not Nursery Rhymes' and 'Not Not Lullabies': How Carol Ann Duffy and Þórarinn Eldjárn Refurnish the Nursery

Olga Holownia

Nursery rhymes, like the material chairs, tables and beds that make the nursery environment, never fall out of fashion and out of use. Their ubiquity and utility are evident (Goldthwaite, 1996; Styles, 1998), as is the fact that they involve an uncanny reiteration of common internationally-recognised motifs and patterns. Alongside the canonical repertoire exists an equally long-standing tradition of nursery-rhyme parodies which is being continuously replenished by new inventions epitomised by such collections as Michael Rosen's *Hairy Tales and Nursery Crimes* (1985) and Roald Dahl's *Revolting Rhymes* (1982) (*cf.* Livingston, 1971). By comparing the children's poetry of Carol Ann Duffy and Þórarinn Eldjárn, I aim to show how such playful and subversive refurnishing of the body of nursery poetry is far from confined to the British Isles. Furthermore, although such poetry is bound to be embedded in local traditions, the internationally-familiar aural qualities of nursery rhymes may obliterate language and cultural barriers.

This presentation of two contemporary examples of nursery poetry underlines the way these two poets from different backgrounds share an approach indebted to the masters of literary nonsense, Lewis Carroll, Edward Lear, but also Halfdan Rasmussen and Lennart Hellsing. Furthermore, it points to the existence of parallel trends in children's verse which have been developing since the mid-1970s. Bearing these features in mind, one is drawn to suggest a tentative comparison with IKEA nursery furniture, which shares key characteristics with the rhymes chanted around such furniture: simplicity, popularity, practicality, global presence and nonsense – indeed the product names resemble gibberish outside Scandinavia. Even when a nursery is refurnished with these familiar stock elements, it is still going to offer room for wild games and satisfy the imaginations of children as a furniture series introduced in the 1990s aimed to do. It was in that same decade that Duffy and Eldjárn turned to writing for young audiences to such a prolific degree that, to date, their respective oeuvres for children surpass their poetry for adults. In what follows I will be looking at their attempts to refurnish the nursery with new uses of stock elements. I will be focusing on parodies of *Mother Goose* rhymes (Duffy) and anti-lullabies (Eldjárn), also discussing the poets' original inventions.

Duffy and Eldjárn belong to the same generation; both came to prominence in the 1980s and '90s, and their poetry, both on and off the page, has since enjoyed unprecedented popularity in their respective countries. Noteworthily, they have been involved in, or influenced by, the poetic revivals of the 1960s and '70s and their works share preoccupations with the irreverent and innovative children's verse which has been conspicuous in Britain and Iceland since the mid-1970s (Styles, 1998:262-81; Kristjánsdóttir, forthcoming). Like Roger McGough, Brian Patten and other popular poets of that time, Duffy and Eldjárn are crosswriters. In the spirit of the carnivalesque, this new poetry builds on reversals and teases authority figures by siding with young readers. It plays with conventions, creatively exploits incongruity, humour, absurdity, and indulges in wordplay or even plain jokiness. The realm of the commonplace often serves as the inspiration for both the diction and imagery of their poems. However, the most familiar linguistic expressions, subjects and forms are presented in a way that lets us see them anew. This 'regaining of a clear view' is captured both by the concept of defamiliarisation, especially in nonsense verse, and, in relation to retellings of traditional material, by the concept of 'recovery' (Tolkien, 2001:56-7; Northrup, 2004). The latter is related to a sense of wonder similar to that experienced by a child revelling in things that for us have lost their heuristic pith. Although this poetry never avoids dark themes, what comes to the fore is the poets' preoccupation with language and their frequently self-reflective reliance on 'the revaluation of cliché' (Henri, 1968:80). Such revaluations, common in Duffy's and Eldjárn's poetry, which achieve a distancing effect (Whitley, 2007), provide a source of humour but also make one reflect on what we have come to take for granted. Clichés needn't be only linguistic. Indeed, we may speak of clichéd motifs, plots, forms or imagery which undergo revaluation.

Interestingly, Duffy's involvement with children's literature started with non-parodic revaluation. In her rewriting of the Grimm tales, first published in

1996, the poet aimed to recover the original language and imagery of the tales which had been bowdlerised and Disneyfied over the years. Although her first collection for children appeared only in 1999, the decade of her devotion to children's verse resulted in an impressively versatile and substantial edition of *Collected Poems for Children* (2009) and has become the subject of critical examination (Müller-Zettelmann, 2003; Whitley, 2007). As these critics have pointed out, in many respects Duffy's poetry for adults and works for children overlap, beginning with her Grimm tales and continuing in *Meeting Midnight* (1999), *The Oldest Girl in the World* (2000), *The Good Child's Guide to Rock 'n' Roll* (2003), *The Hat* (2007) and also *The Stolen Childhood and Other Dark Fairy Tales* (2003). Duffy started writing for children after the birth of her daughter in 1995. Bearing in mind the aforementioned aspect of 'recovery', it is interesting to hear the poet say that motherhood gave her access to early memory and imagination, which she describes as 're-being a child' (Duffy, 1999).

Re-being a child entails re-facing all manner of horrors which are evoked and simultaneously dispelled in poems such as 'Don't Be Scared', 'Be Very Afraid', and 'Tales of the Expected'. However, natural or innocuous sounding titles such as 'Quicksand', 'Whirlpool', 'Late' and 'Jamjar' in fact foretell the grotesque fate that meets their protagonists. The grotesque may be entwined with humour, as in the charm-like poem 'Irish Rats Rhymed to Death'. Among the lighter verses reminiscent of traditional nursery rhymes, we find an exclamatory ABC ('The Alphabest') and rollicking rock'n'roll rhymes. In many cases, the play with word sounds, the rhythm, and particularly the rhyme tend to dominate the poem's content. Moreover, familiar tunes resound in meta-textual riddles and unconventional tongue-twisters. Jemima Riddle 'plays the fiddle/hey-diddle-diddle/d' (Duffy, 2009:30) in a poem that is a minimalist dialogue comprising riddles reminiscent of nonsense verse. Seemingly simple, it can be treated as 'a stimulating introduction to the mechanisms of language and thought' (Müller-Zettelmann, 2003:191). The same rhyme is reconfigured in a poem about Bo Diddley who 'got fiddly on a diddley bow' (Duffy, 2009:18). Duffy's poems about the rock'n'roll heroes resemble tongue-twisters, started off by the name of a particular singer. Thus 'Little Richard was a twitcher' (p16) and 'Chuck [Berry] walked like a duck' (p16), both of which seem to echo playground jeers (cf. Opie and Opie, 2001: 175-205). 'Jerry Lee Lewis (b. 1935)' who 'leerily/woogied' (Duffy, 2009:21) tops the other ones in the quality of a true tongue-twister. Each poem is spun around a line from, or a title of, a known song. Snatches of pop songs indeed belong to the revolutionarily updated and broadened language of today's poetry for children (Styles, 1998:267). A revaluation occurs, however, when such quotations occur in children's verse. Short, snappy lines, rhymes and refrains place these poems between song lyrics and nursery rhymes. The imitation of both seems deliberate, as does the way they are allowed to overlap, thus becoming mnemonic verses about the heroes of Duffy's childhood to be memorised by children living today, but which also sneakily address the adults.

Interesting revaluations on various levels take place in Duffy's cycle 'Not Not Nursery Rhymes' (Duffy, 2009:175-7). They tap into the trend of reworkings of nursery rhymes in which the hypotext 'provides a 'coathanger' for new wit and experimentation' and the new nursery rhymes display dual appeal (Styles, 1998: 100). They tend to retain the unbowdlerised flavour of the original rhymes or folktales and aural qualities are crucial to the way the reworkings play with our expectations. Duffy's cycle includes versions of such classics as 'Humpty Dumpty', 'Jack and Jill', 'Three Blind Mice,' and 'Hey Diddle Diddle.' The last one opens with 'Ho Doodle Doodle' (Duffy, 2009:176). 'Ho' sounds like a dwarf's response to 'Hey' and triggers the alternation of vowels in the words that follow, so 'doodle' becomes the natural counterpart to 'diddle'. As a result, the rhyme pattern rather than the story itself seems to prompt the transition from 'fiddle' to 'poodle'. The poem's dynamics depend on how the new rhyme nears and departs from its hypotext. It stays – with one exception – within the original rhyming scheme, but the iconic trio, cat-fiddle-cow, is replaced by rat-poodle-elephant. Instead of the three unrelated images of the original comes an inconclusive story about the quarrelling rat and the poodle, communicated via a text message by the elephant, and the poem does fit into a 160-character limit of such messages. The poodle's appearance promises a story – two animals suffice to build the conflict – but nothing happens. Duffy introduces syntactically logical links between the lines, but the fact that the syntax of the new poem seems more logical merely makes one reflect on the lack of coherence between the images of the hypotext. The new version matches, if not supersedes, the familiar one in exposing 'unresolved tension between [the] presence and absence of meaning' which defines literary non-sense (Tigges, 1988:55).

We find a more radical revision of the hypotext in 'Three Sharp-Sighted Mice'. The innocent sounding antonym brings not only the reversal of cause and effect, but also changes the victims in the Grimm-esque scenario of the rhyme: the mice run away from the farmer's wife, who had used a carving knife to slit her husband's throat (Duffy, 2009:175). The verse echoes the hypotext, but the introduction of 'sharp-sighted' reverses its meaning. No longer about blindness, the poem tells of what the mice *see* and witness. Furthermore, Duffy plays with the literal connotation of the modifier. Appearing in the beginning, 'sharp' anticipates the events – and images – of the lines that follow. The full rhyme of 'wife-knife-life' preserves intact the poem's overall structure but contains a gruesome story which, incidentally, may allude to a lesser-known version of the round (cf. Opie and Opie, 1997:361). Instead of the original question in the final line comes the image of spilled blood, an image ironically less absurd than that of three blind mice with cut-off tails. One may object to the presence of such a poem in the refurnished nursery, but it is possible to defend it. Duffy recovers the crudeness of traditional rhymes (*cf.* Ronald, 1994) just as she did in her retellings of the Grimms. This 'robust comic defiance of grown-up pieties' (Warner, 1995) seems to appeal to the wild imaginations of the young audience (Warner, 2007:17). Secondly, as often happens in nonsense verse, the prominence of rhyme and metre deflates the horror (Kennedy, 1989). At any rate, children used to cartoons such as *Tom and Jerry* may be less shocked by the horrific image than the three sharp-sighted mice are.

Similarly, horrors and crudeness of the traditional repertoire are recovered and subsequently subject to 'new wit and experimentation' in Eldjárn's verse for children. Child-gobbling ogresses, human-abducting horses, hair-raising monsters and blood-thirsty warriors are mocked and tamed by means of recontextualisation, wordplay and rhyme. His poetry is grounded in traditional metrics and shares certain preoccupations with his works for adult readers, especially with regard to revaluation of common expressions and the transposition of themes from the Icelandic myth-kitty into contemporary reality. His children's poetry has been described as 'pioneering' (Aðalsteinsdóttir, 2006:606). The key collections started coming out in the 1990s, including *Óðfluga* (*Fastfly*, 1991), *Heimskringla* (*The Circle of the World*, 1992) and *Halastjarna* (Comet, 1997). These were followed by *Grannmeti og átvextir* (*Froots and Vegedibles*, 2001) and *Gælur, fælur og þvælur* (Lullers, Scarers and Twaddlers, 2007) which became a bestseller, outstripped only by the last volume of *Harry Potter*.

It is worth noting that in *Gælur* the poet uses one of the most traditional poetic forms called *rímur* – an Icelandic type of metrical ballad – to tell the fantastical stories that lurk in everyday reality. Eldjárn, who translated *Alice's Adventures in Wonderland* (1996), is an exponent of the nonsense genre in Iceland who challenges the claim that only English writers delight in nonsense (Cammaerts, 1925:76). In his best rhymes he exploits the wide possibilities offered by Icelandic word formation rules to create genuine tongue-twisters and provoke a sense of wonder about commonplace reality. Thus, for instance, he defamiliarises fruit and vegetables with the likes of 'chucknuts' ('*hentihnetur*'), 'vulcherries' ('*gammsínur*') and '*beancucumberries*' ('bauna-gúrkur'). Or he composes tongue-twisting sounds in a poem comprised almost entirely of words containing clusters of identical consonants such as *klarinetttittré* (clarinet-peg-tree), *rabbböndin* (chit-chat cords), *hammmáll* (hum-spoken) or *krosssauminn* (cross-stitched). In his lullabies, however, the poet complies with the international and traditional conventions required by the form but subverts them from within, as it were, thus creating verses akin to Duffy's 'Not Not' cycle.

'Vökuvísa' ('Wake-a-by') (Eldjárn, 2008:529) is Eldjárn's variation of vögguvísa (lullaby, literally cradle verse). Its setup is simple enough: a grandfather sings his granddaughter a lullaby. Yet, the transgression of the genre is signalled already in the poem's title, since in Icelandic the difference between the state of dreaming and vigil hinges on one voiceless consonant. The poet effectively uses paronomasia, based on the similarity between *vagga* (a cradle; to rock) and *vaka* (vigil; to stay awake) in order to subvert the primary purpose of a lullaby. The regular rhythm created by the traditional type of stanza called *dverghenda*, with its full end rhymes and regular alliteration, maintains perfect melodic serenity throughout a poem within which horror lurks. Inconspicuously, a discord sneaks in half-way through the poem as the grandfather realises that his singing in a 'husky and hoarse voice' proves to be a hair-raising experience for the baby. Ultimately, the lulling song becomes a waking one, as the title forewarns. The lullaby's main function is thus reversed and the authority figure is ridiculed.

Similarly, in the rhythmically titled 'Vöggumaggarugga' ('Cradle Maggi Rock') (Eldjárn, 2004:36-7) not only is the genre's prime purpose mocked but so is the authority of the parent. Maggi, the lullaby's addressee, is to be sent to sleep. The poem consists of two parts that differ crucially in their rhyme – schemes and diction. The beginning appears fairly conventional, consisting of lines such as 'Magga í ruggu ruggar/ruggumamma' (Maggi is in a cradle cradled/by cradling-mummy) and 'Mamma mamma dúlla/Maggi fara að lúlla' (Mum mum humming/Maggi going lulling). No knowledge of Icelandic is needed to discern how the clusters of soothing 'gg' and 'll' and the regular rhythm organising this part make it resemble a perfect cradle song. The language mimics and simultaneously mocks baby-talk. The characteristic shift in viewpoint occurs after a telling ellipsis placed between the two parts of the poem. This pause suggests that the singing ceases, as is indeed the case. Maggi's mother falls asleep and we hear the boy speak instead: 'Í hjarta finn ég fögnuð:/FRÁBÆRT, HÚN ER ÞÖGNUÐ!' (I feel jubilation in my heart:/ GREAT, SHE'S QUIET!) The boy can play in peace once his mum, whom he irreverently calls 'the old diehard', is pacified. The role-reversal depends for its effect on the initial use of simple, baby-talk syntax by the mother whereas Maggi's diction is strikingly coherent and eloquent. 'Motherese' or baby-talk plays an important, and soothing, role in this type of verse, one purpose of which is language acquisition (Warner, 2007:231). Conversely, in 'Vöggumag-garugga' such language is described as getting on the boy's nerves while he proves to be able to communicate in a grown-up way.

Eldjárn's lullabies tend to develop contrary to the reader's expectations. Firstly, despite a suitable form, they fail to send children to sleep and secondly, the poems mock, even if only benignly, the singing adults and encourage us to sympathise with the victims of parental inadequacy. Although conveyed in a humorous manner, these poems are reminiscent of Carroll's parodic lullaby performed by the Duchess (Carroll, 1993:77), which, as Marina Warner argues, captures the inherent ambivalence and contradictory nature of traditional cradle songs (Warner, 2007:222). In this context Warner actually discusses an Icelandic verse with the lines: 'Sleep, you black-eyed pig/Fall into a deep pit full of ghosts' (Warner, 2007:222). One can also recall 'Ný vögguvísa' ('New lullaby') by Káinn (Kristján Níels Jónsson, 1860-1939) whose soothing opening words segue into 'Shut up, obey and be good' (Vísnabók, 1965:65). Indeed, Eldjárn's lullabies expose similar exasperation and impatience, encapsulated in the exclamation: 'GREAT, SHE'S QUIET!' Significantly, however, in the new Icelandic lullabies, which in the style characteristic of urchin verse flout con-ventions, these emotions are expressed by children, not adults.

What is the nursery refurnished by Duffy and Eldjárn like? It allows plenty of room for wild games of sense and nonsense. We find familiar stock elements, but they are reconfigured in witty and challenging ways, forcing us to enjoy them anew. The poems of Duffy and Eldjárn play with readers' expectations by investigating and defamiliarising the commonplace, coining words, invert-ing metaphors, and allowing poetry to 'run wild' (Cammaerts, 1925:57). The contemplation of meaning, regardless of the possibly absurd message it carries, is what the revaluation of familiar forms and cliché-metaphors hinges on. In most cases the revaluation takes place at the phraseological level. But Duffy and Eldjárn also deploy the most formulaic of verses or borrow their structures in order to refill them with new content. Revaluation relies on the reader's expectations and the failure to fulfil them. Both adult and child audiences remember the original rhymes, so the more altered the content, the more humorous or shocking the effect brought by the new poem. This is what happens in Duffy's 'Not Not Nursery Rhymes'. Eldjárn's lullabies, on the other hand, rely on no specific hypotext, but the form itself makes us expect something different to what is delivered. Arguably 'every one of us could recite a string of nursery rhymes before we knew the meaning of the words which form them' (Opie and Opie, 1997:42). These rhymes insidiously lodge themselves in our memory. Thus grown-up readers may be disconcerted when no cow jumps over the moon, as is the case in Duffy's 'Ho, Doodle Doodle'. But new readers of new nurseries may find comfort in knowing that the cow did not disappear from the nursery. The cow has successfully transgressed cultural and linguistic barriers to land in 'Haikow' (Duffy, 2009:99), a four-line poem which consists of seventeen repetitions of the all-conveying and internationally understandable language of bovine sublime: 'Moo.'

Works Cited

Aðalsteinsdóttir, S (2006) Icelandic Children's Literature, 1780-2000. In Neijmann, DL (ed) A *History of Icelandic Literature*. Lincoln and London: University of Nebraska Press

Cammaerts, E (1925) *The Poetry of Nonsense*. London: Routledge and Sons

Carroll, L (1993) *Alice in Wonderland*. Wordsworth Editions: Ware

Duffy, CA (1999) *Interview with Carol Ann Duffy. Work in Progress*. London: BBC Radio 4

Duffy, CA (2009) *New and Collected Poems for Children*. London: Faber

Eldjárn, Ó (2004) *Óðhalaringla* (Madcomhere). Reykjavík: Vaka-Helgafell

Eldjárn, Ó (2008) *Kvæðasafn* (Collected Poems). Reykjavík: Forlagið

Goldthwaite, J (1996) *The Natural History of Make-Believe: A Guide to the Principal Works of Britain, Europe, and America*. Oxford: Oxford UP

Henri, A (1968) *Tonight at Noon*. London: Rapp and Whiting

Kennedy, XJ (1989) Disorder and Security in Nonsense Verse for Children. *The Lion and the Unicorn*, 13, 28-33

Kristjánsdóttir, D (forthcoming) Bókabörn. Reykjavík: University of Iceland Press

Livingston, MC (1971) *Speak Roughly to Your Little Boy: A Collection of Parodies and Burlesques*. New York: Harcourt Brace Jovanovich

Müller-Zettelmann, E (2003) 'Skeleton, Moon, Poet'. In Michelis, A and Rowland, A (eds) *The Poetry of Carol Ann Duffy: 'Choosing Tough Words'*. Manchester: Manchester University Press

Northrup, CB (2004) The Qualities of a Tolkienian Fairy-Story. *MFS Modern Fiction Studies*, 50, 814-37

Opie, I and Opie, P (eds) (1997) *The Oxford Dictionary of Nursery Rhymes*. Oxford: Oxford University Press

Opie, I and Opie, P (2001) *The Lore and Language of Schoolchildren*. New York: New York Review Books

Ronald, R (1994) The Generative Power of Nursery Rhymes. *Children's Literature Association Quarterly*, 19, 100-04

Styles, M (1998) *From the Garden to the Street: An Introduction to 300 Years of Poetry for Children*. London: Cassell

Tigges, W (1988) *An Anatomy of Literary Nonsense*. Amsterdam: Rodopi

Tolkien, JRR (2001) *Tree and Leaf*. London: HarperCollins

Vísnabók Káins (1965), Reykjavík: Bókfellsútgáfan

Warner, M (1995) Shitzee, spitzee! *TLS*, January 6

Warner, M (2007) *Monsters of Our Own Making: The Peculiar Pleasures of Fear*. Lexington: University Press of Kentucky

Whitley, D (2007) Childhood and Modernity: Dark Themes in Carol Ann Duffy's Poetry for Children. *Children's Literature in Education*, 38, 103-14

12

Humpty Dumpty and the sense of an unending

David Rudd

Antony Easthope (1991) once performed some 27 different readings of Gerard Manley Hopkins' poem, 'The Windhover', and Rod McGillis (1996) showed a similar facility interpreting 'Jack be Nimble'. My analysis of Humpty Dumpty, particularly as he appears in *Through the Looking-Glass*, follows this tradition – rather than that of Frederick Crews' *The Pooh Perplex* (1964). The standard nursery rhyme is as follows:

> Humpty Dumpty sat on a wall,
> Humpty Dumpty had a great fall.
> All the king's horses and all the king's men,
> Couldn't put Humpty together again.

But the character has become irrevocably associated with Lewis Carroll, especially as illustrated by John Tenniel. Like the other traditional rhymes in the *Alice* books, many think that Carroll penned them himself. The same is true of the parodies, the originals of which have largely been forgotten. Yet there is a key difference between the parodies and the rhymes, which lies precisely in the fact that the former work internally, changing the words themselves, whereas, with the latter, the text is lexically constant; it is external elements that change: the context, or lens, through which the text is framed.

This difference has interesting implications for what nonsense is. For in Carroll's case there are good arguments to suggest that rather than disrupting sense, he was, in fact, seeking more of it. In showing up the messy slippage of figurative language through nonsense, Carroll actually seems to be trying to establish what we might term *known-sense*. Thus he resolutely tries to undo language's ambiguities, to restore it to the literal; the simile 'as mad as a hatter', for example, becomes, indeed, a Mad Hatter; a 'grin like a Cheshire Cat' becomes similarly transmogrified, and so on (*cf.* Sewell, 1952).

Humpty Dumpty is the avatar of this; he is renowned for his power to establish a monologic sense:

> When *I* use a word, Humpty Dumpty said, in rather a scornful tone, it means just what I choose it to mean – neither more nor less ... The question is ... which is to be master – that's all. (Carroll, 1970:269)

He seems to epitomise what Carroll was himself about, refashioning phrases and idioms so that their signification could be shut down to a verbal monotone: no metaphor, no simile – no metonymy even – but, rather, *mono-nymy*. And I use the name Carroll, here, rather than Dodgson, as the author also worked hard to establish a clear division between the two, to the extent of demanding that a cross-reference in the Bodleian Library catalogue, linking the two, be removed.

However much, then, that Dodgson wished for some final disambiguation of language, so that one could talk precisely of cabbages and kings, he also realised the impossibility of this, given the process of signification. He realised how the individual tokens of language operate in different contexts – as shown by the way the jury in the *Alice* court scene rides roughshod over these very distinctions: 'the jury eagerly wrote down all three dates on their slates, and then added them up, and reduced the answer to shillings and pence' (Carroll, 1970:146).

In Humpty Dumpty, then, as Jacques Lacan observes (2001:60), we have a figure who takes it upon himself to be a master of discourse, despite delinquent words:

> They've a temper, some of them – particularly verbs: they're the proudest – adjectives you can do anything with, but not verbs – however, *I* can manage the whole lot of them! Impenetrability! That's what *I* say! (p269)

This sounds quite a dangerous thing for someone with an eggshell skin to say, until he defines his terms:

> I meant by 'impenetrability' that we've had enough of that subject, and it would be just as well if you'd mention what you mean to do next, as I suppose you don't mean to stop here all the rest of your life. (p269)

As Alice responds, 'That's a great deal to make one word mean'. She then gets Humpty Dumpty to explain 'Jabberwocky' in his own terms, it perhaps being logical that someone who can make nonsense out of normal words might be able to make sense out of nonsense ones. He confidently sets about the task of unpacking the meanings of its opening stanza:

'Twas brillig, and the slithy toves
    Did gyre and gimble in the wabe:
All mimsy were the borogoves,
    And the mome raths outgrabe. (p270)

Thus, to give one example, 'a '*borogove*' is a thin shabby-looking bird with its feathers sticking out all round – something like a live mop' (p272).

The way that Humpty Dumpty masters language, then, is by imposing a god-like singularity of meaning on words, similar to the way that God has Adam name all the animals in Genesis. Humpty Dumpty, sitting on high on his wall, seems to incarnate this sense of plenitude, of a *fons et origo*, while the wall also suggests notions of an enclosed, Edenic space. It is only when Humpty Dumpty has his own fall, 'a very heavy crash shook the forest from end to end' (p276) – which is foretold in the nursery rhyme – that the normal communicative function of language is restored. It is this democracy of signs, of common tokens, that Humpty Dumpty not only despises – 'You've been listening at doors – and behind trees – and down chimneys' (p264) – but which he is keen to stop; for, if things mean in the normal way, then that which he cannot even bring himself to enunciate – '*The King has promised me – with his very own mouth* – to – to ... ' (p264) – in other words, his downfall, will come to pass.

With a verse form, this sense of language's inevitable victory is even more powerful, which is perhaps why Humpty Dumpty objects so much to Alice starting to quote his rhyme, since verse lays more emphasis on iterability, on repetition; in short, full rhyme has a sense of fatalism.

So, as with the chicken and egg problem of which came first, Humpty Dumpty clearly sides with the egg: he wants to be in control of language, rather than recognise that it pre-exists, and thus pre-empts him. If his existence is called forth by the very rhyme that names, or nominates him, it just as readily ex-nominates him.

How far the Humpty Dumpty nursery rhyme did indeed pre-exist him is controversial, as indeed is its original meaning. The Opies, though, make a strong case that the rhyme was originally a riddle, to which the answer is 'an egg':

> There is a girls' game called 'Humpty Dumpty' ... In this game the players sit down holding their skirts tightly about their feet. At an agreed signal they throw themselves backwards and must recover their balance without letting go their skirts ... Perhaps the rhyme was not originally a riddle. Eggs do not sit on walls; but the verse becomes intelligible if it describes human beings who are personating eggs. (Opie and Opie, 1951:215)

However, I think that they might have noted one more element: that the final word of the rhyme, 'again', turns the rhyme into a round – pun unintended – sending the reader back to its beginning. This would not only emphasise the cyclic nature of things, which the egg symbolises, but it would also tie the rhyme more closely to notions of woman's time, of cycles and eggs forming on walls of wombs, only then, in most cases, to fall away. Moreover, this female mystery is one that men, regardless of their power – regardless, that is, of 'all the king's horses' and 'king's men' – can neither comprehend nor recreate.

If the rhyme was initially about women's fertility, then Carroll's version distinctly makes it more male-centric, particularly evident in Carroll's variant final line, 'Couldn't put Humpty Dumpty in his place again'. As Alice comments, this line's 'much too long for the poetry' (p262), but, for this very reason, draws attention to Humpty Dumpty's gender, and perhaps aligns the author more closely with this orotund figure. One could even argue that the lack of scansion lessens the emphasis on 'again', on the round, instead pointing out how Humpty Dumpty, just like the verse, has lost his form. As a yolky mess might, it runs on. Moreover, if one wanted to push the connection between Humpty Dumpty and Dodgson further, one might also point out that the author was himself destined to remain childless, having only his own creative outputs to engender, many of which, we are told, he invented to dispel disturbing night thoughts.

But going back to the original rhyme, we could also give its feminist emphasis more of a queer inflection, seeing Humpty Dumpty as having both male and female characteristics *in potentia*, as Plato argues in the *Symposium*. Consequently, the oral rhyme becomes more explicitly gendered only when Humpty is pictured, or the rhyme's words changed. In these terms, Humpty Dumpty's fall, keeping the various connotations of this word, is precisely into a patriarchal society where *he* always takes precedence, as Carroll makes explicit in referring to 'his place'.

Of course, for many Victorian readers, like the exemplary Duchess, a moral is obligatory, and it is easy to discern one: once broken, something cannot be fixed; or, in more Biblical terms, we cannot return to the Garden, to that place where word and thing were once conjoined. Slippage of meaning is an inevitable consequence of the Fall, which Carroll both bemoans and exploits. But it is equally possible to see more challenging morals in the verse, to see it as commenting on the hierarchical ordering of society, which we might frame in Marxist terms. Indeed, the very name, Humpty Dumpty, has connotations of uppity-ness, of getting above one's station – which is just what Humpty Dumpty might be seen to have done, positioning himself on top of a wall. He wants all to know about his associations with Royalty: 'Now, take a good look at me! I'm one that has spoken to a King, *I* am: mayhap you'll never see such another: and, to show you I'm not proud, you may shake hands with me!' (p264). He seems to have the pretensions and deferential manner of working-class royalists like Alf Garnett. In this reading, labour is effectively represented by the wall, constructed by workers who might regularly be seen balancing precariously on tall buildings and towers, constructing the very factories and chimneys that would enslave them.

However, Humpty Dumpty's uppity-ness is so overblown that it could be ironic, in which case the verse's second line is particularly interesting: there has been an elision; that is, the reason for Humpty Dumpty ending up off the wall has been glossed over. We are told only that this person 'had a great fall' – the fate of so many workers. Whereas owners would tend to blame labourers for their clumsiness, being drunk or whatever – *Humpty Dumpty*, the dictionary says, was a nickname for a clumsy person – the workers would point to the dangerous, unsafe conditions under which they laboured. We have a traditional, ideologically mainstream reading, then, and a more subversive alternative. In the former, we appear to hear the point of view of the ruling class: this clumsy, humpty dumpty figure has raised himself onto the wall without due care and attention – and he's clearly overweight, perhaps from overindulgence – so it's small wonder that he gets his come-uppance, or come-downance. After this presumption of standing above society, the forces of law and order are quickly on the scene, stressing the proper order of things, with the king at the top, and his emissaries, the cavalry, clearly visible below. The fate of people stepping out of line is underlined: they are likely to meet an unpleasant end. Alternatively, though, we might wish to draw attention to the fact that, in the third line, the horses precede the men – not the normal order of things. Furthermore, the men are not even seen to be riding, for the two groups are introduced separately, as though, perhaps, the horses – a metaphor for the workforce, maybe, as in the term 'workhorses' – have unseated their riders, the king's men, and risen up against them. If we follow this line of thought, we may then wish to revisit the opening line, and see Humpty Dumpty not as a commoner but, in fact, as the monarch, being the only named person in the rhyme. His 'great fall' would then suggest that there has been a revolution, in which the king's men, also unseated from their positions of power, are unable to re-establish traditional law and order. This gives the rhyme another moral, as a cautionary tale for royalty.

All these interpretations, as noted earlier, are context dependent. To some extent writers provide the context themselves, both within the text – place, character, period, imagery, content – and through their own historical location, as gendered, ethnic, class-based, national beings. But readers are also historically situated, thus adding more idiosyncratic dimensions: they have a reading-history, an awareness of other texts and discourses, which inflect their interpretations accordingly. Stanley Fish (1980), associated with reader-response criticism, argues that these 'interpretive communities' not only give a contextual framework for our interpretation of a text, but that they also delimit our reading; thus we will physically see certain things and not others. Fish – who sounds like he could have stepped straight out of Alice, and indeed, Humpty's own poem has the line, 'I sent a message to the fish' (p274) – thus recommends that the reader '*slow down* the reading experience' (Fish, 1980: 28), so that one can go with the temporal flow of having meaning arrive one word at a time, rather than being imposed magisterially at the end.

Reading 'Humpty Dumpty' in these terms, we might then come up with a very different interpretation, and not be restricted by the temporal unfolding of the clauses: Humpty sat on a wall first; then, at some later point, he fell off it. Indeed, it is quite possible that there is a gap here. It could be, therefore, that this character had a fall in the past, but is now back on the wall again. The king's horses and king's men would then simply have demonstrated their incompetence after his earlier fall, in that, at that time they couldn't put Humpty together again. However, others, more competent, might have succeeded in doing so; or, indeed, Humpty Dumpty could well have achieved this feat of pulling himself together on his own. Given the way that the coordinates of time and space are distorted in the Looking-Glass world, such a reading has some provenance.

Shifts in the ordering of events are common, too, in psychoanalytical readings: earlier events are retroactively interpreted, and some events – traumatic ones especially – are repeated *ad nauseam*. The rhyme might then be seen to re-enact that stage in life when the child has to separate from its mother, coming to see itself as a separate being. DW Winnicott, in fact, thought

Humpty Dumpty such a good illustration of this process that he actually used the term 'Humpty Dumpty stage' to characterise how a child must learn to balance inner and outer worlds, to avoid the very psychic disintegration – a falling apart – that Humpty enacts. The child, in negotiating this stage, draws on transitional objects (Winnicott, 1971) – things like teddy bears or security blankets as symbolic stand-ins for the absent parent. Humpty Dumpty, lacking these supports, therefore becomes a victim, his ego failing to develop properly. It is thus significant that Humpty Dumpty is so often pictured as an egg, the shell being a suitable metaphor for the ego, something that is seen to hold a person together, providing a unified, public self, although less palatable contents might lurk within.

However, for other psychoanalysts, such as Jacques Lacan, the ego is not something to protect and cultivate; rather, the ego is seen as more like the pearl of an oyster: it might be highly prized, but is in fact the product of external irritants. For Lacan, the ego provides us with a false sense of self, representing social conformity. The ego originates at what Lacan calls the mirror stage, when we are shown a falsely whole image of ourselves in a looking-glass, which we then try to live up to. But in order to function more successfully we need to see through this mirror image, to recognise that we never really possessed the coherence that greets us. Rather than this outer casing being a real self, it is, in fact, more like what Lacan calls an *hommelette* – ie *homme-lette*, or little man, punning on the word *omelette*, which suggests that it more resembles a shapeless mass of egg (Lacan, 1977:197). In these terms, it is the socially-adjusted self that the king's men – representatives of the Other – cannot put back together. This still does not exclude the possibility of Humpty Dumpty, whose very name captures a fractured sense of self, with its taunting, echoing rhyme, starting a new life, one less constricted by social convention, by the official structures and institutions of society. The descent of Humpty Dumpty would then be a *felix culpa*, a fortunate fall, allowing the birth of a new man – or woman.

Let me suggest one other reading, though, for it feeds into my in-conclusion. This draws on Derrida's work, which is centrally concerned with the inability of language to contain sense within discrete categories. Walls of course, by their very existence, create a divide, an either/or. But Humpty Dumpty, sitting on the fence, so to speak, suggests a wish to be both/and, to fend off any commitment to one thing rather than another. His situation brings to mind Derrida's notion of *différance* (Derrida, 1982), which argues that sides are never distinct; rather, they are connected at the very point of their divide, the wall; categories, in other words, always inter-depend. Humpty Dumpty's very name, as noted above, suggests a state of fracture, of being broken in two – which is what rhymes do: they seem to unify difference, but in sound only. Not just Humpty Dumpty, either, for the horses and men are also talked of separately: horses first, men after, as if the latter might have fallen off the former – mimicking what Humpty has done. The phrase 'couldn't put Humpty together again' is, then, particularly noteworthy, for 'Humpty', as such, never was together, in being separated from his rhyming other half, 'Dumpty'. The name intimates something that was always already fractured.

This might lead us to see the text as lacking any coherence, despite the fact that, as readers, we always strive to achieve some final sense of textual wholeness. So, we move linearly through it, word by word, perhaps seduced by the full rhymes into thinking we might attain some sort of satisfactory conclusion – as readers might hope from my chapter; yet final meaning is always deferred, always just escaping us. We come armed with the tools of analysis; and we are certainly aware of the rules of grammar – those officials that police texts as assiduously as the king's emissaries – but, just like them, we find that once the text starts to unfold, we can never draw a tidy line round it and declare interpretation finished. In fact, it can only be put together – again! Each new construction is also a deconstruction, an *hommelette* that lacks clear boundaries, the signifiers spreading meaning as fast as we try to delimit it.

Humpty Dumpty seems to realise this with his own poem that he recites for Alice. It concludes:

> 'And when I found the door was shut,
> I tried to turn the handle, but –'
> There was a long pause.
> 'Is that all?' Alice timidly asked.
> 'That's all,' said Humpty Dumpty. 'Goodbye.' (p275)

It's tempting to end there: 'That's All Folks', as Bugs Bunny or Elmer Fudd might say. But Alice's response, 'Good-bye, till we meet again!' suggests, once more, that – indeed – there must be more.

Context, then, is all. Nonsense is created by words out of place, or words existing in more than one place simultaneously, as do puns, or words with bits of their make-up – their morphemes, phonemes, graphemes – missing, awry. Isolate a word and its meaning falls away: is it 'important – unimportant – important – unimportant', as the King of Hearts tries to decide in *Alice*. Without context it doesn't much matter, for the latter, 'unimportant', will always win. Carroll demonstrates this, following the very illogic that he finds language permits – though I think he'd prefer it didn't. But he is most careful to isolate such nonsense through his framing devices. It is contained within a looking-glass and bound by the rules of chess; and lastly, it is enclosed within the persona of that humorous children's writer, Lewis Carroll, from whom the mathematician and logician distances himself.

It seems appropriate to end this engagement with Humpty Dumpty as Alice herself does, with the sense of an unending, to adapt Frank Kermode's phrase. As Alice puts it, in true Derridean style: 'of all the unsatisfactory people I ever met –' She never finished the sentence ... ' (Carroll, 1970:276).

Works Cited

Carroll, L (1970) *The Annotated Alice* (ed) Martin Gardner. Harmondsworth: Penguin

Crews, FC (1964) *The Pooh Perplex: A Student Casebook.* London: Arthur Barker

Derrida, J (1982) *Margins of Philosophy* (trans) Alan Bass. Chicago: Chicago University Press

Easthope, A (1991) *Literary into Cultural Studies.* London and New York: Routledge

Fish, S (1980) I*s There a Text in this Class? The Authority of Interpretive Communities.* Cambridge: Harvard University Press

Kermode, F (1968) *The Sense of an Ending.* Oxford: Oxford University Press

Lacan, J (1977) *The Four Fundamental Concepts of Psycho-Analysis* (ed) Jacques-Alain Miller (trans) Alan Sheridan. London: Hogarth

McGillis, R (1996) *The Nimble Reader: Literary Theory and Children's Literature.* New York: Twayne

Opie, I and Opie, P (1951) *The Oxford Dictionary of Nursery Rhymes.* Oxford: Oxford University Press

Sewell, E (1952) *The Field of Nonsense.* London: Chatto and Windus

Winnicott, DW (1971) *Playing and Reality.* London: Tavistock

13

'If it rhymes, it's funny': Theories of Humour in Children's Poetry

Karve Coats

Karen Coats

One day while walking to school, my daughter and I were discussing a headline we had recently seen that she found funny even though it had no humorous content. 'It just rhymed,' she said, 'and I think if it rhymes, it's funny.' She's right, according to Alastair Clarke's study on the pattern recognition theory of humour. Clarke sets his theory apart from theories proposed and debated in philosophical and literary discourse by asserting a neuroscientific basis for humour that disregards content altogether: for Clarke, 'The humorous response is evoked by the surprise recognition of a pattern' (2008:27). Content is important for Clarke only insofar as it forms the individual entities that are first apprehended and then recognised as repeating in adapted circumstances. Pattern recognition is obviously a crucial facet in a child's developing cognitive arsenal; it enables a child to access and find order in a world that would otherwise present itself as a kind of terrible randomness of individual events or entities. As sequences of entities develop into patterns, children can act on expectations of pattern repetition, and this produces a kind of reward or sense of mastery. Humour, on the other hand, produces a different kind of reward, because it is based not on the expectations of the repetition of a familiar pattern, but on the surprise of discerning a pattern despite altered circumstances or in an unexpected place, and thus rewards our ability to parse innovation.

In the case of the headline, for instance, my daughter expected the linguistic pattern to be resolved in a non-rhyming way in keeping with most serious or ordinary language, and was therefore surprised and rewarded to recognise another linguistic pattern, that of rhyme, in an unexpected place. Children's poetry, on the other hand, is a place where we often expect to find rhyme, repetition, rhythm, and other established and easily discernable patterns. Indeed, Kieran Egan (1988) points out that this particular type of word play facilitates and augments a child's cognitive abilities by helping her recognise patterns and generate pattern completion or continuation. For a poem to be humorous, though, there must be some sort of innovation on an expected pattern that evokes surprise, such as when ordinary syntax or a recognised poetic form is violated, or when words are used in an unfamiliar or punning way, or when subtler cultural patterns dependent on content unexpectedly appear.

In the following limerick of unknown origin, we find such a surprise based on violating the expected rhythm of a familiar form:

> There was a young man from Japan
> Whose limericks never would scan.
> When asked why this was,
> He replied, 'It's because
> I always try to fit as many syllables into the last line as ever I possibly can.'

Likewise, this anonymous limerick, which includes a play on two meanings of the word 'meter', enabling a semantic as well as a formal level of pattern recognition that contributes to its humour:

> A decrepit old gas man named Peter,
> While hunting around for the meter,
> Touched a leak with his light.
> He arose out of sight,
> And, as anyone can see by reading this, he also destroyed the meter.

These playful deviations of the limerick form are so ubiquitous as to have become an established subgenre of their own – the anti-limerick. As with any parody, however, some level of familiarity with the original is necessary for readers to get the joke or, in Clarke's terminology, to recognise the pattern that is being innovated. In this parody of Lear from W.S. Gilbert, the deviance from the pattern is so significant that for children, who either are not familiar enough with the limerick form to find the pattern or who don't recognise the original, the effect is likely to be confusion rather than humour:

> There was an old man of St. Bees,
> Who was stung in the arm by a wasp;

When they asked, 'Does it hurt?'
He replied, 'No, it doesn't,
But I thought all the while 'twas a Hornet.' (Wells, 1903:xix)

Deviations and surprise recognitions of new patterns are not just limited to form. Ogden Nash, for instance, often created nonsense words in his limericks, such as 'wearance' and 'tearance', to continue the pattern of the rhyme he had established with 'Clarence' and 'parents'. There's no reason why the words shouldn't exist – they are pronounceable and their form doesn't violate any conventions of spelling or root-suffix adhesion – but they just don't, and therefore their use is surprising, incongruent, and humorous. Another example of more complex pattern recognition can be found in Douglas Florian's 'The Monarch Butterfly'. In this poem, Florian establishes a subservient formal pattern of rhyme and repetition, but also a dominant semantic one of stately formality in his description of the butterfly. He positions his monarch as the leader of 'great migrations' and uses inverted syntax such as 'Past nations he wings' to evoke high seriousness and dignity of purpose and carriage. The final word, 'puke', then evokes surprise because, while it continues the subservient patterns of rhyme and rhythm, its position as slang and its reference to an abject bodily response violates the dominant pattern of lofty description that the poem has established. With the surprise comes the recognition of dissonance or pattern cessation that then evokes a humorous response.

While I find Clarke's work useful for analysing linguistic forms of humour such as those illustrated above, I find myself wanting to put both cultural and psychological meat on its very bare bones. After all, his condition for humour does not, by his own admission, account for why not everyone laughs at the same things, and thus I think an interdisciplinary approach that takes into account social interaction, cultural norms and psychoanalytic theories of development is a necessary supplement for a truly comprehensive understanding of why some poems are funnier than others. For instance, in Clarke's discussion of the evolutionary functions and benefits of humour, he asserts that humour gives us a physical reward for cognitive perception in difficult circumstances that is, the release of endorphins, hormones and neurotransmitters; and alterations in levels of stress hormones (2008:51-56). In other words, humour makes us feel as though we have won something. This accords with professor of speech communication Charles Gruner's (1997) comprehensive claim that all humour, no matter what form it takes or content it contains, can be explained through the superiority theory first articulated by philosopher Thomas Hobbes. Hobbes observes:

Men laugh at mischances and indecencies, wherein there lies not wit or jest at all ... Also, men laugh at the infirmities of others ... I may therefore conclude that the passion of laughter is nothing else but *sudden glory* arising from a sudden conception of some *eminence in ourselves* by comparison with the infirmity of others, or with our own formerly: for men laugh at the *follies* of themselves past, when they come suddenly to remembrance, except they bring with them any present dishonor. ... (as cited in Gruner, 1997:13)

In all humorous utterances and situations, there is an element of competition, adds Gruner, which sets the stage for there to be a winner and a loser. Take away the possibility of winning and losing, and you take away the humour. He stresses, interestingly, that unlike gambling, where the possibility of winning is what keeps the gambler going, the possibility of losing is what keeps us in the game of humour. If you had a magic formula, for instance, that ensured that you would always bowl a perfect game, bowling would soon lose interest for you; the excitement and incentive of any game is the hope that you will triumph against the possibility that you won't. In life, likewise, as the country song goes, sometimes you're the windshield, and sometimes you're the bug, and this uncertainty is one of the conditions that make humour possible.

Even theories and explanations of humour play into the superiority theory. Gruner claims that his is the only theory of humour we need; Clarke does likewise. Likewise, we assert our superiority whenever we offer an explanation for an individual instance of humour. If I can explain it, I prove that I have understood it – in other words, my perspicacity has won out over the ambiguity of language or the incongruity of the concept. If I have to explain it, say, to someone else who didn't understand it, not only have I won out over the joke, I've also won out over the person who didn't get it – getting something that someone else didn't is *de facto* a form of winning, unless, of course, what you get is the flu or something equally unpleasant. At any rate, it's a common cliché that if you have to explain a joke, it isn't funny. Well, maybe yes and maybe no. You might not think it's funny because you weren't able to discern the pattern upon which it innovates – which means you didn't win, either over the meaning of the joke itself or over the butt of the joke. She who laughs last, after all, might just think slowest.

If we avoid fiddly pedantic competitions among theorists and accept the idea that the thrill of victory is either one of the necessary conditions or one of the rewards for humour, then the question becomes what would count as a win when it comes to linguistic humour, such as that which we find in much children's poetry. I would argue that through language, and specifically through the patterned language play of poetry, we win out, to some degree, over the randomness and terror evoked by the two inevitabilities of life identified by Bataille and closely linked to embodied experience: 1) I am insufficient, and 2) I will die (1988:xxxii).

Lacanian psychoanalysis teaches that the child's separation from the mother inaugurates a sense of lack, of insufficiency, first on the part of the child herself, but soon on the part of the mother as well. Language, especially a patterned language full of metaphors and rich imagery, substitutes in some way for that lack by enabling both social connection and an imaginative connection between the world of words and the world of things. Poetic language, with its formal structures and its ability to metonymise entities and pattern experience, enables children to erect structures of predictability over which they have an illusion of control, allowing them to exercise a form of linguistic mastery over a physical world they can't always comprehend and certainly cannot control. Hence it separates them from their embodied experience at one level, while its rhythms and sonorous music reconnect them to that body in pleasurable ways.

Examples of how this works come in the many short humorous treatments that I might call paeans to the skin. For instance, Max Fatchen, in his quatrain 'Hullo, Inside,' and Colin West, in his quatrain 'Insides' both express gratitude to their skin for enclosing their innards and holding their parts together (Prelutsky, 1991). Tedd Arnold (1997), on the other hand, expresses anxious sentiments about the same phenomenon. In his picturebook, *Parts*, a boy discovers that bits of him – hair, skin, boogies, belly-button lint, teeth – are falling off. His concern is that 'The glue that holds our parts together isn't holding me!!!' (n.p.). His anxiety is both expressed and expelled by his use of a tightly controlled meter and through the deployment of humour. What he demonstrates without realising it is that, to a large degree, *words* are what hold his body image together; his parents eventually explain the processes of exfoliation and tooth loss, thus partially alleviating his anxiety, which has already been contained through the use of rhyme, just as Dr. Seuss created controlled anarchy through the tight containment of chaotic action within a fixed, regular metre. The humour comes through the reader's winning out over the things that trouble the protagonist – the reader recognises in this boy's fears ones that she herself has put aside, but she also enjoys the process of bouncing along in a pattern that surprises her with its linguistic innovations.

Children come hardwired with a range of diffuse emotions that need to be organised and developed according to cultural and social norms and ideologies. Children's literature plays a huge role in helping in that project, as it provides images and language that carry the values and possibilities for identity construction in a given culture. Along with adult and peer interaction, children's literature and culture shape children's identities by giving them the discourses and images to identify with. Children's poetry plays a crucial role in this project by helping children regulate embodied experience; they must transition from and combine the rhythms of their own bodies into the rhythms their cultures and languages value. They have a basic emotion of fear or anxiety; their stories teach them what to be afraid of; their poems help them contain those fears by manipulating their emotional states and containing them in metre. When they realise their essential separateness from other people and things in the world, they develop longing and desire; their stories teach them both what is missing and what is desirable; their poems ameliorate those longings by transforming them into aesthetic pleasures.

Stories and poems organise diffuse emotions into narrative and formal contexts that allow us to manage reality; this is an historical constant. But the values people live by change over time and across cultures. I would argue that contemporary western culture requires certain dispositions for people to flourish: among these are mental flexibility, a high tolerance for ambiguity, a capacity for moral decision making in the face of complex and competing ideologies, and divergent thinking. These are all, according to philosopher John Morreall (1999), a result of a comic, as opposed to a tragic, way of viewing the world. In Clarke's terms, they result from the evolved ability to discern patterns across varied circumstances. Children's poetry, especially the nonsense tradition inaugurated by Carroll and Lear, demands that sort of mental flexibility and facilitates its development through the manipulation of patterns of rhythm and rhyme set against absurd rearrangements of the physical as well as the linguistic world.

Deploying our interdisciplinary model, we might say that the appreciation of nonsense verse or humorous poetry represents the fruition of a victory won in stages. In psychoanalytic terms, the use of language is a triumphant response to the trauma of expulsion from the maternal body because it aligns the child with the paternal Law as it is represented in the written word. Indeed, Kristeva asserts that the child's 'entry into syntax constitutes a first victory over the mother' (1980:289) and just as he rejects his indebtedness to the body of the mother, he also uses language to recast embodiment *per se*. Poetic language has a somatic dimension that enables the child to re-find a

126

bit of the *jouissance* he has lost in his replacement of immediate embodied experience with imaginary and symbolic representations of experiences. It involves the body emotionally with its rhythms and its patterns of sound, and gives the material world back to the child in images. However, the achievement of language is an incomplete victory for the child, as it simply asserts a new, paternal master who could potentially swallow the child up in its own straitened and lockstep rhythms that affirm the hegemony of a patriarchal symbolic order. A disruption or unexpected alteration cracks the pattern up, allowing for movement and innovation. In other words, if the acquisition of syntax is a victory over the mother, then the acquisition of a sense of humour is the child's first victory over the father.

From victory unto victory the child progresses through the stages Freud outlined in the development of a sense of humour, which correspond handily to Erikson's stages of development as well; each win enables a child to enjoy yet another level of humorous poetry. Freud's stage of play, for instance, challenges the congruity of objects with their names or uses and concepts with their meaning. Humour at this stage consists in calling people and things by names that aren't theirs, or using objects in innovative ways – calling mommy daddy, say, or using a pan as a hat. This kind of play aligns with Erikson's stage of trust vs. mistrust in that children have to acquire a sense of consistency in regard to the things and people in their world. Once they are assured of that consistency, they can test it through playful manipulation that produces humour rather than anxiety – just because I call mommy daddy doesn't mean she changes. Poems that challenge identity and imagine alternative uses for everyday things, often playing out absurd consequences, participate in that sort of humour.

Scatological or scandalously gross poems that challenge adult rules of propriety find favour with children who are in Freud's jesting stage. Freud emphasises that the key factor in this stage is an audience who will in fact be scandalised. Erikson's more nuanced account of this stage indicates that children will experience conflicts between autonomy versus shame and doubt, and initiative versus guilt. Poems such as those found in Adam Rex's Frankenstein books (2006, 2008), that explore the abject, disgusting, and monstrous or that blatantly violate parentally approved conventions, correspond to the issues of the child asserting himself against the strictures of his culture, the rejection of which might induce shame or guilt. On the other hand, if you take the initiative and make a sandwich from the garbage your neighbors throw at you, or find a husband after you're dead, or craft a hat from carrots to stave off carnivorous zombies, you can meet the challenges with humour rather than shame, doubt, or guilt.

In Freud's final stage, children (and adults) use jokes to expound upon problematic themes, without expressing hostile and sexual feelings. Playground poetry, which is often competitive, sexual, and aggressive, evolves at this stage in which, according to Erikson, competence is at stake against a sense of inferiority. Aspiring wits invent and recite poems that display their linguistic finesse while containing anxiety over their bodily prowess. Dirty limericks, suggestive jump rope rhymes and wicked parodies of old favorites dominate the poetry slams of the playground set, sublimating emergent sexual and hostile feelings that may not even be understood through a medium young poets have successfully mastered.

Obviously, theoretical models such as those I have discussed and put forth are attempts at mastering the complexities of lived experience, destined to remain inadequate to that experience. Indeed, the most important thing to remember when discussing any sort of stage theory is that the stages are persistent and recursive; anxieties that seemed long overcome may resurface at any time, and victories must be renegotiated. And while competence in all aspects of life is what we aspire to, the certainties of life – our insufficiency and our mortality – have stacked the decks against us. With children's humorous poetry, however, we can find and play with the cracks in the ideological systems, the linguistic codes and patterns, and the pretentiousness of the pretence. We can crack wise, and we can crack ourselves up, thus finding the truth in the song by Leonard Cohen: 'There is a crack in everything: that's how the light gets in' (1992).

Works Cited:

Arnold, T (1997) *Parts*. New York: Dial

Bataille, G (1988) *Inner Experience*. LA Boldt (Trans.). Albany, NY: SUNY Press. Originally published as L'Experience Interieure, Editions Gallimard: 1954

Clarke, A (2008) *The Pattern Recognition Theory of Humor: An introduction*. Cumbria: Pyrrhic House

Cohen, L (1992) *Anthem. On The Future [LP]*. Canada: Sony Music Entertainment

Egan, K (1988) *Primary Understanding: Education in early childhood*. New York and London: Routledge

Erikson, EH (1968) *Identity, youth, and crisis*. New York: Norton

Florian, D (2004) *Omnibeasts: Animal poems and paintings*. New York: Houghton Mifflin Harcourt

Freud, S (1961) *Humour. The Standard Edition of the Complete Psychological Works of Sigmund Freud*. J Strachey (Ed.). London: Hogarth Press

Freud, S (1963) *Jokes and Their Relation to the Unconcious*. New York: Norton

Gruner, CR (1997) *The Game of Humor: A comprehensive theory of why we laugh*. New Brunswick, NJ: Transaction

Kristeva, J (1980) *Desire in Language: A semiotic approach to literature and art*. LS Roudiez (Trans). New York: Columbia University Press

Morreall, J (1999) *Comedy, Tragedy, and Religion*. Albany: SUNY Press

Prelutsky, J (Compiler) (1991) *For Laughing Out Loud: Poems to tickle your funny bone*. New York: Knopf

Rex, A (2006) *Frankenstein Makes a Sandwich*. New York: Harcourt

Rex, A (2008) *Frankenstein Takes the Cake*. New York: Harcourt

Wells, C (1903) *A nonsense anthology*. New York: Scribner

14

Children's Oral Poetry:
Identity and Obscenity

C.W. Sullivan III

Folklorists have been collecting poetry from children for over 100 years, and antiquarians for even longer. Adults in general, though, have only vague and probably overly-sentimental memories of the rhymes that they circulated. Children's oral poetry, however, is the creation of a culture significantly different from the adult culture around it, and it is interesting and enlightening to examine the ways in which the members of this culture use poetic forms to create, first, an identity separate from the adult culture and, second, especially through the medium of obscenity, an identity in opposition to the adult culture.

Simon Bronner asserts that the division between adult authority and the children under adult control is reflected in children's folklore in general:

> For children, we must remember, do not simply ape the mores of adults. They want to declare their own identity, and lore is their protected expression of cultural connection to one another ... Besides rebelling against adult norms, children's folklore reflects children's concerns about their rapid growth, the appropriate responses to adult society, and traditional roles and values in a nation being modernised. (1988:29-31)

Oral poetry, whether handed down traditionally to deal with recurring situations or created and circulated in response to contemporary cultural stimuli, forms a very large part of younger children's folklore.

Children use traditional rhymes in what Iona and Peter Opie call 'oral legislation' (1959:121-153); that is, they use rhymes in the way older children and adults use books of rules. Counting-out rhymes, for example, such as 'Eenie, meenie, miney, moe' or 'One potato, two potato', are considered un-biased ways of selecting the first 'IT' in a game, the sacrifical person who has to be 'IT' without having been caught. Game or play rhymes are not always legislation, but they do structure children's activities; examples include game rhymes, 'The Farmer in the Dell', hand-clapping rhymes, 'I'm a pretty little Dutch girl', ball-bouncing rhymes, 'My name is Alice', and the largest category of all, jump-rope rhymes, 'Cinderella Dressed in Yellow', 'Teddy Bear, Teddy Bear, turn around', and 'Policeman, Policeman do your duty'. Such rhymes have been circulated by children for generations as they organised their own play, without direct adult supervision, long before they were whisked off to such regulated activities as adult-organised football or baseball leagues, Boy Scouts, or Girl Guides.

In addition to regulating their own games, children have a series of rhymes that attempt to enforce conformity. Children have their own ideas, independent of – but to some extent derived from – the adult culture that surrounds them, and they have rhymes which make fun of or insult transgressors within the group. Overweight children hear 'Fatty, fatty, two-by-four,' a child hastily dressed might hear, 'I see London, I see France/I see [name]'s underpants,' informers to authorities hear, 'Tattletale, tattletale,/Hanging on the bull's tale,' liars hear 'Liar, liar, pants on fire,' and, of course, immature or sensitive children hear, 'Cry, baby cry, stick your finger in your eye.' There are many more such rhymes, and the point is that they are circulated by children, not taught by adults, and address what the child's folk group considers proper or, more to the point, improper behaviour.[1]

On a slightly more complex level, and more obviously influenced by the adult community, perhaps especially by the family, are rhymes that insult people outside the child's immediate peer and age group. The Opies, collecting in the 1950s, included the following rhymes in a chapter entitled 'Partisanship'. Some rhymes have historical origins:

> The Irishmen ran down the hill,
> The Englishmen ran after,
> And many a Pat got a bullet in his back
> At the Battle of Boy'an Water. (1959:343)

Other kinds of partisanship can be directly religious. Protestants may say, 'Catholic, Catholic, ring the bell,/When you die you'll go to hell' and be answered by the Catholics, 'Protestant, Protestant, quack, quack, quack,/Go to the Devil and never come back' (p344). Still other rhymes can be political, this one based on an Oscar Meyer bologna commercial jingle:

My peanut has a first name
It's J-I-M-M-Y
My peanut has a second name
It's C-A-R-T-R (*sic*)
Oh, I hate to see him every day
And if you ask me why I'll say
'Cause Jimmy Carter has a way
Of messing up the U-S-A (Sullivan, 1980:9)

What are serious matters to adults – war, religion, and politics – become fodder for children creating parodies of that adult seriousness.

There are also national and ethnic attitudes in some children's rhymes. When I was young, we caught 'a Nigger by the toe', although later and more sensitive versions of 'Eenie, Meenie, Miney, Moe' change the offensive 'Nigger' to 'Tiger'. In *One Potato, Two Potato: The Folklore of American Children*, Herbert and Mary Knapp, collecting and publishing some twenty years after the Opies, include, in addition to political rhymes, what I would call derisive rhymes about Polish people (denigrated as 'Polacks'), African-Americans, Asian-Americans and Jews (pp190-206). One that the Knapps collected covers several bases:

Franklin said to Eleanor,
'Eleanor, how are you?'
Eleanor said to Franklin,
'I've got some advice for you.
Roses are red, violets are blue,
You kiss the niggers,
I'll kiss the Jews,
And we'll stay in the White House
As long as we choose.' (p201)

Rather than reinforcing internal conformity, these rhymes solidify the folk group's identity in opposition to what anthropologists and sociologists, as well as folklorists, would call 'The Other'; i.e., those people who are obviously and demonstrably not 'Us'.

Another way in which children assert their own identity is through parody. This seems to me a more subtle kind of partisanship or derision in which children take what is presented to them by the adult culture and parody it; that is, they take something serious and change it to make it humorous. Bronner suggests that 'Children are fond of parodying the standard and familiar, especially when in the process of doing so they can establish that they have a world of their own making' (p77). Nothing is out of bounds as far as children are concerned. They will parody religious materials from evening-meal grace, 'Good bread, good meat,/Good God, let's eat' to evening prayers, 'Now I lay me down to sleep,/A bag of peanuts at my feet', to Christmas carols, 'Joy to the world, the school burned down'. School is a particular target; 'The Battle Hymn of the Republic' becomes 'Mine eyes have seen the glory of the burning of the school' and in a parody of 'On Top of Old Smokey', we hear 'I shot my poor teacher/With a forty-four gun'. Commerical jingles, too, are prime targets: 'MacDonald's is your kind of place,/They throw french fries in your face', 'Pepsi Cola hits the spot,/Smells like vinegar, tastes like snot', or 'Sani-Flush, Sani-Flush,/Cleans your teeth without a brush'. And there are many more parodies of this sort.

While most parodies serve to establish children's identity as separate from the adult world, some parodies indicate different levels within children's folk culture. By parodying the theme song from the television show, *Barney and Friends*, older children can indicate that they have outgrown a program directed at the very young viewer. In 'I Hate You, You Hate Me'; Children's Responses to Barney the Dinosaur, Elizabeth Tucker, while also acknowledging timely references to topics like the AIDS epidemic, asserts this very point. The original theme song, which begins 'I love you, you love me', becomes in parody versions:

> I hate you, you hate me.
> Let's go out and kill Barney
> And a shot rang out and
> Barney hit the floor
> No more purple dinosaur. (Tucker, 1999:28)

And as Judy McKinty (2000) points out, there are similar songs about the Teletubbies, set to the Barney tune:

> I hate Po, Po hates me,
> We're not a happy family,
> With a dagger in his back and a bullet in his head,
> Uh-oh Laa Laa, Dipsy's dead. (p49)

The older child's execution of Barney or one of the Teletubbies signals his or her rejection of that earlier stage of life.

By far, the most popular area of parody is the nursery rhyme. Nursery rhymes are among the earliest rhymes to which children are exposed, the earliest rhymes they learn themselves, and the earliest rhymes they parody. Moreover, the parodies show both the separation from the adult world and the development of the child within his or her folk group. The earliest of these, that is, those said by the youngest children, are usually innocent:

> Mary had a little lamb,
> It was a greedy glutton,
> She fed it on ice cream all day,
> And now it's frozen mutton. (Opie, 1959:90)

And one of my favourites:

> Mary had a little lamb,
> Her father shot it dead,
> Now Mary takes her lamb to school,
> Between two hunks of bread.

But as children get a bit older, the parodies become somewhat more daring:

> Mary had a little lamb
> She tied it to a heater
> Every time it turned around
> It burned its little peter. (Bronner, 1988:80)

And then more sexually suggestive and linguistically complex:

> Mary had a little lamb,
> And, boy, was the doctor surprised.

And:

> Mary had a little lamb,
> She also had a bear;
> I've often seen her little lamb,
> But I've never seen her bear [bare].

What is true of the 'Mary had a little lamb' parodies is also true of other nursery rhymes. Parodies tell what Jack burned when he jumped over the candle stick, what Jack and Jill were really doing up on that hill, what happened to Mother Hubbard when she went to get her dog a bone from the cupboard, how having so many children affected the Old Woman who lived in the shoe, and what Jack Horner was eating in the corner, just to name some of the most popular – and children love circulating these parodies with naughty words in them.

Children's rude or obscene humour has been a problem for folklorists for some time. On the one hand, publishers would not accept such material in the 1950s. The Opies' collection was not published till the end of the 1950s and, even then, Iona Opie has since told me in private conversation that Oxford University Press would not publish some of the ruder material she and Peter collected. By the time of the Knapps' *One Potato, Two Potato* in 1976, things had changed, and racier materials could be published. When Simon Bronner published *American Children's Folklore*, in 1988, it seems as if anything was allowed. However, the Opies said, 'Genuinely erotic verse ... is unusual' (p95), and the Knapps echoed that sentiment; 'Little erotic verse shows up in grade school' (p85). However, as the Knapps admitted on the very next page (p86), it wasn't easy, and was sometimes impossible, for adults to convince children to tell them such materials – and for obvious reasons. Such material does exist at the junior-high and high-school levels, where it is recited or told perhaps expressly for its erotic value (the basic knowledge of sex and sexuality being fairly well understood by the tellers at that age).

As the Knapps suggest and Bronner's examples reinforce, such erotic materials become plentiful among junior high school age children. As with the 'Mary had a little lamb' parodies, children's obscene humour is developmental within the folk group; that is, as the children get older, their obscene verse changes. The first subject of such verse is faeces. One of the first insults a child learns is to call someone else a 'doo doo head', and there is an attendant verse, 'Nanny, Nanny boo boo/Stick your head in doo doo'. The very first obscene verse I learned from an older boy in the neighborhood was:

> 1944
> The monkey climbed the door
> The door split
> The monkey shit
> 1944

Why this made me laugh heartily, I now have no idea. A rhyme reported by the Knapps may illustrate its age with a reference to a chain-pull toilet, 'Push the button, pull the chain,/Out comes a little black choo-choo train' (p62). Bronner includes:

> The night was dark
> The sky was blue
> Down the alley
> A shit wagon flew
> A bump was hit

> A scream was heard
> A man was killed
> By a flying turd

and remarks that 'These rhymes comment on children's growing understanding of taboos on certain images and words' (p81). They are also opportunities for children to engage in what Mechling might call 'obscene play' or 'forbidden play' (1986:94), a kind of play which is their own and in which they engage in direct opposition to the attitudes of the adult folk group. And faeces is just the beginning.

In addition to faeces, there is a general interest in all excretory functions. A rhyme in which the reciter points to the general areas of chest, crotch, and buttocks creates interesting food metaphors:

> Milky Milky,
> Lemonade,
> Around the corner,
> Hot dogs made.

As the title of Donna Lanclos' article, 'Bare Bums and Wee Chimneys' indicates, there is a great deal of children's lore-rhymes, jokes, sayings and songs about those two areas of the body. In addition, underwear, which covers those body parts, is another topic of more than passing interest to children, and in addition to the 'I see London, I see France' admonitory rhyme, there are others; and most of the rhymes in this category involve someone's having lost his or her underwear. One such rhyme begins:

> Tarzan, Tarzan, through the air
> Tarzan lost his underwear
> Tarzan say, 'Me don't care –
> Jane make me another pair' (Bronner, 1988:78)

In that rhyme and its many variations, Jane, Boy and Cheetah are also naked. These rhymes about body parts and underwear, as well as the jokes and songs and sayings about them, allow children to engage in some forbidden language play and, because adults would find at least some of that language play objectionable, the children have, once again, delineated and taken possession of something that is not only their own but in opposition to adult norms.

From a focus on body parts and their excretory functions, it is probably not a huge step to focus on body parts and their reproductive functions. The information children have about sex and reproduction is often incomplete, hazy, and/or erroneous; but as soon as they are aware that babies come from women's bodies, their lore begins to reflect this. The Knapps report the following recitation by a ten-year-old boy: 'Now I lay her on the bed,/I pray to God I'll use my head' (p172), both a parody of 'Now I lay me down to sleep' as well as a rather vague rhyme about sexual activity. More familiar, but no less vague, is a parody of 'My Bonnie Lies Over the Ocean':

> My Bonnie lies over the ocean
> My Bonnie lies over the sea,
> My daddy lies over my mommy,
> And that's how they got little me (p185)

About a variation of the song, Bronner reports that the person from whom the song was collected learned it in second or third grade; he comments: 'Within the apparent innocence of this ditty, the singer is declaring her astute awareness of sexual knowledge supposedly kept hidden from children' (p218, n.22). Children's questions about where babies come from show that they are, indeed, interested in the subject, and the rhymes, songs, jokes and sayings indicate not only a sort of innocent knowledge, but also a willingness to know and share whatever information they have.

While it may be obvious that children know what they are talking about in the immediately previous examples of innocent sexual rhymes, it may be that they are saying more than they know in others. According to Roger Abrahams (1969:31-32), the single most popular jump-rope rhyme is:

> Cinderella
> Dressed in yellow
> Went upstairs
> To kiss a fellow
> Made a mistake
> And kissed a snake
> How many doctors
> Did it take?
> 1, 2, 3, 4, 5 ... (Bronner:70)

In a variant reported by the Knapps, Cinderella 'Came downstairs with a bellyache', a line inserted between 'Kissed a snake' and 'How many doctors did it take?' (1976:125). Mechling argues:

> One way to account for the popularity of this rhyme is to see in it a disguised discussion of sex and pregnancy. The rhyme begins innocently enough with a fairytale character, probably known to children through the Disney film and storybooks. But the Cinderella story itself is about the sexual awakening of a

young woman. In the jump-rope rhyme, the young woman goes upstairs to kiss her boyfriend, but she kisses a 'snake' instead, and one way to interpret the meaning of 'kissing a snake' is in sexual symbolic terms. In the child's vague understanding of reproduction and the difference between the womb and the stomach, sexual contact could result in a 'stomach ache' – that is, pregnancy. (p101)

The 'bellyache' figures in numerous hand-clapping, jump-rope, and other game rhymes; and it is important to note that these are girls' game rhymes, making the sexual interpretation even more convincing.

At some point in the growing up process, children become adolescents, and their folklore, especially the humorous narratives, and even more especially, their obscene narratives, changes dramatically. Folklorists often talk about age-group folklore (Brunvand, 1998:54-56), ending childhood at twelve and beginning adolescence at thirteen, but some children learn things sooner and others later. Perhaps it might be better to look at the intent with which obscene materials are circulated among children.

In other words, the intent of the adolescent teller is different from the intent of the child teller. The adolescent teller intends to be erotic; the child teller, generally, does not. On the first level – *identity* – the child tellers are creating and passing on verses that are their own, outside of and sometimes in opposition to what they hear from and see in the adult community; and it is difficult to tell just how important it is for those who are essentially powerless to have something of their own, something that they can control. On the second level – *obscenity* – the child tellers are also asserting their independence from the adult culture, especially with the verses about bodily functions and the like; but they are also beginning show an awareness of, in their own language – both direct and metaphorical – that most secret of all adult knowledges, the knowledge of sexuality. But the child's intent, whatever else it is, is not to be erotic.

We will read our children poems from *A Child's Garden of Verses, When We Were Very Young*, and *Now We are Six*, and our children will love those books and poems, but when they are on their own, on the playground or in the woods, it is more likely that they will be reciting some of the materials, or variations thereof, mentioned above. And this is as it should be; they are entitled to their own poetry and to their identity as children as they express it in that poetry.

Note

1 Examples, unless otherwise noted, are from my own experiences or collections.

Works Cited:

Abrahams, R (ed) (1969) *Jump Rope Rhymes: A Dictionary.* Austin: University of Texas Press

Bronner, S (1988) *American Children's Folklore.* Little Rock: August House

Brunvand, J (1998) *The Study of American Folklore.* 4th ed. New York: Norton

Fine, G (1979-1981) Pre-Adolescent Male Slang, I-VII. *Children's Folklore Newsletter* II.1, II.2, III.1, III.3, IV.1, IV.2, and IV.3.

Knapp, H and Knapp, M (1976) *One Potato, Two Potato: The Folklore of American Children.* New York: Norton

Lanclos, D (2000) Bare Bums and Wee Chimneys: Rudeness and Defining the Line Between Child and Adult. *Children's Folklore Review* 22.2 p7-48

McKinty, J (2000) E-Contributions. *Children's Folklore Review* 22.2 p49

Machling, J (1986) Children's Folklore. In E. Oring (ed) *Folk Groups and Folklore Genres.* Logan, Utah: Utah State University Press pp91-121

Opie, P and Opie, I (1959) *The Lore and Language of Schoolchildren.* London: Oxford University Press

Sullivan, C (1980) *Peanuts and Baloney.* Center for Southers Folklore 3.1 p9

Tucker, E (1999) 'I Hate You, You Hate Me': Children's Responses to Barney the Dinosaur. *Children's Folklore Review* 22.1 p25-33

15

Poetry in Children's Annuals

Victor Watson

My aim in this chapter is a modest one – to demonstrate that a number of children's annuals have played a significant part in introducing poetry to children and children to poetry.

Annual is a slippery term. It usually refers to publications associated with story papers or comics, such as *Dandy* (1939-) or *Film Fun* (1938-61); or publications associated with a newspaper (*Daily Mail Annual*, 1945-55?), or radio and television programmes (*Children's Hour*, 1928?-58?), *Blue Peter*, 1964-). The term also covers free-standing miscellanies such as *Joy Street* (1923-41) or *Blackie's Children's Annual* (1905-41?). A further complication is that until the beginning of the last century weekly or monthly magazines were often bound into single volumes, also referred to as annuals. They include the *Boy's* and *Girl's Own* (1879-1940, 1880-1941) and *Little Folks* (1875-1933, bound in six-monthly volumes). So we have to accept that the word *annual* is used loosely to refer to almost any kind of miscellany, published on a roughly annual basis, usually in the months before Christmas.

By the start of the twentieth century annuals had established their trademark range of contents – stories, poetry, information articles, puzzles, competitions, black-and-white illustrations, together with colour plates and fold-out pages. Annuals such as *Leading Strings, Little Folks*, the *Girl's Own* and the *Boy's Own* took it for granted that poetry should naturally form part of their material. Even the rollicking *Greyfriars Holiday Annual* had a good deal of verse, including this characteristic parody of Wordsworth's 'We Are Seven' by 'Dick Penfold' –

I met a little Greyfriars Boy
    Fifteen years old, he said . . .

The poem proceeds with witty tonal and parodic exactness as the poet questions the little boy, and concludes -

'You say there's four in Study One,
    And you hang out elsewhere;
And yet you tell me you are seven!
    There's some mistake I swear.'

Then did the youthful Bob reply,
    'Seven worthy chums are we;
There's Wharton, Nugent, Inky, Bull –
    And I'm as good as three!'
(1926, 338)

Most annuals included poetry, and though poems were undoubtedly used in some publications as space-fillers , there were others whose editors saw it as their role to introduce their readers to a sustained variety of poetry as well as articles about poetry and poets – in fact, to provide an introduction for children to literary criticism and comment. It is those – to be precise, five of them – that this chapter will consider, beginning with *Joy Street*, which appeared in 1923 and from then on roughly annually until the start of World War 2, and its sister monthly paper, *Merry-Go-Round* (1923-35?). Both were published by Basil Blackwell.

The annual was dedicated to Rose Fyleman the poet associated with fairy poetry, and much better known in her own time than she is today and its title-page included some very distinguished names – Walter de la Mare, Eleanor Farjeon, Hilaire Belloc, Laurence Housman, Edith Sitwell, Hugh Chesterman and Fyleman herself. In fact de la Mare contributed stories, not poems; A.A. Milne eventually began to contribute, but also only stories, as did Eleanor Farjeon. Norman Hunter contributed a story, illustrated by Eve Garnett, as well as many stories published in *Merry-Go-Round*, including an early *Professor Branestawm* serial (1929). In addition, there was poetry by some distinguished figures – Hugh Chesterman, Edith Sitwell, Madeleine Nightingale, Hilaire Belloc, the Irish poet Katharine Tynan, E.V. Rieu, Laurence Housman, L.A.G. Strong, Hugh Walpole and Algernon Blackwood.

The monthly magazine published 'The Dormouse and the Doctor' and 'Heigh Ho, The Holly' by A.A. Milne, more poems by Rose Fyleman, and songs (with music) by Eleanor Farjeon, as well as poems by Hugh Chesterman, Laurence

Housman, E.V. Rieu and John Drinkwater. 'The Four Brothers' by de la Mare was published in the May issue for 1929.

There clearly seems to have been an implicit policy. *Joy Street* and *Merry-Go-Round* set themselves apart from other children's annuals and magazines of the day by resolutely excluding non-fiction. There were only stories, plays and poetry, with many illustrations. The poetry was mostly lyrical, magical, and ballad, but there was also a considerable emphasis on comic verse, especially nonsense. The tone was very much influenced by de la Mare and Milne.

It was probably the onset of war that killed off *Joy Street*. But, afterwards, in 1948, a new children's magazine and its annual appeared. Since as early as 1910 there had been a *Collins Children's Annual* – E. Nesbit had been published in it. But in 1948 this changed to the *Collins Magazine Annual*, a compilation of work chosen from the new monthly periodical, *The Collins Magazine*, which in 1953 changed its name to *The Young Elizabethan* later *The Elizabethan*. The annual, however, retained its title, and was issued for eight years. The editor was Patricia Whitlock, co-author of *The Far Distant Oxus* and its two sequels.

From the start this magazine/annual featured major children's writers of the period – Noel Streatfeild, Eve Garnett, Barbara Euphan Todd, Lorna Lewis, Monica Edwards (pony stories), Ian Serraillier, Patricia Lynch, Barbara Willard, Rumor Godden, Captain W.E. Johns (*Biggles* stories) and Eleanor Farjeon. It included illustrations by John Verney, Edward Ardizzone and Fritz Wegner, and poetry by Ian Serraillier (e.g. 'The Tale of the Spoilt Boy Prince') and comic verse by Eleanor Farjeon. Virginia Graham's 'A Cautionary Tale' is characteristic –

> An ass of a boy named Augustus Mountjoy
> While playing about on the strand,
> Selected a spade
> And commenced with the blade
> To bury his Dad in the sand.
>
> While engaged on this ploy this ridiculous boy
> Was peremptorily summoned away,
> And forgot as he ran
> Where he'd buried the man,
> Who hasn't been found to this day.
>
> My children, a toy can both wound and annoy,
> So be wise where another has erred,

And mark I beseech
Any place on the beach
Where your relatives may be interred.

(*Collins Magazine Annual* Vol 2, 1949, 63)

There was also a regular column entitled 'The World of Books' by Viola Garvin. The emphasis was on fiction, concentrating on recent and contemporary publications. The first of them was a recollection of childhood, beginning with this impressive and uncompromising declaration of faith, almost a manifesto:

> . . . this is a confession of faith – I loved books then, and now, 40 years later, I love them still and turn to them, sure that whatever I need, be it comfort or happiness, excitement, thought, romance, rest, refreshment, escape from dullness, or adventure, I shall be able to find it by reading. So I read a bit every day of my life, and it is this habit of reading as regularly as you wash or eat that makes books the delightful happiness they are to everyone who has grown used to using them so. (*Collins Magazine Annual Vol 1*, 1948, 40)

There is poetry too. One article introduces its young readers to Edward Lear – his life, his publications (with dates) and how to find out more about him. That leads the writer to Lewis Carroll and J. M. Barrie. The way she starts this article is by quoting Wordworth (from the 'Intimations' Ode: 'There was a time when meadow, grove and stream . . .'). Another article is entirely devoted to poetry. Again she begins by quoting, this time from *The Tempest*. She then in a quiet and scholarly vein goes on to compare two anthologies, Walter de la Mare's *Come Hither* and Lord Wavell's *Other Men's Flowers*, commenting on – and quoting from – Traherne, Keats, de la Mare, Browning, Coleridge, Tennyson, and Robert Bridges. That is not all: she concludes with a paragraph summarising the appeal of eight further anthologies for young readers. This is a substantial literary review.

In another, her intention is to write about *Robinson Crusoe* but – yet again – she introduces it with poetry, this time quoting William Cowper on Alexander Selkirk ('I am monarch of all I survey,/My right there is none to dispute.'). She follows this with a paragraph about Addison and Steele and early 18th century London; and that leads her neatly to Daniel Defoe. It is clear that the use of poetry – not primarily for itself but to provide points of critical or historical reference – was common.

Collins Magazine was very much of its age – gently and humorously authoritative in tone, explanatory and celebratory in approach, and rural and conservative in its assumptions. The tone of its reviews and articles on literature was adult and teacherly – accurate, enthusiastic and explanatory. Most importantly, the magazine clearly saw itself as having an important role as intermediary between the young reader and the wider literature. Poetry was part of that. In addition to including whole poems, its writers demonstrated how poetry – and quoting poetry – were and ought to be a natural feature of intelligent discourse with its young readers.

The Collins Magazine Annual ceased publication after 1955. But as the Annual ceased publication, the *Collins Magazine* was taken over by Kaye Webb as editor. Its *Young Elizabethan Poetry Award* for poetry by its readers was established by her in 1957 and became an important feature. She also established a Book Page in every issue, the first of them written by Noel Streatfeild. As before, the writing of young readers was given particularly strong emphasis.

Although *The [Young] Elizabethan* continued to be published for almost another 20 years, until 1973, the editorial letter in the eighth, final, annual had an elegiac and slightly forlorn tone.

> A word before you begin ... There is not so much published these days for the younger generation's spare time reading which does not fall into the category of 'comic' or 'strip cartoon' – a medium of expression which is all very well now and again but is in danger of becoming the staple diet of many young people today. In this Annual we are aiming to do something rather different, to provide *a full diet of reading* and entertainment: to encourage you to think, and act, for yourself, and not have all your 'visualising' done for you by comic strips, and people with balloons coming out of their mouths ...
>
> Well, well! Very few people read editorials anyway ... (my italics) (*Collins Magazine Annual* Vol 8, 1955, [7])

This was a reference to the fact that there was a good deal of concern in the 1950s and 1960s that some long-established annuals and magazines – such as *The School Friend* and *Girls' Crystal* – that had in the 1930s and 1940s provided a consistently popular diet of prose fiction (and, rarely, poetry), had now gone over entirely to pictorial strip stories.

Perhaps that was one of the factors that Ann Thwaite had in mind when, in 1968, she edited the first of a new miscellany entitled *Allsorts*. According to the dust-wrapper for Number 2, she could see no reason why there shouldn't be 'an annual containing some *real writing*' (my italics). *Allsorts* provided, every year until its demise in 1975, a mixture of exceptionally high quality. Only the best contemporary writers were invited to contribute; they included Christianna Brand, Catherine Storr, Margaret Drabble, Penelope Lively, Joan

Aiken, Ruskin Bond, Jill Paton Walsh, H.E. Todd, Dorothy Edwards, Gillian Avery, and K.M. Peyton. There was poetry by Stevie Smith, Anthony Thwaite, Elizabeth Jennings, Michael Frayn, Alan Brownjohn, D.J. Enright, Vernon Scannell, George MacBeth, Peter Porter, and Ted Hughes ('Stag Hunt').

Roughly contemporaneously with *Allsorts* came a series of six annual anthologies called simply *Miscellany*, edited by Edward Blishen for Oxford University Press. Here, the emphasis was firmly on the best fictional writing of the day, backed by the best contemporary illustrators. There was writing by Rosemary Sutcliff, Gillian Avery, Henry Treece, Mary Treadgold, Leon Garfield, Kevin Crossley-Holland, Joan Aiken, K.M. Peyton, Noel Streatfeild, Molly Hunter, Alan Garner, Ruskin Bond, Ian Serraillier and Nicholas Tucker; and illustrations by Charles Keeping, Brian Wildsmith, Victor Ambrus, Glenys Ambrus, William Stobbs, Raymond Briggs and John Lawrence.

There were also extracts from writers of the past, notably Juliana Horatia Ewing. There was a poem by John Clare, and work by living poets including Charles Causley ('Ballad of the Frog Princess'), Geoffrey Summerfield, Nancy Smith, R.C. Scriven (a poem loved by teachers of choral verse, 'The Thingummyjig'), Hans Baumann, Andrew Salkey, Leonard Clark, Anthony Thwaite and R.D. Lancaster.

Each of these annuals seems to have been a fresh start, a new venture inspired and sustained by a gifted and determined individual or group, often prompted by social or cultural changes (the perceived decline of quality fiction in magazines), and put an end to by random or contingent events (paper and staff shortages during World War 2). It is not possible to argue with any certainty that there was a conscious continuity of influence linking them, except that their editors all presumably shared a belief in the value of poetry and the importance of literary education.

Nothing better illustrates this than the publication I have left till last, a Victorian magazine/annual which pre-dated all of them, called *Atalanta* and issued for eleven years from October 1887, co-edited for most of its life by L. T. Meade. None of the twentieth-century editors and contributors mentioned above ever referred to it and no debt or continuity was acknowledged. Whatever its subsequent influence or lack of it, *Atalanta* was a weighty magazine in its own time, and with serious artistic pretensions. L. T. Meade was best known as a prolific writer of novels for older girls. She was an active member of the all-female Pioneer Club, well-known for its commitment to social equality for women and the education of girls. It is not surprising that the main concerns of *Atalanta* were contemporary art and the history of art, along with a strong commitment to literature.

Take the first issue, for example. It opened with a poem by Edwin Arnold.

> Greek Atalanta! girdled high;
>> Gold-sandalled; great, majestic maid;
> Her hair bound back with purple tie;
>> And in her hand th' Arcadian blade,
> To doom the suitor who shall choose,
> Challenge her to the race – and lose.

> (*Atalanta Vol 1*, 1887/8, [3])

The tone has been set and the audience defined – intelligent girls aged from about ten to thirty, capable of responding to high Victorian sentiments and understanding classical imagery and poetic syntax. It was not unlike its more famous and long-enduring rival, the *Girl's Own Paper*, but more solidly intellectual and highbrow.

Overleaf in that first issue was the first installment of a story by Mrs Molesworth, *Neighbours*; a poem by Mary B. Dodge; a play-script; several more articles; and the first part of a story by Ryder Haggard, *A Tale of Three Lions*. That was not all. There were three more poems, more stories, an article on embroidery and lace – and finally 'Search Passages in English Literature', in which there are four substantial quotations which readers are invited to identify: from Chaucer's *The Legend of Good Women*, Shakespeare's *All's Well That Ends Well*, a recently published poem by Austin Dobson, and a passage which I think is from Bunyan. Throughout its eleven years, *Atalanta* published fiction by George MacDonald, Charlotte Yonge, and R. L. Stevenson.

The second issue included an article on Sir John Millais, and another on Coleridge. This was to be a main characteristic of *Atalanta* – features on artists and writers. These were substantial and scholarly articles, demanding of their readers a serious commitment to reflect and analyse. Here, for example, is Richard Garnett rounding off a nine-column essay on Coleridge:

> He may not quite equal Shakespeare and Milton as a master of verbal music, but his metres and his effects are more varied. Tennyson is more varied still, and not less exquisite, but he is rather a great artist than a natural fountain of melody, and it is difficult to imitate his blank verse at any rate, without falling into mannerism; while Shelley, the third great modern master of musical speech, can hardly be imitated at all. The contrast between Coleridge and Shelley is

instructive. The natural bent of Coleridge is to blank verse; of Shelley to lyrical poetry ... (*Atalanta Vol 1*, 1887/8, 110)

Young readers were being introduced to literary discourse with a vengeance! Thereafter, there were similar features on George Meredith, Sir Walter Scott, Charles Lamb, Jane Austen, Charles Dickens, L. M. Alcott, J.M. Barrie (a decade before *Peter Pan*), Charlotte Brontë, George Eliot, W. M. Thackeray, Oliver Goldsmith, Charles Kingsley, Rudyard Kipling and Elizabeth Gaskell.

The poets given this critical attention included Robert Browning, Elizabeth Barrett Browning, H. W. Longfellow, S. T. Coleridge, and W. E. Henley. Furthermore, throughout its eleven years *Atalanta* published poems by Laurence Housman, Christina Rossetti ('Yes, I have a goodly heritage'), Katharine Tynan, Susan Coolidge (a ballad), two by Everard Hopkins (brother of Gerard Manley), Anna Letitia Barbauld, and R. D. Blackmore. Poetry from the canon was regularly published and included work by Heywood, Herrick, Spenser, Raleigh, Sidney, Keats, Shelley and Scott.

Finally, here is a poem about fairyland and a young child's imagination:

> My little one, so grave and wise,
> With wistful mouth and dreaming eyes,
> And soft chin on your dimpled hand,
> How goes the world in Fairy-Land?
>
> You see the lovely fairy-land,
> That grown-up folks can't understand;
> Where all the pretty things are true,
> And life rhymes as it ought to do.
>
> There Cinderella turns a Queen,
> There live the merry men in green . . .

There are three more verses in this vein; and the poem concludes:

> For you the rhymes of long ago
> Grow real, because you love them so.
> Love lends them voice and shape and hue,
> And makes a fairy-land – for you!
>
> (*Atalanta Vol 6*, 1892/3, 354)

Readers might be surprised to learn that this is a poem by Edith Nesbit. Although she had two stories published in *Atalanta*, most of her early contributions were poetry. (Incidentally, the first word on the wooden cross marking Nesbit's grave is *Poet*.)

The significance of children's annuals has long been neglected. However, from an educational point of view their importance is incalculable – if only because for 150 years they penetrated thousands of homes where there were few other books and little interest in poetry. They have in my view made a major contribution to the history and development of children's reading.

I would go further and argue that the annuals I have described saw beyond the role of entertainment by making a serious and sustained attempt to mediate between literature and the child reader. They introduced the best contemporary writers alongside writers of the past. Furthermore, they provided models for literary discourse, suggesting implicitly how it might be possible to enjoy and discuss reading in terms of a changing and developing canon.

They were, of course, paternalistic, uncompromising and assured in their role as gate-keepers of literary excellence. There is nothing like them today in a pluralist culture when such certainties are no longer possible. Nor should there be. But their role as literary educators to three or four generations of young readers should at least be documented and acknowledged.

Works Cited:

Arnold, E (1887/8) *Atalanta* Vol 1. (L T Meade [Elizabeth Thomasina Meade Smith] and Alicia A Leith, eds) London: Hatchards

Garnett, R (1887/8) *Atalanta* Vol 1. (L T Meade [Elizabeth Thomasina Meade Smith] and Alicia A Leith, eds) London: Hatchards

Garvin, V (1948) *Collins Magazine Annual* Vol 1. (Pamela Whitlock, ed) London: Collins

Graham, V (1949) *Collins Magazine Annual* Vol 2. (Pamela Whitlock, ed) London: Collins

Nesbit, E *Atalanta* Vol 6. (L T Meade [Elizabeth Thomasina Meade Smith] and A B Symington, eds) London: 'Atalanta' Office, Paternoster Row

'Penfold, Dick' [George Richmond Samways] (1926) *Greyfriars Holiday Annual for Boys and Girls.* (C M Down, ed) London: The Farringdon Press Ltd

[Whitlock, Pamela] (1955) *Collins Magazine* Annual Vol 8. (Pamela Whitlock, ed) London: Collins

16

Wicked Thoughts: Fairy-tale Poetry for Children and Adults

Laura Tosi

The title of this chapter was inspired by Judith Viorst's poem 'Wicked Thoughts' (1981), which has nothing to do with fairy tales but effectively describes the elation of the poem's speaker as s/he fantasises about the despicable Mary Ellen Write being eaten by a lion in one bite:

> I'd cry and cry and cry and cry.
> (But just to be polite).

I think this short poem captures and represents quite remarkably the irreverent strain that can be found in many poems inspired by fairy-tale models. As the parenthetical aside illustrates, contemporary fairy-tale poetry often voices politically incorrect, and occasionally wicked, thoughts of fairy-tale characters, that traditional fairy tales do not reveal. I would like to to use the word 'wicked' in the widest possible sense, to describe the characters' subversive attitudes, gender-specific bad behaviours, sarcasm and irony – as well as downright disillusion about fairy-tale models. In other words, any form of overtly oppositional stance voiced by characters who question the fairness of their destiny or the happiness of fairy-tale endings.

As Max Lüthi (1981:34) has observed, folktale characters lack the dimension of depth: they 'are figures without substance, without inner life ... completely beautiful and good or completely ugly and bad'. If we ever imagine fairy-tale characters thinking, we expect them to think in character. For example, we do not expect to be too far from the poetical truth when we imagine the dwarves regretting Snow White's departure, or the grandmother's fear in the wolf's belly, or, again, Cinderella's joy at seeing her dainty foot fitting the slipper perfectly. However, when poems let us into the characters' inner world, what we see is often unexpected, or even shocking. In Sara Henderson Hay's 'One of the seven has somewhat to say' (1963), a dwarf thinks with nostalgia of the time when he could enjoy a happy bachelor's life with his brothers, with irregular meal times and clothes flung on the floor:

> Remember how it was before she came? ...
> Those were the days, if you know what I mean.

In Laurence Snydal's 'Grandmother' (2003) the old lady is happy and snug inside the wolf:

> I let each sighing lung
> Massage the ache from these old bones.

In Judith Viorst's poem ' ... and then the prince knelt down and tried to put the glass slipper on Cinderella's foot', (1981) Cinderella is planning to change her mind about the prince:

> He's not nearly as attractive as he seeemed the other night.
> So I think I'll just pretend that this glass slipper feels too tight.

Fairy-tale poetry offers the extraordinary opportunity of stopping to listen to an individual voice in the plot-ordained world of folktale and fairy-tale. Transposing a well-known fairy tale of the Western tradition into a contemporary poetic form may appear to be problematic. Traditional storytellers rely on the inevitable unfolding of a plot with a clear opening situation, various complications and an act of closure of some kind. In contrast, modern poetry frequently resorts to metaphors, stylistic surprises as well as flashbacks and epiphanies: genre conventions that may appear foreign to the linear sequence of traditional tales. In this paper I would like to investigate both contemporary fairy-tale poetry addressed to an adult audience and poetry addressed to a child audience and discuss the unexpectedly similar ways in which they illuminate the moment in which characters decide to reconsider their fixed destiny.

Of course, fairy-tale poetry is not a contemporary phenomenon. One only needs to think of the narrative poetry of the Romantic and Victorian Age (from the Lambs to Christina Rossetti, from Tennyson to Browning). The twentieth century has appreciated the fact that the fairy-tale has been able to accommodate alternative versions which have challenged and subverted formal conventions as well as ideological configurations. In comparison with the abundance of contemporary fairy-tale poetry for an adult audience, fairy-tale poetry exclusively for children appears relatively scarce – more poetry seems to be addressed to a double audience, in contrast to prose, where re-visionist fairy tales, primarily for children, are a well-researched and common occurrence.

Fairy-tale poetry appears to be a typically hybrid genre, as it relies on a body of written prose works for its very existence but also encourages oral delivery as well as silent reading. Like folktales, fairy tales and ballads, passed on from generation to generation and from person to person, fairy-tale poems lend themselves to being either read or performed. However, modern lyric poetry based on fairy-tales may also encourage us to concentrate on the particular resonance of words and imagery, suggesting new ways of looking at familiar things (as when Anne Sexton in 'Red Riding Hood', 1971, describes the cutting of the wolf's belly as 'a kind of caesarean section' and the rescuing of Little Red Riding Hood and her grandmother as 'a little death' and 'a little birth').

Often we hear the characters' wicked, or worried, thoughts as they pause before some crucial event in the story. These are moments of revelation and insight in which the character reveals inner conflict, or even resistance to the pre-ordained plot. Stevie Smith's Frog Prince (1962), for example, is not look-ing forward to his imminent disenchantment as he appears to have enjoyed his hundred years as a frog by the river:

> I am happy. I like the life,
> Can swim for many a mile.

In recent years women authors have experimented widely with re-writing fairy tales, both in prose and poetry. In a highly perceptive essay that has now become a classic, Karen Rowe (1986:57) uses the image of Philomela in the Ovidian myth as the prototype of the storyteller. She suggests that

> In the history of folktale and fairy tale, women as storytellers have woven or spun their yarns, speaking at one level to a total culture, but at another to a sisterhood of readers who will understand the hidden language, the secret revelations of the tale.

Women poets have challenged stereotypical gender roles through voices that express firm views about patriarchal domination in society. Through the appropriation of the subjectivity of traditionally undeserving and wicked characters like the witch, these poems have also functioned as critical readings which investigate gender as a social and political construction. Some female poets have specifically chosen to appropriate the witch's role in their verse: Sexton, for example, opens her adult collection *Transformations* with a poem,

'The Gold Key' (1963), in which she defines herself as a 'middle-aged witch', 'ready to tell you a story or two'. Similarly, Sara Henderson Hay closes her collection of poems intended for a mixed readership with 'The Witch' (1963), a powerful female figure who asks readers to look at themselves in a mirror, where

> ... you will see my features
> Inextricably mingled with your own.

Hay's witch is celebrating her capacities as 'a plotter, a plot-maker, a schemer, a witch, an artist, an impersonator, a woman of almost infinite creative energy, witty, wily, and self-absorbed as all artists traditionally are', as Gubar and Gilbert (1984:38-39) have described the Queen in Snow White. This is a model (or anti-model) of female assertiveness and manipulative inventiveness that, as Hay suggests, is a part of ourselves.

Modern fairy-tale poetry often investigates possibilities for identities that disrupt the traditional equation between beauty and goodness, frequently dispensing with marriage-dominated plots (see, for example, Herman, 1974, Williams, 1978 and Cole, 1986). Carol Ann Duffy's 'Bad Princess' (2000) is 'looking for trouble' as she meets her double in the forest. After the verbally violent confrontation that occurs with her enigmatic and frightening alter ego the Tree Girl, the Bad Princess decides that she is not up to the fight. The poem ends conventionally, with the Bad Princess running for her life 'into the arms of the dull young Prince' whom she marries eventually. The Bad Princess appears to have given up her forceful ways (and wickedness) in order to comply with the unwritten social rules of princess-like behaviour.

In Stevie Smith's 'Cool as a cucumber' (1950), the fairy's curse by the wishing well has changed Mary, the protagonist, from a prototype of calm self-possession to a 'nervy grim and bold' creature who 'looks over her left shoulder and does not do as she is told'. There is no way to establish whether Mary is indeed under a spell, or whether this is her more authentic self, which she has been able to liberate from her pre-curse, 'cool' identity. As the narrator reminds us, after the curse has made her unfit to marry, 'she grows worse and worse'. Like the Bad Princess, Mary at some point runs for her life, but this time it is not to meet a prince but to escape from the miller's son who has asked her to go back to him. The wicked thoughts here are what the (potentially unreliable) speaker expresses – in their opinion, Mary has obviously strayed from the model of obedience and calm that she used to embody. The fact that we never get to hear Mary's own voice – as she is described, judged and possibly misunderstood by what we could call the collective voice of the village – leaves all interpretation open (Huk, 1997:164). As with Duffy's princess, we are left to wonder how cursed or bad these female characters really are. How grumpy or intractable and bold do they need to be if they want to explore other possibilities than marrying a dull prince?

Laura Whipple's child oriented *If the Shoe Fits* (2002) fragments the plot of 'Cinderella' into 33 poems which intersect with one another, with a strong musical and theatrical flavour. The illustrated collection is framed by two poems related by Cinderella's father's ghost; while the opening poem voices the restless father's remorse – 'What a fool to take that woman into our lives ... I cannot rest' – the closing poem has achieved resolution and the father is at peace at last. In this concerto of tunes and rhythms, some voices are heard more than others and at different moments, the poems following the chronology of the story in a fragmented form. Before he meets Cinderella, for example, we hear the prince grumbling about having to be at the Ball – 'I dance, mechanically, clock-watching'. Later he expresses regret at Cinderella's disappearance, and is even disconcerted at the prospect of having to try the glass slipper on all the girls in his realm.

Whipple also brings to life the voice of figures whose perspective on the story has never been disclosed, like Cinderella's cat or the glass slipper itself. In Whipple's version Cinderella's uncertainty about her own happily-ever-after destiny – one of the poems is called 'Cinderella's doubt' – reveals an acute awareness of the impracticability of the fairy-tale model of happiness that can also be found, in more dramatic terms, in poems for an adult audience. It is undeniable that most fairy-tale poems directed to a young audience speak, in fact, to a double audience. This is not, obviously, an exclusive feature of contemporary fairy-tale poetry – again, one thinks of *Goblin Market*, a cross-audienced classic (Lanzen Kooistra, 1997). It is, in fact, quite difficult to find fairy-tale poetry written exclusively for a child audience. Whipple is an exception in this respect, as are Roald Dahl's collections *Revolting Rhymes* (1982) and *Rhyme Stew* (1989), but Judith Viorst's collections *If I were in Charge of the World* (1981) and *Sad Underwear* (1995), which include sections on fairy tales, are subtitled 'poems for children and their parents'. Stevie Smith's 'Cool as a cucumber' and 'The Frog Prince' are collected in *Our Bog is Dood: Selected Poems for Young Children* (1999), but these poems reveal uncommon subtlety and complexity and lend themselves to the investigation of adult subtexts, as do Gwen Strauss's poems, *Trail of Stones* (1990) also marketed to a young audience. The author of the text on the front flap of Hay's *Story Hour* seems to be ambivalent, to say the least, about readership: after stating that the poems can be enjoyed by a schoolgirl, they quote Hay's own words that these poems, 'though based on nursery tales, are definitely not for children'. We have to take into account that often the distinction between children's poetry and adult poetry is not terribly clear-cut – Morag Styles (1998) has shown that many poetry collections throughout the centuries have made a point of including poetry not written specifically for children.

As many commentators have noted, fairy tales are not really children's stories at all, which can pose problems for modern adaptors with a strong sense of a child audience. If we take 'Hansel and Gretel', for example, we cannot deny that it is a story that speaks to our innermost fears, of bad mothers and worse stepmothers, who cross the boundaries of propriety and want to devour what they are supposed to protect and cherish. Poetry versions of this tale have tried to come to terms in various ways with its disturbing combination of malnutrition, child abuse, gluttony, and survival. Dahl's way of dealing with the issues of hunger and abandonment, in *Rhyme Stew* (1989), is to stress in a surreal and comical way the mother's selfish distress at having to feed the children. Both parents are depicted as heavily overweight:

> My motto is that *we* come first,
> Them kids should *always* get the worst.

Dahl's parents actually jeopardise their children's chances of survival, so that they – the adults – can thrive. In sacrificing the children to the remorseless drive of their own needs, their behaviour is little different from that of the witch. Similarly, Sexton, inspired by mother games of kissing and playful nibbling in her poem 'Hansel and Gretel' (1971), has this innocent practice turn into a potentially cannibalistic drive, when the mother's voice announces:

> I have a pan that will fit you.
> Just pull up your knees like a game hen.

She then suggests taking the baby's pulse to set the oven at the correct temperature.

Although children's poetry and adult poetry address similar issues, children's versions, not surprisingly, tend to downplay the grim details of the stories or try to reframe them in humorous ways. In contrast, adult poems, like 'Hansel's Game' by Agha Shahud (2003), celebrate the children's overcoming the witch in more morbid terms, as the children appropriate the witch's cannibalistic impulse, announcing in the happy-ever-after ending that the witch is kept – refrigerated – in the basement:

> Now and then we take portions of her
> to serve on special occasions.

As Jan Montefiore observes (1987:39), fairy-tale poetry seems to attract writers – especially women – whose language is closest to ordinary speech. These poets do not seem, on the whole, to be drawn to formal experiments – Hay chooses the traditional sonnet form, for example. They communicate their experiences of the fairy-tale world as storytellers do, and even if free verse can be deceptively easy – as in Stevie Smith's poetry – and often displays the simplicity and directness that can be found in children's verse, poets can turn the scenario of fairy tales into a web of dangerous relations, dark symbols and unexpected meanings. Those children's authors who have tried their hand at fairy-tale poetry, however, use linguistic devices and narrative strategies that are often surprisingly similar to those employed by poets writing for adults. For example, authors as diverse as Dahl and Sexton use a distinctly contemporary tone and diction, mixing anachronisms and modern parallels for characters and situations of the fairy tale in deliberately satirical ways. They employ more than a hint of irony to challenge the ending of 'Cinderella', both deploying characteristically slangy language to project a dis-illusioned voice that describes the fate of their modern-day heroines. Dahl's 'Cinderella' (1982), or rather Cindy as she is called in the poem, feels 'as rotten as can be' and tells her fairy Godmother rudely to get her to the Ball imme-diately as her friends have all gone to the Palace disco and she does not want to miss it.

In her collection *Transformations*, Sexton always prefaces her poems with an introductory section, which has the function of translating the Grimms' plots into our own experience. 'Cinderella' (1971) opens with the story of the plumber who wins the lottery:

> From toilets to riches.
> That story.

Both poets juxtapose a fairy-tale past with contemporary plots and with destinies that are transfigured by parody, implicitly dismissing the original Cinderella story, and its ending, as mechanical and impossibly happy. Sexton's own ending uses similes to create witty and cruel comparisons, like that be-tween the supposedly happy situation of the couple and the lifeless and slightly dusty appearance of old dolls on display in a museum case, untouched by the passing of time: 'their darling smiles pasted on for eternity'. Not to be outdone, Dahl goes as far as rejecting the traditional ending completely: Cinderella cannot possibly marry a prince who, like the Queen of Hearts in *Alice*, roars 'Off with her head!' each time a stepsister's foot enters comfortably into the slipper. No longer interested in marrying such a prince, Dahl's Cindy asks her Godmother to find her 'a lovely feller, a simple jam-maker by trade', with whom she lives happily ever after. This is her only chance of happiness, which has nothing to do with the magical journey from rags to riches on which the Grimms' improbable and – in the poem's view – phoney plot is built, 'Just to keep the children happy'. 'That story', as Sexton would have put it.

Both Cinderellas, Sexton's and Dahl's, are defined by parodic hyperrealism and the tragicomic dismissal of the magic and romantic elements. While Dahl intersperses his fairy-tale poems with ironic and often wickedly funny comments on the originals, adult poems occasionally reflect more deeply about what fairy tales do to grown-up readers and explicitly address the issue of re-writing fairy tales for a contemporary audience. It is true that most poetry which uses fairy-tale material, rather than transport us into the world of magic and make-believe, tends to perform disenchantments (as in the title of a famous anthology of fairy-tale poetry by Wolfgang Mieder, 1985) on a reading public or audience. However, the fact that many poets and prose writers still find fairy tales inspiring as a stimulus for their own work, thus revitalising fairy-tale motifs and conventions, is evidence of both the stylistic plasticity and the symbolic resonance of this genre (Tosi, 2006). In 'Reading the Brothers Grimm to Jenny', Lisel Mueller (1985) explores a child's response to the wonderful world of fairy tale, where 'death is a small mistake, where the kiss revives'. The mother's voice initially wonders whether it is wise to indulge her daughter's desire to believe in fantasy worlds, but eventually chooses to trust that what fairy tales have to offer is often more real and meaningful than most everyday experiences. Indeed they may help us come to terms with reality, perhaps by appropriating precisely that utopian dimension of fairy tale which Ernest Bloch described. According to Bloch (Zipes, 1979:135), the unwritten maxims of fairy tales are: 'consider yourself as born free and entitled to be totally happy, dare to make use of your power of reasoning, look upon the outcome of things as friendly'. So Jenny's mother brushes away her qualms and 'wicked thoughts' about lying to her daughter and ends, like this chapter with a celebration of the fairy-tale world of beyond, to which a mother can indeed provide the golden key. She becomes ready to learn from her daughter 'the terror and the bliss, the world as it might be'.

Note

I am indebted to Lisa Sainsbury for an enlightening lecture entitled 'The Female Voice of Fairy-Tale Poetry' which was delivered at the University of Venice on October 29th, 2008, for ideas regarding the relationship between fairy tales and poetry.

Works Cited:

Cole, B (1986) *Princess Smartypants*. London: Penguin

Dahl, R (1989) *Rhyme Stew*. London: Penguin

Dahl, R (1982) *Revolting Rhymes*. London: Penguin

Duffy, C A (2000) *The Oldest Girl in the World*. London: Faber and Faber

Gilbert, S and Gubar, S (eds) (1984) *The Madwoman in the Attic. The Woman Writer and the Nineteenth-Century Literary Imagination*. New Haven-London: Yale University Press

Henderson Hay, S (1963) *Story Hour*. New York: Doubleday and Company

Herman, H (1974) *The Forest Princess*. Berkeley: Rainbow Press

Huk, R (1997) Poetic subject and voice as sites of struggle: toward a 'postrevisionist' reading of Stevie Smith's fairy-tale poems. In Y. Prins and M. Shreiber (eds) *Dwelling in Possibility. Women Poets and Critics on Poetry*. Ithaca and London: Cornell University Press

Janzen Kooistra, L (1997) Goblin Market as a cross-audienced poem: children's fairy tale, adult erotic fantasy, *Children's Literature* 25:181-204

Lüthi, M (1981) *The European Folktale: form and nature*. Bloomington and Indianapolis: Indiana University Press

Montefiore, J (1987) *Feminism and Poetry: Language, Experience, Identity in Women's Writing*. London and New York: Pandora

Mueller, L (1985) Reading the brothers Grimm to Jenny. In W. Mieder (ed) *Disenchantments. An Anthology of Modern Fairy Tale Poetry*. Hanover and London: University of Vermont

Rowe, K (1986) To spin a yarn. The female voice in folklore and fairy tale. In R. Bottigheimer (ed) *Fairy Tales and Society: Illusion, Allusion and Paradigm*. Philadelphia: University of Pennsylvania Press

Sexton, A (1971) *Transformations*. Boston: Houghton Mifflin

Shahud, A (2003) Hansel's Game. In J. M. Beaumont and C. Carlson (eds) *The Poets' Grimm. 20th Century Poems from Grimm Fairy Tales*. Ashland, Oregon: Story Line Press

Smith, S (1962) 'The Frog Prince' and (1950) 'Cool as a Cucumber'. In *Our Bog is Dood. Selected Poems for Young Readers*. London: Faber and Faber, 1999

Snydal, L (2003) Grandmother. In J. M. Beaumont and C. Carlson (eds) *The Poets' Grimm. 20th Century Poems from Grimm Fairy Tales*. Ashland, Oregon: Story Line Press

Strauss, G (1990) *Trail of Stones*. London: Walker Books

Styles, M (1998) *From the Garden to the Street. Three Hundred Years of Poetry for Children*. London: Cassell

Tosi, L (2006) Did they live happily ever after? Rewriting fairy tales for a contemporary audience. In P. Hunt (ed) *Children's Literature: critical concepts in literary and cultural studies*. London and New York: Routledge

Viorst, J (1981) *If I Were in Charge of the World and Other Worries*. New York: Aladdin Paperbacks

Viorst, J (2000) *Sad Underwear and Other Complications*. New York and London: Alladin

Whipple, L (2002) *If the Shoe Fits. Voices from Cinderella*. New York: Mc Elderry Books

Williams, J (1978) *The Practical Princess and Other Liberating Fairy Tales*. London: the Bodley Head

Zipes, J (1979) *Breaking the Magic Spell. Radical Theories of Folk and Fairy Tales*. Austin: University of Texas Press

17

Anthropomorphism Dressed and Undressed in Beatrix Potter's Rhymes and Riddles

Lorraine Kerslake

Anybody who has opened one of Beatrix Potter's little books will undoubtedly remember her pictures of animals for years to come for, like other great children's writers, she has the power of creating immortal characters that remain with us throughout our lives. Although Potter's work has been widely documented and critically acclaimed, her apparently simple rhymes and riddles have more often taken second place beside her animal stories. Like Lewis Carroll's most memorable verse, many of Potter's rhymes and riddles are embedded within the stories, adding a subtle flavour to their overall meaning. This chapter focuses on the theme of nature and animals as a source of Potter's inspiration, and investigates how the form of poetry enables Potter's work to connect child readers to the animal world, particularly through the use of anthropomorphism in her nursery rhymes and riddles.

Potter's engagement with nature – her careful observation and reflection about the natural world, as well as her wish in later life to preserve the landscapes of the Lake District – are closely linked to the concerns of contemporary ecocriticism. Her art, in other words, is connected to the challenges offered by environmentalism and ecology. Moreover, Potter experienced enough repression in her life as a female naturalist for this to be relevant to the perspectives of ecofeminism, which attempts to link the oppression of women with that of nature. The pre-eminence of the theme of nature in Potter's work and life takes on new significance, seen from this perspective.

At the turn of the century Potter's observational skills and artistic talent in mycology were not recognised, causing her to turn to writing animal stories for children, first as a diversion, and later to earn her long overdue independence. She was, as Barbara Gates has put it: 'especially well equipped for this enterprise' since 'from an early age, she knew her animals as she would come to know her fungi – from a scientific perspective' (1999:231). Potter was both an acute observer and a detached scientist, as can be seen in her drawings, where her major concern was to remain as accurate and faithful to the true nature of animals as possible.

Potter's authentic love for nature may have been stimulated partly by her isolation as a child. Although her confined childhood and strict parents have often been thought to be responsible for her solitary nature, her upbringing did provide opportunities that were, in some respects, unusual for children of her time. The fact that, from the age of five, she was allowed to keep her own menagerie of both live and dead animals in her nursery, not to mention the experiments she carried out with her brother, Bertram, suggests that in many ways her upbringing was more progressive than that of many of her contemporaries. Her own pets were often models for many of her characters. Amongst her favourites are her many rabbits, including Benjamin Bouncer and Peter; her mice (including Appley Dapply and Hunca Munca); and her hedgehogs (Mrs Tiggy-Winkle, or Old Mr Pricklepin), which appear in many of her tales and books of rhymes.

As a child, much of her inspiration came from her frequent visits to both Kew Gardens and Kensington Gardens, as well as to the Natural History Museum and the South Kensington Museum (later the Victoria and Albert Museum), where she would quietly observe and make her first sketches and scientific drawings. She describes one of her visits in her journal dated Dec 20, 1895:

> Went to the Museum, very empty and quiet. Studied fossils peaceably, and afterwards the insects again, but investments and a general twitch got too much for me. I never saw anything so fearful as the stuffed animal; I had not been in that gallery for a long time till the other day. Cousin Alice wanted to see them. We got as far as the walrus and then both turned back. It is like eating pork on Sunday. (in Linder, 1989:412)

This passage exemplifies some of Potter's more complex and contradictory feelings towards the way nature was represented in her society. Alongside her 'peaceable study' of fossils and insects displayed in the museum, there is a disturbing apprehension and sense of 'fearfulness' upon contemplating the lifeless taxidermic representations of dead mammals. What exactly got too much for her? Was it the oppressive sight of unclothed death in the form of stuffed animals? Potter's own relationship with animals shows that they are both like and at the same time not like us: on the one hand we have her pets and on the other we have the dissections and skeletons that also fascinated her – along with rabbit pie! Potter's feelings also point to her early sense of empathy with nature and the non-human. From an ecocritical point of view, empathy is key to the development of an environmental ethic. The term 'anotherness', as applied to ecocriticism by Patrick Murphy, is also relevant in Potter: the recognition of the other, the non-human, not just as a self-existing entity that is respected, rather than exploited, but also as fellow beings with which to engage and interact. For humans, animals are always the other, and always remain the observed. But in Potter, imaginative engagement with the natural world is shown as a bond of respect, which, along with her realism and subtle subversiveness, prevents her offering too sentimental a view of nature. In this sense her scientific study is accompanied by a sensitivity to 'anotherness'. Her awareness of this allowed her a privileged understanding of animal behaviour, from a different angle to other children's writers and illustrators of the Golden Age.

Potter's distinctiveness, in this respect, springs in large part from her finding new ways to bring poetry, story and illustration together as integrated wholes. Already by 1902 she had begun planning her own book of rhymes; however it was delayed by other work and the sudden death of her fiancé, Norman Warne. It finally metamorphosed into an abridged collection which came out in 1917: *Appley Dapply's Nursery Rhymes*, followed by *Cecily Parsley's Nursery Rhymes* in 1922. One of the main differences from her tales, which were originally written as picture letters, is that the nursery rhymes and pictures that appear in her two books of rhymes are more of a compilation of material recycled from different sources, rather than an original work, since they date back long before *Peter Rabbit* was published. The nursing mouse is a good example of how Potter recycled her illustrations: she appears in 'The Old Woman in a Shoe', the only traditional rhyme included in *Appley Dapply*, and as Hunca Munca in the *Tale of Two Bad Mice*. Many of the images that accompany Potter's book of rhymes have been critically acclaimed as being some of her finest art work. Speaking of *Old Mister Prickly Pin*, Mrs Tiggy-Winkle's uncle, Potter wrote in 1920: 'I considered the hedgehog was about the best drawing I ever made' (Stevenson, 2005:122). Details are drawn with accuracy, as can be seen down to the tiny tags of Appley Dapply's cupboards or the old woman mouse, whose shoe has changed from ordinary footwear to a much more elaborate *Cinderella* slipper. The vitality of Potter's drawings also demonstrates her aesthetic principle of grounding the potentially senti-mental or anthropomorphic aspects of her books within more realistic and closely observed settings.

Rhymes intrigued Potter from an early age. She had been brought up on nursery rhymes, many of them illustrated by Walter Crane and Randolph Caldecott, whose style she had originally tried to follow in *Appley Dapply*. Her imagination also fed off the fairy tales told to her by her governess and fantasy literature. For example, *Little Pig Robinson* has references to strong childhood impressions left by Edward Lear's *Owl and the Pussy-cat* and John Tenniel's sheep illustrations from *Alice's Adventures in Wonderland*. Potter's love for traditional rhymes and riddles can be appreciated from the fact that she wove them into her writing through the voices of her animal characters whenever she could. *The Tailor of Gloucester*, her favourite story, contains many snip-pets of quoted rhymes including the 'Three Little Mice', which was also printed separately as a booklet; *Squirrel Nutkin* has nine rhyming riddles, in-cluding 'Hickamore, Hackamore', 'Hitty Pitty', and 'Arthur O'Bower'; 'Tom, Tom the Pipers Son' is the basis of *Pigling Bland*, which also includes the rhymes 'To Market, To Market' and 'This Little Pig', which later appears in *Cecily Parsley.*

Potter's imaginative use of such traditional sources – fables, folktales, riddles and rhymes – never occludes a sense of the real animal involved. Instead, by transforming traditional nursery material originally about humans or fairies, and putting this into an animal context, she gives the rhyme a new meaning. Several examples of this can be seen in *The Tailor of Gloucester*, particularly in the scenes where the mice tauntingly recite nursery rhymes to the cat. 'Four-and-twenty tailors went to catch a snail' takes on a new relevance here, as the mice have taken over the tailor's work and, effectively, his identity:

> There was a snippeting of scissors, and snappeting of thread; and little mouse voices sang loudly and gaily –

> 'Four-and-twenty tailors went to catch a snail,
> The best man amongst them durst not touch her tail;
> She put out her horns like a little Kyloe cow,
> Run, tailors, run! Or she'll have you all e'en now!'

In addition to the obvious connection forged between the mice and tailor, the rhyme takes on other meanings that are developed through multiple analogies and figurative play with size and perspective. The 'tailors' (even in their trans-formed role as mice) are much bigger than the snail they chase of course, but much smaller than the metaphorical cow who terrifies them. Thus, the tailors' 'snail hunt' undergoes a comic reversal when the snail's horns emerge, so that with delightful absurdity, the human snail hunters are now being pursued by a dangerous snail-cow. Potter uses the licence of verse to build on her own observational skills, focusing on the minute details of the snail's horn and tail writ large.

The last verse links back to the mice's current situation, with the cat's desire to 'have them all e'en now' keeping the reality of natural instincts very much in play. What is particularly interesting here is how anthropomorphism enables her recontextualised rhymes to function in multiple ways. This can also be seen in the famous verses of 'Three little mice sat down to spin', accompanied by six drawings in the original sequence that are considered to be among Potter's finest art work:

> The little mice only laughed, and
> tried another tune –
> 'Three little mice sat down to spin,
> Pussy passed by and she peeped in.
> What are you at, my fine little men?
> Making coats for gentlemen.
> Shall I come in and cut off your threads?
> Oh, no, Miss Pussy, you'd bite off our heads!'

Once again the last line has a particular relevance to the mice's relationship with Simpkin the cat, since, despite their taunting, and the fact that the tables of predator and prey have been turned in the poem, the mice still remain potential victims. The poem – with its sardonic closing rhyme of 'threads' with 'heads' – keeps us conscious of the violence inherent in the natural order. The cat's helpful offer to cut off 'threads' is a thinly disguised metaphor for killing the mice, a likely reality should the door that separates them in the story be opened.

It is evident then that, although mice, together with squirrels, may appear to be the most light-hearted reciters of nursery rhymes in Potter's tales, their real roles often provide a darker undercurrent to this playfulness. *Squirrel Nutkin*, 'a Tale about a tail – a tail that belonged to a little red squirrel' is very much an anthropomorphic story of squirrels indulging in human-type behaviour, and can be read as a moral tale of disobedience and the consequences this brings. The fact that Potter invests the moral fable with details of an authentic and localised nature is also apparent here, however: the lake surrounding the island the squirrels regularly venture out to is identifiable as Derwent Water.

After provoking Old Brown the owl, Squirrel Nutkin is caught, but, like Peter in Mr McGregor's garden, he manages to escape at the price of losing his tail, and with it his desire to tell riddles. Old Brown, the owl, has a status of superiority that distinguishes him from the other animals. He appears as a kind of god figure, invested with authority and power: the other squirrels ask for his permission to gather nuts, reminiscent of medieval pagan animism, and he is placated by offerings from them and worshipped as a symbol of wisdom. However, his instinct to kill smaller animals with ruthless efficiency, when sufficiently provoked, remains a source of implied dramatic tension, and is indeed enacted at the end of the story. In contrast to the owl, Nutkin is anthropomorphised as a trickster, who breaks the rules without any regard for authority. Nutkin's rhyming riddles – which he uses to taunt the owl – are the main form this rule-breaking takes. Nutkin's trickster role is similar to that found in *Uncle Remus* and the Brer Rabbit stories, where, in both cases, the creatures talk and behave 'de same ez folks'. However, Nutkin's 'naughtiness' relates to both his human and animal nature. His lack of regard for authority is central to the human, moral fable; but as a squirrel he also ignores the basic rules of nature, when he fails to show respect for the predatory instincts of an owl. Yet Potter treats the consequences of his double transgression relatively lightly, letting Nutkin off, like Peter Rabbit, with a cautionary warning. This can be seen as a strategy encouraging readers to develop empathy for the other, by playing on the dual animal-human nature of her characters.

In Potter, the human world is often blurred with that of animals but, although her creatures may appear as humans, they never lose their real animalness. The smokescreen of mixing human with animal behaviour and the metaphor of clothing are devices used to narrow the gaps between the human world with that of animals. In *Three Little Mice*, and in *Squirrel Nutkin*, none of the animals appear clothed, whilst the mice in *The Tailor of Gloucester* – where the theme itself is the making of clothes – are portrayed wearing elaborate costumes. Even when her characters wear clothes, however, they frequently appear in their natural state too, as if to recall their real appearance and remind us of their true nature. To a large extent, they appear as real animals when they are unclothed and only act like humans when dressed. As Lane observes, when 'animals appear without their clothes: it is never done by accident, but always to stress and as it were recall their true natures ...' (1985: 117).

Potter's rhymes have a similar function to the shifting semiotic of clothes in the stories, in that they operate in between the realms of the human and natural. The rhymes are placed in natural settings that are rich in fauna and flora, as can be observed in her sketches of trees and woodland in *Squirrel Nutkin*. Traces of her earlier expert knowledge of mycology can also be seen in her rhymes and tales: clearly differentiated forms of fungi, agarics, appear in the background settings for Squirrel Nutkin; while in the 'Toads' Tea Party' the toads are seated on bun-shaped boletes. In this way, the expertise drawn from a lifetime of observation is woven into her tales, since Potter provides accurate details and names different species of plants and trees to help young readers distinguish and identify their local environment. Her anthropomorphism can thus be read as a literary device used to make us attentive to the detail of the natural world. She plays with the boundaries between the human and animal in forms that both reconfigure and accentuate environmental awareness and education.

From an ecocritical perspective, Potter's rhymes and riddles are also particularly effective in creating metaphorical links to animals' behaviour and habitats. For example, Nutkin 'bobbed up and down like a little red cherry' and later he 'danced up and down like a sunbeam'. These metaphors function at multiple levels, since they also contain the 'answers' to Nutkin's riddles and are marked with italics to help young readers solve them. Overall though, the metaphors serve to extend the interconnectedness of the animal figures with their real environment and to ground the whole in a larger imaginative truth:

> All her little hedgerow, farmyard and wainscot animals are conceived with imaginative truth, though they are shrewdly humanised, and their stories told throughout in human terms, there is, imaginatively speaking, not a word of falsehood. We close the books, knowing more about animal and human nature than we did before. (Lane 1985:116)

The careful observation and reflection found in Potter's tales engage children with the natural world in a way that combines empathy with respect for essential otherness. In this sense, she builds on our environmental imagination. From an ecocritical perspective, her work can be read as looking at nature from the animal other's point of view, while her rhymes and riddles play a key role in weaving a sense of this otherness into the reader's consciousness. In this way, Potter stimulates environmental imagination in young readers and invites them to reconsider our relationship with today's damaged natural world.

Works Cited:

Blount, M (1977) *Animal Land: The Creatures of Children's Fiction.* New York: Avon-Hearst

Gates, B (1999) *Kindred Nature: Victorian And Edwardian Women Embrace The Living World.* Chicago and London: University of Chicago Press

Lane, M (1985) *The Tale of Beatrix Potter: A Biography.* London: Frederick Warne

Linder, L (1989) *The Journal of Beatrix Potter 1881-1897.* London: Frederick Warne

Potter, B (2006) *The Complete Tales.* London: Frederick Warne

Stevenson Hobbs, A (2005) *Beatrix Potter: Artist and Illustrator.* London: Frederick Warne

18

Once upon a time in the realms of Eden: Children's Poetry in Brazil

Telma Franco Diniz

... we walked around, admiring the river whose waters run deep and wide ... stayed a while, drinking and resting alongside the riverbanks and under the trees, of which there are so many, so tall and so exuberantly crowned, that no man can get them counted; streams are plentiful; infinite; and the land is so bountiful that, if cultivated, all crops will bloom, for water springs are good and abundant ...

The first thing that came to mind when I began to consider how Brazilian poets respond to Nature, was the text above, written over 500 years ago. It comes from a letter by Pero Vaz de Caminha to the King of Portugal in 1500, written from a ship moored off the northeast coast of Brazil. He not only told the King about the discovery of the New Land, but also lingered in colourful detail on descriptions of the scenery, the natives' physical build, their feathery headdresses, what they ate, how they sang, danced and laughed and how innocent they seemed, even as they went about naked. According to Caminha, the crew had found some kind of Eden.

Many explorers and travellers – before and after Caminha – compared the new continent to a Promised Land (Zilberman, 1994). Nevertheless, Caminha helped graft perceptions of Brazil onto a recurrent image, thriving in European minds since the Greeks: the idea that an earthly Paradise really existed; a mystical, hidden land, where men and women could find spiritual renewal and live peacefully in harmony with the fertile earth (Rouanet, 2000:16-17). This idea of a paradise on earth was encouraging for the Portuguese Crown, not only serving a religious purpose – that is, to catechise the natives – but also

for exploitation of the land, which was made to appear rich and easily cultivated with little effort. So for two hundred years the image of Brazil as *locus
amoenus* was passed on to Portuguese travellers and settlers alike: the image
would sail from Brazil to Europe in travellers' and merchants' reports, returning to Brazil within the minds and hearts of the settlers and priests. Consequently, the hetero-image – the image seen from outside Brazil of a paradisiacal land of incomparable natural beauty and inexhaustible resources –
developed into some kind of self-image for Brazil, too. Later, this Eden-like
image moved from the travellers' prose to poetry written by Brazilians, who
continued to praise the surrounding landscape and the land's abundance and
profitability (Sousa, 2004).

An early poem of this kind was '*Descrição da Ilha de Itaparica*', composed by
Fray Santa Maria Itaparica in the eighteenth century. Here the poet praises his
birthplace, the Island of Itaparica, in Bahia, northeast Brazil, and all the things
that exist there: the exotic fruit (*pitomba, pitanga*), the shoals of fish and the
'shiny metal', attracting legions of explorers lured by easy wealth (Stegagno-
Picchio, 2004). Another poem written in the same period is 'Uraguay', by
Basílio da Gama, an epic about the Guarani War between the Jesuit/Indians
and the Portuguese/Spanish forces. In this poem, the Guarani are portrayed as
good, honest and wise – an image comparable to that of the noble savage.
Itaparica and Basílio da Gama greatly influenced Brazilian authors who
followed them. Moreover, they were praised by European critics, who saw their
poems as containing ideals that Brazilian writers were recommended to embrace if they wanted to be authentic nationalists (Zilberman, 1994), an objective of Romantics in the nineteenth century.

Gonçalves Dias, Romantic and heir to the Eden-on-earth imaginary, was one
of the most celebrated poets of the mid-nineteenth century. His most famous
poem, '*A canção do exílio*' (2002), sings of nostalgia for his homeland. This
poem has been anthologised for children again and again ever since its first
publication in 1843. It may be relevant that Dias had moved to Portugal for
college education at a time when Brazilians were experiencing a surge of
patriotism in the aftermath of Independence in 1822. Even so, the poem has
remained popular and has inspired many rewritings. Here are the first and
second stanzas, translated into English by Nelson Ascher (2008):

> My homeland has many palm-trees
> and the thrush-song fills its air
> no bird here can sing as well
> as the birds sing over there.

> We have fields more full of flowers
> and a starrier sky above,
> we have woods more full of life
> and a life more full of love.

Casimiro de Abreu also produced poems praising homeland, such as the seven-stanza poem '*Meus oito anos*' (Abreu, 2002), in which the poet longs for his childhood, when he played on the fields, mountains and waterfalls of Brazil. The fifth stanza goes like this:

> Carefree son of the mountains
> I lived happily and blessed
> resolute and open chest
> – barefooted and naked arms –
> running around the waterfalls
> meadows, valleys, hills and highs,
> chasing the fast brief wings
> of blue, deep blue butterflies!

As seen above, from Arcadia to Romanticism, the most successful poets extolled the symbolic image of Nature and Brazil as twin entities, as though they were mirrors of one another.

Brazil became a Republic in the late nineteenth century. A flourishing urban middle-class pressured for changes (Zilberman, 2005), including demands for better public education. The government reacted favourably and developed campaigns to improve literacy. Journalists, teachers and intellectuals took on the task, and the first books written exclusively for children were released to a precise group of addressees: the body of students who had enrolled in the recently built schools. One of these intellectuals was Olavo Bilac, whose collection *Poesias infantis* [Childhood poetry], published in 1904, was very successful. Passages of his most quoted poem, 'A pátria' (Bilac, 1929), are still recited by Grandmas and Grandpas nowadays. Encomiastic and full of civic enthusiasm, Bilac exhorts children to love their homeland:

> Love, with faith and pride, thy nation and homeland!
> Child! Thou wilt never see a country this grand!
> What skies! what seas! what streams! what forests!
> Nature here is in an endless jest!

> Emulate the grandeur of thy nation and homeland!

In the preface of *Poesias infantis*, Bilac confirmed that the book dealt with simple issues and promoted moral behaviour in children. He was an influential person, a man of letters, and his literary criteria for what was good for children remained valid for many decades.

In February 1922, the city of São Paulo hosted the Modern Art Week, which would become a watershed in the history of Brazilian art, with fine art exhibitions, lectures, concerts and poetry readings. The event broke with Academicism and introduced Modernism to Brazilian society at large. Before long, modern poetry had adopted the use of colloquial terms and free verse. However, this did not extend to children's poetry, which took many years to embrace these new ideas.

In Brazil, poetry for children was strongly related to the context of schooling. As a result, children's poetry remained didactic and laudatory, advising young readers to be good citizens and extolling the virtues of the country (Camargo, 1999). Poetry for children started to loosen its ties with school and shed its pedagogical concerns around 1943, when Henriqueta Lisboa published *O menino poeta*, a lyrical collection whose intense use of metaphor differentiated it from earlier poetry exemplified by Bilac. Lisboa also showed love for nature and her country, but in a more subtle way. In the poem 'Cantiga de Vila-Bela', for instance, she urges the cotton-pickers to come and celebrate the harvest along the banks of São Francisco River, the 'father river', and build there a new 'green-and-yellow' city (colours in the Brazilian flag), where 'the maiden and the braggart might live happily ever after' (Lisboa, 2008). Lisboa also made use of children's games, incorporating references to Brazilian traditions into her poems, such as 'vamos todos cirandar', a popular verse equivalent to the dancing game 'ring-around-the-roses', reproduced in the three-stanza poem 'Ciranda de Mariposas'. The poem shows how, for Lisboa, animals and plants are one with human beings, all part of the cosmos; men and women are brothers and sisters to the stars, the moths, and the moon.

Right from the start, we are invited to join the moths in a circle. The poet then traces a parallel between the moths out there in the cold night, and the stars in outer space. Readers are encouraged to sympathise with their longing for warmth and light. Here are the first and last stanzas:

> Let's all ring around,
> Around the moths let's ring.
> Moths at the glass window
> Are jewels, are gold earrings ...

Bright stars are heavenly moths
(the street is so cold, so soon!)
flying their wings of hope
into the glass window of the moon.

As we have seen, not all nature-related poems for children had civic purposes or boasted openly of the country. Animals are frequently protagonists in poetry for children, as they can symbolise the child, or represent the child's inner world. This is very true of the poems of Cecília Meireles. Take the poem 'A égua e a água' (1964). The title translates literally as 'The Mare and the Water', but could also be freely translated as 'The Mare and the Mere', maintaining both the sense and the assonance of the original Portuguese. The poem portrays a mare's search for water. Despite feeling thirsty, the creature just gazes anxiously at the vast nearby lagoon (or 'mere') and goes on, plodding for miles and miles, void eyes upon void spaces, in search of a puddle of water:

Suffice it would a puddle of water
but oh! only many a mile after.

Utter despair!

For a drop of dew is way too scarce
and the mere is so so vast.

The unexpected and innovative open ending allows a variety of readings. We are not really convinced that the mare did not drink from the lagoon due to its vastness alone. Maybe the lagoon represents eternity and the drop of dew the transient aspects of nature. The ephemeral is painful, but it would appear that eternity is also too much for the mare. Likewise, the water in the poem could be interpreted as knowledge, or perhaps love. Whatever it may represent, it does seem that the mare fears having too much of it. Or maybe she does not fear anything, but feels pressured to look for something smaller, due to circumstances beyond her control.

Cecília Meireles doesn't underestimate her young readers' capacity to understand. Moreover, she provides a key in the line 'Utter Despair!', giving the reader the impression that there is more to the mare than the words alone reveal. The poem's complexity is just one of the aspects of its innovation. It also contains wordplay, inner rhymes, free verse, and an echo that reverberates throughout the poem, with the words *água, égua, mágoa, légua, exígua*. In the English version quoted above, this echo reverberates in the words 'mare', 'bear', 'despair', 'scarce', 'ever'.

In Meireles' poem '*O colar de Carolina*', the relationship with nature is emphasised through the child's fluid interactions with vivid colours (Lajolo and Zilberman, 2007). Caroline runs around hilltop columns, but the coral string she wears turns her skin crimson, pink, scarlet. The poet extends the conceit of this dramatic influence of natural phenomena on the girl's body, by imbuing the sunset with the colours of coral too. The effect of this startling image is intensified through the dense pattern of alliterative sounds (Zilberman, 2005):

> Compelled by the carmine colour
> on the string worn by Caroline
> the sun sets its coral crowns
> up the columns at the incline.

In the 1960s and 1970s, Brazilian children and adults witnessed a poetic revolution similar to that which was occurring in England (Styles, 1996): authors who had previously directed their work to an adult audience began writing poetry for children as well, playing with words, and addressing children in a non-patronising way. This is a period of great energy and accomplishment. The public welcomed children's poetry written by Mario Quintana, Vinicius de Moraes, Sidónio Muralha, José Paulo Paes, Ruth Rocha, Sylvia Orthof, Ana Maria Machado, Roseana Murray, Sérgio Capparelli, Bartolomeu de Queirós and Lalau, to mention a few. Here I focus briefly on four of these poets, to illustrate the different approaches towards Nature they have pioneered.

De Moraes' poems are characterised by humour, sound games and the echoing of traditional popular songs. His anthology *A Arca de Noé* is possibly the most famous book of poetry for children in the history of Brazilian literature. He was deeply moved by Brazil's inequalities and made that evident through his verses. In '*Pátria Minha*' (2002) he affirms that Brazil is neither just flowers, nor starry-banners:

> ... my fatherland is thirsty soil
> and white beaches; my fatherland is the great secular river
> that drinks clouds, eats earth
> and urinates sea.

De Queirós grew up in a small mountain village far from the sea. Like most children, at school he read poems that spoke of thrush-songs filling the air, palm-trees, emerald seas and alabaster beaches – a seascape he would only see as an adult. Many of his poems deal with his childhood desire to go beyond the mountains. The title of his book *Sem palmeira ou sabiá* (2006) – 'No palm-trees nor thrushes' – is a clear reference to Dias' *The song of exile*, but also marks his distance from the perspectives of the earlier poet. Queirós' imagery registers strangeness and loss as well as celebration, as when a three-year-old boy throws salt into a puddle to recreate a private ocean. The boy asks his mother:

> 'Mom', I asked, 'I want to see the sea.'
> 'No', she answered, 'look at the river; it flows down to the sea.'

> I looked at the river that crossed town.
> I saw the muddy waters, and salt ran down from my eyes.
>   '*Sem palmeira ou sabiá*'

Lalau focuses on children's apparent unawareness of Brazilian endangered species. The collection *Brasileirinhos* (2001), with illustrations by Laurabeatriz, introduces a range of endangered species to young readers through poems, accompanied by colourful paintings of the animals or their habitat. In '*A harpia e a floresta*' (2008), Lalau voices the harpy eagle's cries about the destruction of its habitat:

> The Amazon is sublime,
> precious as life.

> I beg of you,
> we still got time
> don't destroy the forest
> for it's an awful crime.

Roseana Murray's poems are particularly evocative and spiritual. Nature is present in all of them, be it in similes, metaphors or allegories. In the ebook *Variações sobre silêncio e cordas* (2008), she compares trees and roots to strings that connect and hold Earth to its core:

> When strings break
> and trees no longer can
> probe and shade the ground
> Earth will sway out of tune,
> a lost hot-air balloon.

The poet conveys her environmental message with subtlety. This attitude towards her readers places her work close to that of Meireles, who believes that authors should always leave room for mystery, in order to afford opportunity for young readers to perceive things for themselves (Meireles, 1984).

Currently a profusion of themes and viewpoints is expressed in poetry for children. Many poets are concerned about the environment: some make their commitment obvious, such as Lalau, whilst others, like Murray, are more subtle. The image of Brazil as a land of blessed nature is no longer passed down to children in an absolute, unquestionable manner. However, this image does continue, intrinsic and lyrical, in the work of contemporary children's poets such as de Queirós, who combine this lyrical impulse with a more questioning attitude. Indeed images of paradise, including those conjured by classic writers such as Dias and de Abreu, still pervade the texts recommended in schools, but with more variety in the landscapes evoked and with a greater range of intentions driving the poems. In aggregate, this is perhaps a crucial resource, since, in order to understand who we are today, we need to understand who we were in the past (Coelho, 1993).

The image of what I began by calling this 'paradisiacal land of incomparable natural beauty ... and inexhaustible resources' is rooted in the Brazilian imagination as a founding myth, and perhaps might not be so out of place today if it were not for the word 'inexhaustible'.

Acknowledgments

I should like to thank Andre O. Carvalho for permission to quote my translation of two poems by Henriqueta Lisboa; Bartolemeu C, de Queirós, Roseana Murray and Lalau for permission to quote my translations of extracts of their poems; and Nelson Ascher for permission to quote his translation into English of the poem 'A canção do exilio'.

The author is also grateful to Sarah Rebecca Kersley and David Whitley for their encouragement, excellent suggestions and careful reading.

Works Cited:

Abreu, C (2002) *Meus oito anos*. In Aguiar *et al* (ed.) *Poesia Fora da Estante*, v. 2. Porto Alegre: Editora Projeto

Ascher, N (1999) The song of exile. *Cadernos de Literatura em Tradução* 3 (1)

Bilac, O (1929) *Poesias Infantis*. Rio de Janeiro: Francisco Alves

Camargo, L (1999) *A poesia infantil no Brasil* http://www.blocosonline.com.br/literatura/prosa/artigos/art021.htm (October, 2009)

Caminha, P V (2009) A Carta de Pero Vaz de Caminha http://www.dominiopublico.gov.br/download/texto/ua000283.pdf (October, 2009)

Coelho, N N (1993) *Literatura Infantil*: teoria, análise, didática. São Paulo: Ática

Dias, G (2002) *Canção do exílio* In Aguiar *et al* (ed) *Poesia Fora da Estante*, v. 2. Porto Alegre: Editora Projeto

Lajolo, M and Zilberman, R (2007) *Literatura Infantil Brasileira: história e histórias*. São Paulo: Editora Ática

Lalau (2008) *A harpia e a floresta*. In *Sobre Voos*. São Paulo: Manole

Lisboa, H (2008) *Ciranda de mariposas* In *O Menino Poeta*. São Paulo: Peirópolis

Meireles, C (1984) *Problemas da Literatura Infantil*. Rio de Janeiro: Nova Fronteira

Meireles, C (1964) *Ou isto ou aquilo*. Rio de Janeiro: Nova Fronteira

Moraes, V (2002) *Pátria Minha* In Aguiar *et al* (ed) *Poesia Fora da Estante*, v. 2. Porto Alegre: Editora Projeto

Murray, R (2008) *Variações sobre silêncio e cordas* http://www.roseanamurray.com/ebook/ (October, 2009)

Queirós, B C (2006) *Sem Palmeira ou Sabiá*. São Paulo: Peirópolis

Rouanet, S P (2000) *O exorcismo do bom e do mau selvagem*. Folha de S. Paulo, São Paulo: Caderno Mais

Sousa, C H M R (2004) *Do Cá e do Lá: introdução à imagologia*. São Paulo: Associação Editorial Humanitas

Stegagno-Picchio, L (2004) *História da Literatura Brasileira*. Rio de Janeiro: Nova Aguilar

Styles, M (1996) Poetry for children. In Hunt, P (ed.) *International Encyclopedia of children's literature*. London/New York: Routledge

Zilberman, R (1994) *A Terra em que Nasceste: imagens do Brasil na literatura*. Porto Alegre: Editora da Universidade/UFRGS

Zilberman, R (2005) *Como e Por que Ler a Literatura Infantil Brasileira*. Rio de Janeiro: Objetiva

19

Animal Poems and Children's Rights in America, 1820-1890

Angela Sorby

The Anglo-American children's publishing industry emerged co-terminally with what Lynn Hunt has called the 'revolution in human rights' (Hunt, 2008: 15). When John Newbery adopted Locke's phrase, *Delectando Monemus*, as his motto, he also implicitly endorsed the Enlightenment assumption that all humans, as Thomas Jefferson would put it, are entitled to life, liberty, and the pursuit of happiness. However, because they are not fully capable of self-governance, children have long posed problems for advocates of universal rights. Observing the American scene in her study *Cradle of Liberty*, Caroline Levander has argued that during the nineteenth century the child, in particular, 'reveals a series of manoeuvres through which the idea of the 'authentically human' becomes a part of the machinery of constructing a civic self' (Levander, 2008:9). In this chapter I examine the emergence of animal poems as a major subgenre within American children's poetry, while tracing the changing ways in which such poems construct a civic self by marking but also blurring the boundary lines between authentically human children and animals.

While children's poetry resists strict periodisation, a rough chronology can be sketched. During the colonial period, American children read rhymes, mostly of British origin, that reflected pre-Revolutionary, contractual assumptions about children's rights. Then, during the nineteenth century, American authors began to write animal poems for children while fashioning an historically-specific sentimental vision of the relationship between children and animals. Of course, children's literature from many cultures and historical periods has depicted bonds between children and animals. However, I argue that, in the nineteenth century, a new liberal-democratic subject-position generated new ways of figuring this bond. Specifically, between about 1820 and 1900, sentimental empathy poems taught boys and girls that suffering was a self-evident argument in favour of rights. In other words, rights were intrinsic (as opposed to earned) and visible via the vulnerable bodies of animals. Moreover, it was assumed that children could relate to lame horses or broken-winged birds because children, like animals, were physically and legally powerless. Nineteenth-century children's animal poems thus raised difficult questions related to the revolution in human rights: to what extent are non-citizens also non-persons? Do non-citizens have rights? Do non-persons have rights? In a liberal democracy, what is the difference between a man, a woman, a child, and an animal – and if all are not equal, then do all nonetheless deserve some measure of protection under the law?

To understand how nineteenth-century animal poems are distinctive, it is useful to consider what preceded them. In the transatlantic culture of colonial America, English common law precedents determined children's rights, which were understood contractually: the child's labour belonged to the parent or master, who was in turn obligated to provide for the child. Children (apart from slave children) were not chattel, but they did form part of a working continuum that stretched from the patriarch at the head of the household to livestock at the bottom. The poems in the then-ubiquitous *New England Primer* depict animals as God's working instruments: 'Whales in the sea/God's voice obey' (Ford, 1899:155). These whales have no agency and invite no sympathy, nor are they playthings; rather, they illustrate that authoritarian hierarchies (like the colonial family and the Puritan town) are natural and inevitable. Isaac Watts' 'Verses for Children,' reprinted in the *Primer*, reinforces this worldview:

> When wicked children mocking said,
> To a good man, *Go up bald head,*
> God was displeas'd with them and sent
> Two bears which them in pieces rent,
> I must not like these children vile,
> Displease my God, myself defile. (Ford, 1899:330)

Wild bears were extinct in Watts' Britain, but his poem must have been especially terrifying to children in colonial New England. More significantly, the poem grants the children covenantal duties as opposed to rights. When the children sin, their bodily integrity is immediately violated by the bear, who 'rends' them like prisoners drawn and quartered in a Foucaultian tableau. Readers are not expected to empathise with the children or the bear; both function as disciplinary emblems signifying the power of God, the King, and the colonial Father. Children have civic and spiritual status only when they obey God; their rights are contractual, not natural.

By contrast, nineteenth-century empathy poems assume that children, like animals, have natural or inborn rights based on their capacity for bodily suffering. Fragility is no longer a sign of spiritual weakness but an emblem of purity and a mute plea for protection. As the humane society activist Mrs Fairchild puts it in an 1883 anthology, *Pleadings of Mercy*, 'To the heart which has a moiety of Christian tenderness the appealing face of childhood and the rights of those humble creatures which yield pleasure and profit to the nations cannot lightly be set aside' (1883:n.p.). *Pleadings of Mercy* uses poetry to make its case by printing two verses in succession: 'The Dead Bird' and the 'The Chrysalis: A Dead Baby'. 'The Dead Bird' begins:

> Silent and tiny thing, with folded wing,
>> Frail as the trembling sun-ray on the floor;
> These little plumes of gold will scarcely hold
>> The softest weight of tears that dew them o'er.

The image is meant to excite 'a moiety of Christian tenderness' by stressing the bird's trembling but also the speaker's tears, which literally saturate the avian body, blurring the physical boundary between human and bird. 'The Chrysalis' also begins with trembling as it links a baby and a butterfly:

> Where from this little body, white and saintly,
>> Sweet spirit, hast thou flown?
> That trembled on the verge of time so faintly,
>> And then was gone!

Taken together, these two poems not only imply that winged animals have souls, but that winged animals are souls – that the dead baby's true self is revealed, at death, to be a butterfly. The baby's claim for adult empathy stems from its frail animal nature, just as the bird's claim stems from its infantile helplessness.

Although most nineteenth-century animal poems were not written by Humane Society activists, many nonetheless echo and amplify Mrs Fairchild's agenda. 'Mary's Lamb,' by Sarah Josepha Hale, depicts a bond between a child and an animal that is almost as close as the link between body and soul:

> Mary had a little lamb,
> Its fleece was white as snow,
> And everywhere that Mary went
> The lamb was sure to go. (Hale, 1830:6)

Mary and the lamb are not intellectual equals; when the lamb tries to enter the schoolroom, the teacher ejects it because it is distracting the students. However – and from Hale's perspective, more importantly – Mary and her lamb are moral and emotional equals:

> What makes the lamb love Mary so?
> The eager children cry;
> Why Mary loves the lamb, you know,
> The teacher did reply.

Mary and the lamb – like the dead bird and the dead baby – are interchangeable and bound by a love that inspires mutual kindness and that also inspires the teacher, who ends the poem with a moral:

> And you each gentle animal
> In confidence may bind;
> And make them follow at your will,
> If you are only kind.

The teacher models both animal rights and children's rights; no birch-rod is in evidence although Mary has broken a school rule. Instead, the students are instructed through what Richard Brodhead (1993) has called 'disciplinary intimacy': the strategy of positing and shaping children's emotional responses rather than simply punishing their bodies. Brodhead understands disciplinary intimacy mainly as a means of social control; however, viewed through the prism of children's and animal rights, the teacher's lesson might also be seen as socially transformative precisely because it grants both Mary and the lamb interiority and agency.

An article in the *New York Evangelist*, by 'Aunt' Augusta Moore, makes the connections between 'Mary's Lamb', animal rights, and children's rights more explicit. Moore portrays herself on an outing with some children:

> See the pretty lambs yonder. How innocent are their faces. You've heard the song 'Mary had a little lamb,' I suppose. I have some yarn which that very Mary knit. An acquaintance of mine knew Mary. She is yet alive – a very nice lady – in Boston. How curious some of the sheep and lambs look! ... Just see how much they look like people. Some faces so fair and happy, some so worn and sad. How closely they have been sheared. I am glad they are in such a nice

pasture, where [there] is water, food, and shade. The poor animals that I saw in the grounds of Mr. Baker, the sewing-machine man, were in cages, and though miserably neglected, needing water and food and to be cleaned, they had to stay right in one spot. It was shameful. (1880:6)

Moore reads 'Mary's Lamb' as a text that teaches kindness based on a natural human-ovine kinship: 'Just see how much they look like people!' Like lambs, Moore's child companions enjoy the fresh country air. Because they themselves are autonomous, the children can empathise with Mr. Baker's 'shamefully' confined livestock and understand viscerally that these animal's rights are being violated. Moreover, a sewing machine connotes industrialisation and the spectre of child labour, further cementing the bond between children and sheep.

Herein lies the rub, though: what can the children do about Mr. Baker's abused animals? What can Aunt Moore – a disenfranchised woman – do? Although Fairchild, Hale, and Moore make animal rights seem self-evident and natural, the nineteenth-century American legal system was slow to embrace anti-cruelty measures in part because they interfered with white men's property rights. Moreover, even in 'Mary's Lamb', the lamb is owned by Mary, just as Mary herself is legally owned by her parents and by the teacher in *loco parentis*. Does the property status of children and animals mitigate their rights? Numerous nineteenth-century parodies of 'Mary's Lamb' explore this question by turning the lamb into food:

> What made dear Mary like the lamb,
>   Does any one inquire?
> Because she knew how good it was
>   When roasted by the fire.
> And when served up with good mint sauce
>   And fresh green peas you'll know
> How it is yourself and understand
>   Why Mary liked it so. (1887)

This roasted lamb is discomfitingly funny because it stages a clash between animal rights and the prerogatives of property ownership. The carnivorous Mary and the poem's reader are here united, not by bonds of empathy, but by a shared taste for peas, mint, and of course roast lamb, while the lamb reverts to commodity status. This undermines Hale's basic assumption that lambs are like children, but it also tropes on this assumption: Mary's meal borders on the cannibalistic because the original poem so successfully depicts a moral equivalency between Mary and her lamb.

Nineteenth-century animal poems seldom advocate vegetarianism *per se*, but they do work exceptionally hard to avoid turning animals into stews. Indeed, beginning in the 1820s and continuing through the century, a specific motif emerges that underlines the fundamental legal helplessness of women (like Hale), girls (like Mary) and animals (like the lamb). This motif involves a boy who is inveigled – often by a girl or an animal – to stop fishing, torturing birds, stealing eggs, or teasing pets. For example, in 'The Dead Robin', which appeared in the *Juvenile Miscellany* (1831), a girl chides her brother, who has killed a tame bird:

> See Charles, how little robin lies,
> The film is on his gentle eyes,
> His pretty beak is parted wide,
> And blood is flowing from his side.
> He never, never will come more
> To perch before the open door,
> And never, on the window pane,
> You'll hear him softly tap again.
> Oh! What a very wicked thing
> It was, to break his tender wing,
> And deeper dye his breast of red,
> And kill my darling robin dead.

There is more at stake here than just a robin. Because Charles is a boy, he must learn to exercise power responsibly before he reaches adulthood. The girls and women in his life will always remain – like the robin – vulnerable part-citizens, unprotected by the laws that enfranchise and empower men. The sister's self-protective strategy involves disciplinary intimacy: Charles must be taught to feel bad and to internalise both the robin's suffering and the sister's sadness, so that he can learn to recognise the value of individuals (human and avian) who are not fully valued by custom or law.

In another poem, 'Compassion', also from the *Miscellany*, a boy demonstrates that he has learned his lesson well; he explains to the poem's speaker that he is sad:

> I saw them lead a young ewe lamb
>   Away from all the rest:
> I heard the bleating of the dam –
>   What grief that cry expressed!
> But when I saw the gentle ewe
>   Lay down her head to die –

I wondered men could bear to do
    Such deeds of cruelty.
I think I could not crush a flower,
    That bowed its head so low
It may be pleasant to have power;
    But not to use it so.

Neither Wells nor the *Juvenile Miscellany* advocate an end to farm life or to meat-eating, although the magazine was founded by the abolitionist Lydia Maria Child and later edited by Hale. Rather, the didactic goal of both 'The Dead Robin' and 'Compassion' is to prepare boys for full citizenship by helping them manage power that they alone – not their sisters, their mothers, or their pets – will inherit. At the same time, the robin and the ewe are not purely allegorical: readers are asked to witness, and to interpret, actual battered bodies. Such poems thus raise questions that were often asked in nineteenth-century courts: when does visible suffering trump property-rights? And does it matter whether the sufferer is an animal, a child, or an adult?

Like sentimental culture more generally, animal empathy poems offer coping strategies to children (and women) whose lack of self-determination is assumed. As Mrs. Fairchild's title, *Pleas of Mercy*, implies, the dominant mode in the animal-empathy poem is the entreaty: everyone suffers, everyone deserves compassion and it is the job of the poem to promote universal emotional responses across species. At the same time, poems such as 'The Dead Robin' and 'Compassion' recognise (and do not seriously question) social hierarchies that grant autonomy to men but not women, children, or animals. This reflects a cultural consensus that children, like animals, were dependent creatures at the mercy of their caretakers – a consensus that held until the later nineteenth century, when courts began to use this very idea in order to protect abused children and animals – and the cultural work of empathy became the law of the land.

Indeed, the date can perhaps be pinpointed: in 1873, the New York Society for the Prevention of Cruelty to Animals successfully used the legal system to remove a nine-year-old girl, Mary Ellen Wilson, from her abusive home. As Jacob Riis describes it in *Children of the Poor*, a Methodist missionary wanted to save Mary Ellen, but the police would not help her, so she decided:

> 'I will make one more effort to save this child. There is one man in this city who has never turned a deaf ear to the cry of the helpless and who has spent his life in just this work for the benefit of unoffending animals. I will go to Henry Bergh.' She went, and the great friend of the dumb brute found a way. 'The child

is an animal,' he said, 'if there is no justice for it as a human being, it shall at least have the rights of the cur in the streets. It shall not be abused.' And thus was written the first bill of rights for the friendless waif the world over. (Riis, 1902:143)

The American public sided with Bergh, outraged by a photograph of Mary Ellen's abused body that was widely reprinted. However, as writers like Hale and Wells understood, empathetic responses to children – not to mention 'curs in the streets' – were not automatic but culturally inculcated. People knew how to read Mary Ellen's body because they had been taught to read it. I will not claim that specific poems influenced the case directly, but it seems clear that the discourse of animal empathy, as advanced, *inter alia*, through poems like 'Mary's Lamb', helped to write 'the bill of rights' for that other Mary: Mary Ellen Wilson. Children's poetry, then, did not simply reflect, but actually produced, public sympathy for the cause of children's rights.

Works Cited

Brodhead, R (1993) *Cultures of Letters: Scenes of Reading and Writing in Nineteenth-century America*. Chicago: University of Chicago Press

Fairchild, Mrs. C (1883) *Pleadings of Mercy for the Animal World, and all other Defenseless Creatures*. New York: A.W. Landon

Ford, P (ed) (1899) *The New England Primer: a Reprint*. New York: Dodd Mead

Hall, D (ed) (1990) *The Oxford Book of Children's Verse in America*. New York: Oxford University Press

Hunt, L (2008) *Inventing Human Rights: a History*. New York: Norton

Levander, C (2008) *Cradle of Liberty: race, the child, and national belonging from Thomas Jefferson to W.E.B. DuBois*. Raleigh-Durham: Duke University Press

Moore, A (1880) untitled article, *New York Evangelist* (17 June)

Riis, J (1902) *Children of the Poor*. New York: Scribner

Unattributed (1871) *American Educational Monthly*. (April)

Unattributed (1831) 'The Dead Robin', *Juvenile Miscellany* (July/August)

Wells, A (1829) 'Compassion', *Juvenile Miscellany* (July)

20

'Imaginary gardens with real toads in them': Animals in Children's Poetry

David Whitley

This chapter explores the changing role of the animal in children's poetry. Just as the natural world has always been a kind of bass note for poetry as a whole, so animals have long played a key role in poetry particularly oriented towards children. But the sensibility and culture that poetry addresses has, of course, changed over time. Many would argue that the majority of children's direct experience and knowledge of the wild animals in their immediate environment became progressively more attenuated in the course of the last century, so that children's understanding of real animals' lives is now more diminished than at any point in human history. Given this increasing trend towards the loss of direct sensory experience of the natural world – which, some would argue, is of crucial importance if humanity is to regain its sense of balance and interconnectedness – what role can poetry play in restoring awareness? And, in this context, is the degree to which animal presences are made to feel *real* – however problematic this term may be – within poetry important?

In a brief chapter one can only begin to sketch a few ideas and identify one or two significant issues. But it is possible to gain some sense of shifts in attitude within the domain of poetry by comparing Marianne Moore's mid-twentieth-century definition of poetry as 'imaginary gardens with real toads in them' (1968:266-7) with Christina Rossetti's characteristically playful, incipient awareness of tensions between human and animal perspectives in her poem 'A Frog's Fate.' This is a wry verse pastiche of the traditional Aesopic fable. The poem charts a frog's bathetic attempt to break from the limitations of its froggy nature, as the creature strikes out boldly – with a determination un-characteristic of frogs in general – along the road humans have designed as their highway. As in many of Aesop's stories, the frog's unnatural hubris seals a sorry fate for him, as he is almost immediately crushed under an insouciant driver's cartwheels. But it is the twist Rossetti gives to the expected didactic ending that is of interest here. She imagines a choice – if callous – irony as the waggoner whistles:

> ... (it may have happened so)
> 'A froggy would a-wooing go.'
> A hypothetic frog trolled he
> Obtuse to a reality. ('A Frog's Fate' 1997:98)

The poet then offers the following sententious wisdom as a way of rounding off the unfortunate event:

> O rich and poor, O great and small,
> Such oversights beset us all.
> The mangled frog abides incog,
> The uninteresting actual frog:
> The hypothetic frog alone
> Is the one frog we dwell upon.

Poetry, it would seem – and by extension human consciousness – is taken up with its own song and rides on by, or indeed roughshod over, the real nature that forms its ostensible subject.

It would be too sweeping to claim that poetry in the twentieth century has been consistently taken up with redressing the key terms of the irony Rossetti's poem plays upon, of putting real toads back into the garden of the imagina-tion. Indeed a number of earlier poets – perhaps most notably John Clare – could reasonably be thought of as already developing a realistic imaginative engagement with animal life that operates as a strong ethical, as well as aesthetic, principle in itself. However, it is perhaps fair to say that a number of important twentieth-century poets have also tried to shift the balance decisi-vely in a direction that acknowledges the *real* claims, as opposed to the sym-bolic significances, of animal presences in their poems. McKendrick identifies a characteristic trend in this direction when he praises Elizabeth Bishop's notable poem 'The Sandpiper', for instance, because it 'never, as it were, lets (the sandpiper) leave the ground and doesn't make it subservient to its sym-bolic properties' (2002:131).

This resurgent desire to make the *particular* at least as compelling as the *symbolic* intentions of poems whose subject is the natural world takes place along three major axes, I would suggest. These axes are what determine the relationship between the human speaker – or reader – and the animal figure that is the ostensible subject of the poem. The categories are not mutually exclusive, of course, but most poems, whether for children or adults, organise feelings and perceptions through one or more of the modes of analogy, contrast or identification with the animal subject. Robert Burns' wonderful poem 'To a Mouse', familiar to every schoolchild growing up in Scotland, is perhaps exemplary in using all three of these modes. The poem begins by inviting the reader to join with the speaker in identifying sympathetically with the mouse's trembling state of apprehension: 'Wee, sleekit, cowrin', timorous beastie' (1995:83). The poet then proceeds subtly to draw in analogies between the mouse's situation and his own precarious state; and indeed, by implication, the position of workers on the land generally. Finally, in the closing sententia, this is drawn into a contrast, the mouse's inability to project its consciousness into the past or future heightening the sense that the speaker's precarious situation may evoke even greater suffering and pathos. Although Burns doesn't insist upon this aspect, the particularisation of details of the mouse's life serves as an anchor for the poem's sentiment, providing it with an important realistic edge.

The axis of analogy, aligned as it is with the poet's stock in trade of metaphor, has proved to be particularly fertile in exploring the changing forms of our engagement with animal nature. This is true of children's own inventions, as well as more developed poems by adults. Consider the following children's *insult* poem for instance, from the oral tradition of verse making:

> Birds of a feather flock together,
> And so do pigs and swine;
> Rats and mice will have their choice,
> And so will I have mine. (Iona and Peter Opie, 1992:81. No title)

Since the speaker's intention here is to combine a put-down with an implied rejection of the addressee, the effect of the analogy might be assumed to work in the opposite direction to that of Burns' sentimental identification with the mouse. In fact, however, the blunt assertiveness of this playground rhyme is also founded on a sense of continuity between the animal realms of nature and the principles that determine children's choosing with whom they will associate. No doubt the analogy between animals and humans exercising their powers of discrimination operates in an entirely spontaneous way here.

But it is perhaps worth noting that the issue of animal choice – particularly in relation to sexual partners, of course – became a central concern for Charles Darwin in developing the theoretical underpinning for *On the Origin of Species* (1859).

Contrast is the flip side of analogy, registering difference as more decisive than the forms of association that connect apparently disparate realms. Its usefulness within more recent poetry involving animals is twofold. Perhaps most significantly, it can be used to honour the strange otherness of creatures that might otherwise be sucked up wholesale into the poetic maw of anthropomorphisation. The tendency towards different forms of anthropomorphising – rightly, I think – predominates in the realm of children's poetry especially. But the second function of the contrastive axis is that it can also be used to shape thought and judgments, often of rather unexpected kinds: to provoke readers, in other words. The first function is well-illustrated by Kenneth Grahame's much loved 'Duck's Ditty', where the duck speakers conclude:

> Every one for what he likes!
> *We* like to be
> Heads down, tails up,
> Dabbling free!
> High in the blue above
> Swifts whirl and call –
> We are down a-dabbling
> Up tails all! (1980:30)

The poem's comic celebration of the ducks' distinctive forms of behaviour serves as an effective foil for the poem's carefully attuned observational powers and linguistic vitality. But the contrastive axis also operates, in effect, as a kind of challenge to the reader; an assertion of the ducks' difference, marked by the italicised '*We*', that we are invited both to delight in and to respect. More provocatively, DH Lawrence forces what begins as an apparent celebration of the grace that is inherent in another animal's distinctive movements into a characteristically derisory judgment of the human condition as a whole. Lawrence's subject is a lizard – his admiration of the normally feared or scorned qualities of reptiles is significant in itself:

> A lizard ran out on a rock and looked up, listening
> no doubt to the sounding of the spheres.
> And what a dandy fellow! The right toss of a chin for you
> And swirl of a tail!

If men were as much men as lizards are lizards
They'd be worth looking at. (Lizard, 1982)

The issue at stake here is an ontological one that preoccupied Lawrence in most of his mature writing – how to become authentically human under conditions of modernity that estrange and cripple natural energies. It is interesting how precisely, though, with a touch of philosophical mockery in the 'sounding of the spheres' image, the movement and posture of the lizard needs to be captured in words for the derogatory contrast to become operative. The lizard's presence needs to be made *real*, in other words, for the inauthentic mode of being human in the modern world to be exposed and held up for scorn.

Lawrence's poem suggests that capturing animals in verse is a project directed as much towards enabling humans to reconnect with their *real* animal core as it is towards garnering a renewed sense of respect and responsibility for a threatened and diminishing wild nature. In this context, the axis of identification with animals takes on a particular significance, since it may become not only a way of crossing an emotional gap into the otherness of non-human creatures but also, in some sense, redemptive. It is an attempt to restore wholeness of being, in other words, to a human self-consciousness that has become radically alienated and distorted since the enlightenment. This is certainly one of the most fundamental ways that Ted Hughes has understood his own drive towards 'capturing' animals in words, as he puts it in *Poetry in the Making* (1969:15-31). The redemptive aspect also helps explain why so much of Hughes' creative output has been directed towards children. For children, in this latter sense, have potentialities as yet uncorrupted by the separation from the natural that is so central to modern experience. As Freud suggested, 'Children show no trace of the arrogance which urges civilised men to draw a hard and fast line between their own nature and that of other animals' (1950:126).

The way we understand the *realness* of animals in poetry is critical in this regard. For the animals' real presence must lead in at least two, apparently contradictory, directions. The contrastive dimension must register the actuality of the animals' otherness, must realise this faithfully and scrupulously. But the journey towards the animal – the line of empathy or identification, if you like – must also harness a power that leads towards the articulation of a larger truth than is contained in the literal differences from the human, as these are manifested by external form or behaviour.

To illustrate this I'd like to finish by considering one of Hughes' poems for younger children, 'Shrew' (1995:49). In many ways this might seem a characteristic Hughes lyric, adapted to the ear and sensibility of younger readers; its form – six iambic tetrameter couplets – seems, in itself, to proclaim the virtues of compression and miniaturisation. The poem begins with an evocation of the movement and qualities of the shrew, vividly grounded in the details of its biology. The little animal is 'a famine on four feet', needing to eat several times its body weight each day to survive. The poem then draws this into sharper and more dramatic focus by emphasising the unexpected violence that characterises the social life of a creature whose nature can brook no challenge or competition to its daily discipline of finding enough sustenance to sustain its tiny body. The gentler form of animal greeting that a reader familiar with Burns' quivering mouse might anticipate – 'nose to tender, waggling nose' – is negated by an uncompromising recognition of the shrew's ferociousness in the closing couplet:

> He draws a single furious breath
> And fights the other to the death. ('Shrew')

But it seems to me that, even here, the purpose of the violence is not simply to shake young readers' minds free of the complacent niceties of civilisation, so that their imaginations can countenance the true nature of wildness. The violence is also a spur to think beyond normal categories and judgments – the little shrew is a tiger. And in many ways this dimension of the poem is embodied in its form, which shifts out of rhyming couplets in the penultimate two pairs of lines, where a comparison with the niceties of polite human forms of greeting is drawn into focus, only to return to the full force of epigrammatic closure with the proper couplet at the end.

This potentiality is realised in more explicit ways in many of Hughes' poems for older children. In the collection *What is the Truth?* (1984), for instance, human beings are examined and judged largely on the basis of the truth that inheres in the way they imagine animals that are significant to them. The farmer, whose dream interrogation opens the sequence, is explicitly judged to be wide of the mark. His delight in partridges, whose physical characteristics are rendered as accurately as the culinary pleasure they afford is acknowledged honestly, is considered by God nowhere near the 'Truth' because it remains rooted in what Blake called 'single vision'. The farmer is only in touch with the literal, empirical world in front of him, in other words, with delight registered through the realm of the senses and his functional relationship with partridges as food items. The dream speakers in the collection who get closer to the truth sing their souls into more rhapsodic communion with the animals they most identify with, uncovering fresh insights and valuing the animals' other mode of being in unexpected ways that appear closer to revelation. The machinery for such revelation is generally the metaphor; but the soul's journey that enables such insight to take place shows more kinship with that of the shaman, who must often project him or herself into an animal form to undertake a task and return with wisdom. What is most characteristic about *What is the Truth?* though, is that it does not move towards any single, unitary goal. Whatever the revelation is, it appears to be transitory and provisional rather than ultimate. The animal figures move in and out of focus in a multiplicity of ways: the perspectives linking them to the frame-narrative weave different strands together, rather than seeking a distinct teleological goal.

Perhaps indeed this is the single most important aspect of the enhanced reality sought for animal presences within contemporary children's poetry. Eavan Boland has suggested that poetry can only really ever have one purpose – 'the formalisation of truth' (1995:xv). Although the discipline of *capturing* animal presences in accurate, lifelike ways is a spur, the *truth* inherent within this practice cannot be grasped in any single mode. The interaction of a multiplicity of modes of being may perhaps be taken as an ecological trait in itself. It is a way of respecting what Marianne Moore called 'the raw material of poetry in all its rawness' (*op. cit.*). Whatever that truth is, it is clear that for many of our finest contemporary poets, the presence of animals – real toads in our imaginary gardens – is crucial to our full apprehension of it.

Works Cited

Boland, E (1995) *Object Lessons: The Life of the Woman and the Poet in Our Time*. London and New York: Norton

Burns, R (1995) To a Mouse: on turning up her nest with the plough, November 1785. In *Complete Poems and Songs of Robert Burns*. Glasgow: Harper Collins

Darwin, C (1859) *On the Origin of Species by means of natural selection, or, The Preservation of favoured races in the struggle for life*. London: John Murray

Freud, S (1950) *Totem and taboo: Some points of agreement between the mental lives of savages and neurotics* (translated by J. Strachey). New York: Norton (First published 1913)

Grahame, K (1980) *The Wind in the Willows*. London: Book Club Associates (First published 1908)

Hughes, T (1969) *Poetry in the Making*. London: Faber and Faber

Hughes, T (1969) *What is the Truth?* London: Faber and Faber

Hughes, T (1995) *The Iron Wolf*. London: Faber and Faber

Lawrence, DH (1982) Lizard. In Seamus Heaney and Ted Hughes (eds) *The Rattle Bag*. London: Faber and Faber

Moore, M (1968) Poetry. In *The Complete Poems of Marianne Moore*. London: Faber and Faber. First published in Selected Poems (1935)

Opie, I and P (1992) *I Saw Esau: The Schoolchild's Pocketbook*. Cambridge, Massachusetts: Candlewick Press

Rossetti, C (1997) A Frog's Fate. In Paul Muldoon (ed) *The Faber Book of Beasts*. London: Faber and Faber

21

Poets in the Making:
Ted Hughes, Poetry, and Children

Peter Cook

ed Hughes' interest in writing for children began early in his career. He published three children's books in the space of two years in the early sixties, and acted as one of the judges for the annual *Daily Mirror* Children's Literary Competition (Hughes, 1994a). He also worked with Moira Doolan of the BBC Schools Broadcasting Department on *Listening and Writing,* a series of radio programmes designed to encourage schoolchildren to write poetry. The scripts for the series became *Poetry in the Making* (1967), a work involving all four protagonists in this section of the book: children, teachers, poets and readers. Given the current spate of anxiety about creativity, or the lack of it, in school education, it is salutary to look again at what he has to say, in this work and elsewhere.

Hughes addresses his brief *Introduction* to adults, and particularly to English teachers, referring to himself, in devising the talks, as 'a provisional teacher' (p13). The book is aimed at children 'aged between ten and fourteen' (p11), but Hughes does not see their youth as a limitation: on the contrary, 'I assume that the latent talent for self-expression in any child is immeasurable' (p12). But this sense of limitless aspiration is immediately tempered by a very down-to-earth recognition that 'no teacher could arrange for the psychological crises and the long disciplines that awaken genius in an otherwise ordinary mind':

> by showing to a pupil's imagination many opportunities and few restraints, and instilling into him confidence and a natural motive for writing, the odds are that

> something – maybe not much, but something – of our common genius will begin to put a word in. (p12)

The approach to children outlined here, together with the words 'imagination' and 'natural', and the idea that 'our common genius' will put its word in independently of the conscious mind of the writer, all point to the source of this notion of two levels of 'genius'. Coleridge's famous distinction between 'primary' and 'secondary' imagination in the *Biographia Literaria* of 1817 (p167) is a cornerstone of the Romantic poets' rethinking of nature, and of what is natural to human beings. It has long been recognised that Ted Hughes' ideas about poetry and the poet's role are, as Dennis Walder suggested in 1987, 'fundamentally akin' (p45) to those of Blake, Wordsworth and Coleridge. But the extent of these Romantic tenets in *Poetry in the Making*, and their centrality to the way the book works, have not perhaps been fully explored. Hughes doesn't mention Coleridge here, but treats the ideas of his great predecessor as though they are common property, part of our natural heritage. This is in essence Hughes' aim in *Poetry in the Making*: to persuade us that writing poetry is not only possible, but 'natural', even inevitable. He will achieve this by taking as his starting-point not poetry, or writing, or even words, but the universal urge in children to express themselves, teaching each child 'not 'How to write' but 'How to try to say what you really mean' – which is part of the search for self-knowledge and perhaps, in one form or another, grace' (p12).

An integral part of Hughes' method in *Poetry in the Making* is the inclusion and discussion of poems by a variety of writers, offering 'models' of the type of poetry children could attempt to write without becoming 'false to themselves ... I have stuck to poems where the language is basically plain, modern speech' (p12). Here again we are back with the Romantic poets, with Wordsworth's and Coleridge's revolutionary *Lyrical Ballads* of 1798, written, they announced, 'to ascertain how far the language of conversation in the middle and lower classes of society is adapted to the purposes of poetic pleasure', in order to achieve 'a natural delineation of human passions' (pv). As Richard Holmes notes, 'our modern ideas of how poets actually write' (1989:170) are conditioned by the Romantics' pioneering work.

Hughes never loses sight of these crucial glimpses into the 'natural motive' for writing poetry, and the kind of language best suited to its expression. He starts his first chapter by telling a story of his own childhood. He recalls catching mice at harvest-time, 'till I had thirty or forty crawling around in the lining of my coat' (p15), and stresses the violence of shooting trips with his elder brother, Ted acting as retriever: 'He could not shoot enough for me' (p16). But at fifteen, he says, his attitude to animals changed: 'I began to look at them, you see, from their own point of view. And about the same time I began to write poems' (pp16-17).

Like Hughes' many creation tales in prose and poetry, this opening story is essentially a parable. He was always aware of the influence such a story can have on children, as it 'settles into the mind's foundations as a symbolic map, a template for future psychological growth' (1992:149). But here, unusually for Hughes, the significance is made explicit: 'Maybe my concern has been to capture not animals particularly and not poems, but simply things which have a vivid life of their own, outside mine' (p15). In a direct, almost matter-of-fact way, Hughes has led us to the heart of his own view of poetry, which is an intense re-enactment of William Blake's *Eternity*:

> He who binds to himself a joy
> Does the winged life destroy;
> But he who kisses the joy as it flies
> Lives in eternity's sun rise. (1969:179)

That word 'grace' echoes in the mind again.

But what Hughes wants his young listeners or readers to take from the story is the disturbing and exciting notion that poetry is alive: 'This is hunting and the poem is a new species of creature, a new specimen of the life outside your own' (1967:17). Now he takes us into the practicalities. A poem, he says, is 'an assembly of living parts moved by a single spirit': each word must 'jump to life as you read ... So, as a poet, you have to make sure that all those parts over which you have control, the words and rhythms and images, are alive' (p17). How deftly Hughes gets the reader to begin to think of him or herself 'as a poet'! So we are now ready to get down to the business of 'words that live', that appeal to 'several of the senses at once', as if each word 'had eyes, ears and tongue, or ears and fingers and a body to move with ... It is this little goblin in a word which is its life and its poetry, and it is this goblin which the poet has to have under control' (p18). This image works superbly in its own right, but it also complements the power of the 'Capturing Animals' story, adding another feature to that 'symbolic map' evolving in the child's mind.

Ever practical, Hughes anticipates at this point his young reader's perhaps indignant riposte: 'How do you control all that [?]' (p18). His answer is the most important piece of advice in the whole book:

imagine what you are writing about. See it and live it ... Just look at it, touch it, smell it, listen to it, turn yourself into it. When you do this, the words look after themselves, like magic ... You will read back through what you have written and you will get a shock. You will have captured a spirit, a creature. (p18)

And from there we go straight to 'The Thought-Fox', the poem that embodies everything Hughes has been saying. We notice again how he unifies all his advice within that central parable 'Capturing Animals', gradually building up the features on the symbolic map. But it is also noticeable how closely Hughes' ideas about how poetry should be written again mirror those of the first generation of Romantic poets. When he urges his young readers to 'see' their subject, he wants them to visualise it imaginatively, not physically. Alexander Davis noted this crucial distinction in 1994:

the full capacity of the imagination can be revealed only when the subject frees himself from what Coleridge calls the 'despotism of the eye' ... Their poetry is in large part a record of the quest to free the imagination from what Words-worth, in *The Prelude*, terms the state 'In which the eye was master of the heart', and that which Blake, in *Jerusalem,* calls 'The Eye of Man, a little narrow orb, clos'd up & dark'. (1994:70)

Davis sees this distinction as key to our understanding of Ted Hughes, and goes on to offer a reading of Gaudete and other poems in the light of these ideas. And Keith Sagar has interpreted Hughes' poetry in the light of Blake's 'Fourfold Vision' of 'the wonders Divine/Of Human Imagination' in the poem *Jerusalem* (1983:285-312).

Hughes himself expounded his passionate interest in these ideas, and affirmed their centrality to his views on the education of children, in his 1976 essay 'Myth and Education', which develops the credo behind *Poetry in the Making* in significant ways. Writing here for adults, Hughes suggests that modern society concentrates exclusively upon the 'outer' world of objective reality at the expense of contact with the 'inner' world: the feelings, energies and urges of the human psyche. Yet these inner and outer worlds are 'intri-cately interdependent' (1994b:143); we need to take cognisance of both, and unify them, if we are to achieve wholeness. The imagination is the only power that can do this: it is for Hughes a faculty that all people, not just great artists, need in order to live their lives. It is 'the basis of nearly everything we do', yet 'education neglects this faculty completely' (1994b:142). People who have no imagination are 'dangerous' (p142), as are those who are imaginative but whose imaginings have no grounding in reality: 'Imagination which is both accurate and strong is so rare ... it ought to be education's first concern' (p143).

It is certainly Hughes' first concern in *Poetry in the Making*. With the most simple of words, he devises an exercise in imaginative contemplation, in using the mind's eye and getting the subconscious powers to take over the process of writing, so that the conscious mind will 'get a shock' (p18) when reading it back.

Today there is concern in political and educational circles about creativity in children's education. The National Advisory Committee on Creative and Cultural Education produced its report *All Our Futures* in 1999, and since then we have introduced our teachers to 'Big-C creativity and Little-C creativity' (Craft, 2001), 'empowerment pedagogy', 'possibility thinking', 'play creativity', and dozens of other concepts, not as suggestions, but as requirements. In this respect, the predicament of teachers and the children in their classes brings to mind that of Pip in Dickens' *Great Expectations*, who as a very small child is ushered into the terrifying presence of Miss Havisham, and commanded to 'Play!' (1985:88). There are four areas in which current debate could benefit from Hughes' ideas and I will finish by drawing these out.

The first is to do with integration and integrity. The documents that have formed the basis of recent debate and policy have usually been drafted by committees, with the aim of taking into account a wide range of views, and as a result the level of overall integration is at best superficial. And while the aim is laudable in itself, when it comes to children and creativity, it won't do. Here, a strategy needs to engage with the psyche of the learner at a deep level, and therefore needs to make sense on that level if it is to succeed. This is one of the strengths of *Poetry in the Making*: it is one poet's creativity manual, unified from start to finish by the shaping spirit of one of the most powerful minds of the twentieth century, intensely poetic and practical at the same time, and as such it makes sense on every level.

My second point is to do with language. There is a complete absence of jargon and catch-phrases in *Poetry in the Making*: Hughes has succeeded in writing a classic textbook on creativity without once using the word 'creativity', or indeed many other five-syllable words. This makes it accessible and usable to children and adults alike, in stark contrast to much of the language used in recent debate and policy.

This leads to the third point. *Poetry in the Making*, as we have seen, is underpinned by Hughes' most deeply-felt convictions about human creative processes. And those convictions draw on the accumulated experience and wisdom of English poets of the past, restated by Hughes for his own time and place. He sees those who speak, write and use the English language as a *tribe*, a word he was fond of using, and he identifies passionately with that tribe as a human being and as a writer. This gives *Poetry in the Making*, no less than his poems and fiction, its assurance and authority. Without this grounding we are in danger of repeating old mistakes, and cannot hope to learn even the most basic lessons of history and tradition.

Finally, I believe that we can learn a great deal from Hughes' approach to his audience. Throughout *Poetry in the Making* he assumes that his listeners and readers are intelligent and capable of following a sustained argument. Equally importantly, he is quietly confident that what he has to say is interesting and important to young people. He is refreshingly free of that anxiety which afflicts some contemporary commentators, that poetry and writing cannot possibly interest young people unless they are presented in a self-consciously 'fun' way, an approach which can easily sound superficial and patronising.

I believe that our current anxiety about children and creativity is misplaced. The overwhelming majority of children are innately creative, given the opportunity. But we need to be very sure that our attempts to engage them are based on what we, the tribe, really believe to be the most effective approaches. In the field of language, some recent strategies have tended to treat English as a dead foreign language. It shouldn't need saying that we ought to be encouraging native speakers to revel in their heritage, and urging children for whom English is an additional language to join the world's community of English speakers, readers and writers; it's one of the most precious, rewarding gifts that we can give to anyone. *Poetry in the Making* is a great example of how this can be done.

Works Cited

Blake, W (1969) Jerusalem 1804-20. In G Keynes (ed) *Blake: Complete Writings*. London: Oxford University Press

Coleridge, ST (1971) *Biographia Literaria*. (ed) Watson, G. London: Dent

Craft, A (2001) 'Little c creativity'. In Craft, A, Jeffrey, B and Liebling, M (eds) *Creativity in Education*. London: Continuum

Davis, A (1994) Romanticism, Existentialism, Patriarchy: Hughes and the Visionary Imagination. In K Sagar (ed) *The Challenge of Ted Hughes*. Basingstoke and London: Macmillan

Dickens, C (1985) *Great Expectations*. (ed) Calder, A. Harmondsworth: Penguin

Holmes, R (1989) *Coleridge: Early Visions*. London: Hodder and Stoughton

Hughes, T (1961) *Meet My Folks!* London: Faber

Hughes, T (1963) *How the Whale Became*. London: Faber

Hughes, T (1963) *The Earth-Owl and Other Moon-People*. London: Faber

Hughes, T (1967) *Poetry in the Making: An Anthology of Poems and Programmes from 'Listening and Writing'*. London, Faber

Hughes, T (1992) The Interpretation of Parables. Signal 69 p149

Hughes, T (1994a) Concealed Energies, 1975. In W Scammel (ed) *Winter Pollen: Occasional Prose/Ted Hughes*. London: Faber

Hughes, T (1994b) 'Myth and Education', 1976. In Scammel (*ibid*)

Sagar, K (1983) Fourfold Vision in Hughes. In K Sagar (ed) *The Achievement of Ted Hughes*. Manchester: Manchester University Press

Walder, D (1987) *Ted Hughes*. Milton Keynes: Open University Press

Wordsworth, W (1969) *The Prelude* 1805 (ed) E de Selincourt. London: Oxford University Press

Wordsworth, W and Coleridge, ST (1999) *Lyrical Ballads, with a Few Other Poems*, 1798. Harmondsworth: Penguin Poetry First Editions.

22

Articulating the Auditory Imagination: When Children Talk About Poetry They Hear

John Gordon

I remember an A-level encounter with Gerard Manley Hopkins' 'The Windhover' (1877). We read aloud and in chorus, ten or more of us around desks: I didn't understand. Or at least, not the words, what the poem meant – I couldn't *explain* it. But I do recall its singularity, that it was ineffable, intriguing, frustrating and fascinating: the fragments 'dapple-dawn-drawn Falcon' and 'this morning morning's minion' come back to me now, maybe inaccurately and only half-recalled. Over fifteen years later I recognise the alliteration, am aware of sprung rhythm, but I don't think these points alone are why I still hold the words echoing and alive in my mind. To a degree – maybe this is what the teacher intended – I got a *feel* for it.

The pleasures of poetry and the relationship of these to learning are not lost on other commentators. For Fleur Adcock, heard poetry had an immense impact:

> It was rhythm that seduced me into liking poetry in the beginning: clearly identifiable rhythms at first, in my early childhood, when I fell for nursery rhymes and Sunday school hymns and the Georgian poets my mother read to me at bedtime; and then, in my teens, the more subtle rhythms of poets I was taught at school or discovered for myself: Milton, Donne, Blake, Eliot. (It's sometimes hard to separate rhythm from tone, in its effects ...) (Herbert and Hollis, 2000:199)

It seems difficult for Adcock to explain quite how listening had an impact upon her. When others attempt to describe or define poetry more generally they encounter similar difficulty. An example by Keith Douglas is typical in its openness and reluctance to present a simple summary of poetry:

> anything expressed in words, which appeals to the emotions either in presenting an image or picture to move them; or by the music of the words affecting them through the senses; or in stating some truth whose eternal quality exacts the same reverence as eternity itself. (*ibid*:113)

Central to his definition is the importance of emotions moved in *response* to a text: a poem can only be described with recourse to its effect and affective power, though Douglas does additionally attempt to identify some of the means by which the effect is realised. We may infer the conventional tropes of poetry, figurative language and rhythm, from the first two definitions he essays. Of a different level of significance is Douglas' allusion to poetry's power to evoke 'reverence'. In such a definition, making great claims for the medium, poetry commands awe as a result of its expression of an eternal truth. The value of poetry according to these definitions thus resides in effects of hugely differing scope: the first two imply a test 'on the pulses' (Heaney, 2003), empirical and sensuous experience; the third is an existential jolt, effectively an epiphany. Taken as a triumvirate, the statements provided by Douglas offer up the possibility that in poetry both epistemological and ontological significance are likely to be combined. A poem is knowledge acting on the senses, on being, and vice versa, the senses engaged and collaborating in the construction of meaning. It is a symbiotic balance where subject matter and form not only match but combine.

Poetry has also been described within two broad traditions (Preminger and Brogan, 1993), apparently polar opposites, with any single poem existing somewhere on a continuum between the two. The first inclines towards 'the referential, propositional, and mimetic aspect of language' (p940), where it is assumed that words function predominantly as pure meaning: the associated poetic forms include descriptive and narrative verse, the epic and the lyric. This is poetry where words or their arrangement do not draw attention to themselves, rather they signify extrinsically. In the second tradition however, there is a leaning to words as 'pure sound form or visual form or both' (*ibid*). Words are employed with a self-conscious interest in the words themselves, their phonic or graphic character *per se*, as much as in – even in favour of – the phenomena to which they might refer, if they refer extrinsically at all. This tradition thus entails an investigation of language in itself as much as it does any extrinsic topic or theme.

Two issues presented by these traditions have significance for pupils' responses to voiced poetry in the classroom. For one, the variety of aural and visual poetic modes of the second tradition are said to be unmapped by critics, and it follows that they are neither conceptualised in the curriculum nor in schools, though these modes clearly exist. The second and related concern is that of the 'bivalent entity' of any poem, the 'schizophrenic' nature of poetry that arises from its history in ancient Greece and through the Middle Ages as a predominantly oral and aural medium, then as 'aural-visual mixed' with the advent of the printing press in the fifteenth century (see Ong, 1982: chapter 5). Neither poetry seen nor poetry heard takes precedence; the poem is instead an abstraction which 'may exist in both types of substantial realisation – phonic and graphic' (Fowler, 1966:7). Poetry in the curriculum, however, is not conceived as an abstraction prior to substantial realisation, rather the substantial realisation of poetry is assumed and taken as given: the dominance of printed resources to teach poetry in schools is testimony to the fact. As such, the substantial realisation of poetry in the graphic mode comes to be understood as essential – that is, of the essence. In becoming the convention, it dominates the conception of poetry in the curriculum and therefore often in English lessons which provide an arena for poetic encounters. Furthermore, poetry's realisation in this mode delimits the nature of poetic encounter allowed to pupils in the classroom, with the consequence that the knowledge and experience substantiated *only* in the phonic mode is not available to them.

To respond to this state of affairs has implications both for how pupils respond to poetry and indeed *who* is given opportunity to respond to poetry in any sense that might be regarded as meaningful or educationally worthwhile on their own, personalised terms. It becomes especially important when 'these modes [i.e. phonic and graphic] are apprehended in radically different ways' (Preminger and Brogan, 1993:941). If we do not understand ourselves how the phonic mode is apprehended, not only do we have a wholly inadequate conception of poetry, we also create a situation in which pupils capable of apprehending meaning in sound, are denied potential pleasure and deeper learning. At the same time, those who demonstrate facility with the graphic mode, who think they understand poetry, only actually get the half of it. We must make some effort to understand how poetry is apprehended as an aural medium to do it full justice, and to better serve pupils.

For Eliot, the auditory imagination means 'the feeling for syllable and rhythm, penetrating far below the conscious levels of thought and feeling, invigorating every word' (Eliot, 1933:118). To appreciate its workings in school settings means trying, somehow, to get at those areas *below* consciousness, to understand them a little better and to consider how pupils make meaning from the aurality of a poem rather than from what might be semantically transparent. An interest in the auditory imagination was apparent in *Poetry in the Secondary School* (HMI, 1987), and further informed by Eliot's discussion of the 'music of poetry'. On this Eliot is more specific – the music of poetry is not 'something which exists apart from the meaning' expressed in the semantics of words, but which exists instead 'at a point of intersection' relative to the words adjacent to it, to the context of the whole poem, and to the numerous meanings it has held itself in other contexts 'to its greater or less wealth of association' (Eliot, 1957:25-26). Such multifarious latent meanings recall what Ted Hughes personified as 'the goblin in the word' (Hughes, 1967:18).

Eliot additionally describes the way in which the play of sounds in a poem can come to have meaning:

> I believe that the properties in which music concerns the poet most nearly, are the sense of rhythm and the sense of structure ... [A] poem may tend to realise itself first as a particular rhythm before it reaches expression in words, and that this rhythm may bring to birth the idea and the image. (Eliot, 1957:32)

Eliot contends that rhythm can bring forth an idea, not that rhythms are selected to match an idea. Ideas capable of conventional verbalisation are not then the primary or sole locus of meaning in poetry. It may be, in Eliot's view, that the converse is true: that sound patterns are the dynamic energy and origin of meaning in a given text.

Basil Bunting also describes something akin to the auditory imagination, asserting that poetry aims to do something other than 'mean', it aims to make beauty, which arises from the relationships between lines and patterns of sound, 'perhaps harmonious, perhaps contrasting and clashing, which the hearer feels rather than understands, lines of sound drawn in the air which stir deep emotions which have not even a name in prose' (Herbert and Hollis, 2000:80). It follows from Bunting's remarks that the approach to poetry taken in the classroom must be qualitatively different from the approach we take to prose. We are trying to get at something else when we deal with poetry in school:

> Do not let the people who set examinations kid you that you are any nearer to understanding a poem when you have parsed and analysed every sentence, scanned every line, looked up the words in the Oxford Dictionary and the allusions in a library of reference books. That sort of knowledge will make it

harder for you to understand the poem because, when you listen to it, you will be distracted by a multitude of irrelevant scraps of knowledge. You will not hear the meaning, which is in the sound. (*ibid*:81-82)

Since the inception of the National Curriculum (DES, 1990) in the UK, however, poetry has been presented predominantly as a print-based medium, prescribed mainly in the programmes of study for Reading and Writing. There has been some reference to poetry in the earliest years within the programme of study for Speaking and Listening, acknowledging the pleasures to be had from listening to poetry, though overt reference to similar encounters are lost in curricular details applicable to the secondary phase catering for pupils aged between 11 and 16. The diminishing role of poetry as pupils move through schooling implies a model of progression, where listening to poetry is considered as either a means to the end of reading poetry in print, or a practice inferior in a hierarchy of maturity and sophistication to reading the page. The revised version of the curriculum alters the position of poetry only slightly. The amended Speaking and Listening details (QCA, 2007:69) parallel the prior programme of study (DfEE, 2000) in that poetry is not included in its range and content, though it does receive direct attention, as it has always done, in the details for Reading and Writing.

It appears, then, that the curriculum continues to present poetry as a medium associated with the page rather than with the voice. The wise advice of *A Language for Life* (DES, 1975) has not been absorbed, nor the spirit of *Poetry in the Secondary School* (HMI, 1987). Both encouraged listening to poetry, the former correlating teachers' own confidence and engagement with poetry as an aural medium with effective classroom practice. Sadly, more recent studies suggest a wariness of poetry on the part of English teachers, at least relative to other domains of the discipline (Ray, 1999; Benton, 1999 and 2000; Dymoke, 2002). *A Language for Life* also acknowledged the difficulties many pupils can have when encountering poetry, describing their 'vulnerability' when commenting on texts, and identifying a misguided approach:

> Poetry has great educative power, but in many schools it suffers from lack of commitment, misunderstanding, and the wrong kind of orientation; above all it lacks adequate resources. (para. 9.27)

The resources it recommended comprised 'non-print materials of all kinds', in a context where teachers may 'call freely on record, tape or cassette' (para. 9.25). It implied a causal link between limited opportunity for pupils to hear poems and their difficulties with poetry in general, 'the most exposing element' (para. 9.15) of their English education. The recent Ofsted survey

(2007) described a situation confirming little progress, perpetuating in its own structure and explanations the predominance of poetic encounters around print, albeit with some acknowledgement of good, though relatively unusual, practice that took better account of poetry's aurality. The report's section on pupils' attitudes to poetry indicates that the mode of sound can be a source of pleasure: 'pupils in primary schools, in particular, enthused about opportunities to read aloud and perform poems' and 'also enjoyed learning poems by heart and reciting them' (para. 6). These observations, however, sadly belie the general finding that 'poetry remains a weaker element of provision even where the overall effectiveness of English is strong' (para.3).

In what sort of classroom could the auditory imagination have opportunity to play? This illustration is drawn from research in which middle-school pupils listened to a poem several times over, from a CD and without access to a printed version, and then engaged in conversation about what they heard. In this particular example, the pupils involved are all girls, listening with a female student teacher. The poem they hear is Liz Lochhead's 'Men Talk' (1985). On the page, its opening lines look like this:

Women
Rabbit rabbit rabbit women
Tattle and titter
Women prattle
Women waffle and witter

Men talk. Men Talk.

Women into Girl Talk
About Women's Trouble
Trivia 'n' Small talk
They yap and they babble

Men talk. Men Talk.

It is important to convey something of what the girls heard. Lochhead pauses after the initial utterance of 'women', increasing pace across the rest of the stanza, also varying intonation excitedly, until she comes to the 'men talk' refrains. The pace is broken. These are intoned slowly and deliberately, with elongated vowel sounds. The pattern is repeated across the second stanza, with a marked break at the refrain: this time Lochhead's tone is also lowered as she utters 'men talk'.

The pupils were fascinated with *how* Lochhead read the poem, suggesting their sensitivity to meaning conveyed in sound an awareness of what lies beyond what Eliot termed 'conventional verbalisation'. They did not merely observe that Lochhead spoke with rapidity, but engaged in analytical reflection. First, the rapidity was a source of pleasure through humour – 'it was quite funny, it was fast'. This may be connected to their alertness to the fast-slow variation, speed being associated with women and lack of it with men: certainly they viewed women's rapid talk as positive, while men in their view – and to their detriment – were incapable of keeping up – 'it goes in one ear and out the other'. Furthermore, and no doubt as a consequence of their gendered, subjective standpoint, the speed of Lochhead's reading had for the children veracity and integrity: 'I think it's a serious poem, because it's like true, because like women talk really really fast, and men just talk ... slow'. Intriguingly, this pupil not only engaged with pace as a salient dimension of the poem's capacity to make meaning, she also replicated its manipulation of pace and intonation in her own patterns of speech, increasing speed around the repeated 'really', then lowering tone and pausing before 'slow'. As with other children, it seemed as if the character of the poem in sound suffused her own patterns of speech, below her 'conscious levels of thought' (Eliot) and engagement with the poem. Evident in this instance too is a strong suggestion that the auditory imagination could be gendered: it may be significant whether the heard voice is male or female, depending on your own gender, and it could have a marked impact on your interpretation. A group of boys, incidentally, heard the *same* poem but performed by a man, and offered a very different interpretation.

The phonic mode does seem to be apprehended distinctively from that of print – pupils do different things with it and so teachers need to be attuned to what it is pupils might do and what this can tell us about their learning. Pupils should have more opportunity to appreciate the bivalent nature of poetry. That pupils do not always seem to use a conventional, established literary-critical metalanguage to discuss the poetry they hear does not mean that they cannot make sensitive interpretations, nor that they do not attend to complex ways in which meaning is made within texts. They can construct between themselves subtle understandings of the auditory affordance of heard poems. They do indeed have 'an ear for language' (DES, 1988). If 'poetry embodies delight in expression' (HMI, 1987:1), so do pupils' reactions to it. In this regard, poems – and individual words within them – can indeed become 'sensuous events' (MacLeish, 1960:28), and pupils' responses constitute participation in those events.

Acknowledgements

'Men Talk' from *True Confessions and New Clichés* by Liz Lochhead is reproduced by permission of Polygon, an imprint of Birlinn Ltd.

Works Cited

Benton, P (1999) Unweaving the rainbow: poetry teaching in secondary school 1. *Oxford Review of Education* 25(4) p522-531

Benton, P (2000) The conveyor belt curriculum?: poetry teaching in secondary school 2. *Oxford Review of Education* 26(1) p81-93

DES (1975) *A Language for Life.* (Bullock Report). London: HMSO

DES (1988) *Report of the Committee of Inquiry into the Teaching of English Language.* (Kingman Report). London: HMSO

DES (1990) *English in the National Curriculum.* London: HMSO

Dymoke, S (2002) The dead hand of the exam: the impact of the NEAB anthology on poetry teaching at GCSE. *Changing English* 9(1) p85-93

Eliot, T.S. (1933) *'Matthew Arnold'. The Use of Poetry and the Use of Criticism; Studies in the Relation of Criticism to Poetry in England.* London: Faber

Eliot, T.S. (1957) *'The Music of Poetry'. On Poetry and Poets.* New York: Farrar, Straus and Giroux

Fowler, R (1966) Linguistic theory and the study of literature. In *Essays on Style and Language*, London: Routledge

Hayhoe, M and Parker, S (1988) *Words Large As Apples.* Cambridge: Cambridge University Press

Hayward, J (ed) (1965) *Selected Prose: T.S. Eliot.* Harmondsworth: Penguin

Heaney, S (2003) Staying power – a poetry reading. Lecture given at the Prince of Wales Summer School, Dunston Hall, Norfolk; 30 June 2003

Herbert, W, Hollis, M (eds) (2000) *Strong Words: Modern Poets on Modern Poetry.* Newcastle-upon-Tyne: Bloodaxe Books

HMI (1987) *Teaching Poetry in the Secondary School.* London: HMSO

Hughes, T (1967) *Poetry in the Making.* London: Faber

Lochhead, L (1985) *True Confessions and New Clichés.* Polygon: Edinburgh

MacLeish, A (1960) *Poetry and Experience.* Harmondsworth: Penguin

Ofsted (2007) *Poetry in Schools: A Survey of Practice.* London: HMI

Ong, W (1982) *Orality and Literacy.* London: Methuen

Preminger, A, Brogan, T (1993) *The New Princeton Encyclopaedia of Poetry and Poetics.* New York: MJF Books

QCA (2007) *The National Curriculum.* London: QCA

Ray, R (1999) The diversity of poetry: how trainee teachers' perceptions affect their attitudes to poetry teaching. *The Curriculum Journal* 10(3) p403-418

23

The Affordances of Orality for Young People's Experience of Poetry

Joy Alexander

In this chapter I hope by indirection to find direction out. My central theme is the potential of the spoken word for young people's experience of poetry; there are benefits in enriched understanding to be derived from exploiting the fact that a read poem asks to be simultaneously spoken and heard. Since most children encounter poetry in the classroom, I look back to the 1920s through to the 1940s, as this was the formative period for English as a subject in the school curriculum. I will first of all survey some of the key government documents and books of the time, showing how reading converged with poetry in a way that facilitated oral experience of poems. At this time Longfellow's 'Song of Hiawatha' was a stalwart in the classroom poetry canon, but it is also a poem in which orality itself is a governing concept, and I will briefly discuss it from this perspective. I then focus on a book, *The Child and his Pencil*, which dates from this period and was written by a classroom teacher, RL Russell, in which he describes how he used 'Hiawatha' to get his pupils to enjoy listening to poems and then writing their own. Finally I would like to suggest that this historical snapshot has relevance for young people's experience of poetry in today's very different world.

The Newbolt Report on *The Teaching of English in England* not only broke all sales records of Her Majesty's Stationery Office when it was published in 1921, but it exerted a significant influence on the development of English as a subject. The virtues of reading aloud are a theme to which it returns with some frequency. It is described as 'a method of interpreting literature' (para. 87) and is clearly distinguished from rote learning, mindless repetition and lifeless recitation. Hearing and speaking poetry is purposeful: 'The rendering of literature by the voice is not a mere matter of mechanical correctness, but is the final result of sympathetic entry into the spirit of the writer, and without it no education in letters can be complete' (para. 298). The best reader will be the one who best hears the atmosphere, tone and precise meaning of the phrase or sentence.

The principles that were advanced in the Newbolt Report were worked out and developed in a succession of government-issued handbooks for teachers. As a classroom activity, Reading Aloud is encouraged cogently and practically, but non-prescriptively. It is not advocated as an empty or trite practice, but it acquires a definition rich in meaning, which has particular relevance to poetry. Reading aloud is not the same as acting or elocution. The aim is to make the poem or passage intelligible to others. Proper reading is based on understanding. One Handbook (1924) suggests that when someone in the classroom is reading aloud, the rest of the class should have their books shut. Another claims that reading aloud is 'the most potent means the teacher possesses for awakening in the scholars an appreciation of literature' (1927, para. 17). The 1927 Handbook suggests that young people are more susceptible to understanding through hearing and listening than through language study and close analysis; however this is not a facile process but requires an element of training. In seeking to define Reading Aloud and explicate its function in the English curriculum, it comes to be realised in these documents that it was not an end in itself but was in fact the adjunct of any reading where content and style were evaluated. Reading Aloud more and more overlapped with listening, with what was envisaged being not merely listening *to* but listening *for*, a purposeful listening which was a pre-requisite for understanding. When Reading Aloud is a classroom activity, both reader and hearers are perceived to be participating in a meaningful and worthwhile task, which forms a profitable basis for the discerning appreciation of literature.

It was during this period, in 1933, that TS Eliot gave his celebrated definition of the auditory imagination and, in doing so, explicitly recalled its dominance in oral cultures:

> The feeling for syllable and rhythm, penetrating far below the conscious levels of thought and feeling, invigorating every word; sinking to the most primitive and forgotten, returning to an origin and bringing something back ... fusing the most ancient and civilised mentalities. (Eliot, 1981:108)

The theoretical framework for the exercise of the auditory imagination in the English curriculum, worked out in the 1920s and '30s, was practically exemplified in a number of books in the 1940s (see Works Cited). Contemporary practitioners were strong advocates of reading aloud, but also were interested in choral speaking, with its potential to be counter-productive as a teaching device if performance became an end in itself, and were less enthusiastic about learning by heart, because of its association with rote learning. In a collection of essays on English teaching, one writer insists on reading poetry aloud because 'many children cannot hear the poem when they see it in print' (de Sola Pinto, 1946:15) while another deplores the fact that printing 'made poetry the concern of the eye instead of the ear. Books took the place of bards' (p32). The practice commended in these books is exemplified in the section on 'Teaching Poetry' in a book compiled by a committee of English teachers on *The Teaching of English*, for the Incorporated Association of Assistant Masters in Secondary Schools:

> First we can encourage boys (*sic*) to listen carefully ... When boys have learned to listen, they can enjoy not only a one-effect poem like the ageless gallopers ('Lochinvar', 'Ghent to Aix') but the balance of sounds, the change in 'The Lotos-Eaters' from languor to resented motion. We train their ears by asking what they hear, what sounds remind them of, rather than by encouraging glib use of technical terms like 'onomatopoeic'. Always we must ask what help to the listener each sound-effect gives, or we reduce the poet to the level of the cinema organist showing what tricks he can do ... An alert boy will discover that we are not merely helping him to enjoy poetry – we are also making him alive to the possibilities of all language, not excluding his own efforts in a friendly letter or the efforts of the tub-thumper to work on his emotions. (IAAMSS, 1952:114-115)

Despite the gendered language, this is an extraordinarily astute passage – single-minded, developmental, highlighting the purpose in context of figures of speech instead of regarding them as labels, always relating sound to meaning, promoting the habit of attentiveness, and ultimately showing that careful listening to language is not only a basic part of English as a subject but essential to the full use of language as a human being.

One stock classroom poem at this time was Longfellow's 'Song of Hiawatha.' Extracts appeared in series of Readers and school anthologies and, though not specifically written for this audience, it has generally been regarded as a children's poem. In his introduction, Longfellow says that the poem is for those who:

> Love the ballads of a people,
> That like voices from afar off

Call to us to pause and listen,

Speak in tones so plain and child-like. (1965:203)

It is a poem that is intended to be voiced. Longfellow spent nine months writing 'The Song of Hiawatha' and, when it came to birth in 1855, it sold out its first printing of four thousand copies on the day of publication. It is an epic story of the Ojibway Indians and their great leader Hiawatha. Since theirs was an oral culture, history was transmitted orally: the poem celebrates and exemplifies the art of oral story-telling; the well-known section on the young Hiawatha's education describes a process of observation, naming and memory; the poem tells how Hiawatha introduced picture-writing to his people, a first move away from the prevailing orality. Longfellow's day-job was as Professor of French and Spanish at Harvard; the accuracy with which he incorporates Ojibway vocabulary into the poem reflects both his careful research and his interest in linguistic and literary cultures. The trochaic tetrameter he used was copied from Finland's epic, the *Kalevala*, which was compiled through a long process of oral transmission. I can vouch for how easy it is to listen to and follow the metrical narration, having listened to the four hours it takes to read the poem on my audio-book version. Naturally in a poem of this length the overall quality is patchy but the best passages are very good, such as the story of Minnehaha's death from famine while Hiawatha searches desperately for food in the icy wastes. This is not a poem to be accessed by silent reading. Unfortunately it has lost its status as a poem for the school anthology. Commonly the first thing now that is said about 'The Song of Hiawatha' is not about the poem itself but about the parodies made of it, and then the ridicule by association rubs off on the poem which is too readily dismissed. Another way of saying the same thing, which opens up a less dismissive perspective, would be to say that the poem is easily imitated and this is a feature that can have its attractions and purposes in the classroom.

This was so for RL Russell, as described in his book, *The Child and his Pencil*, which was first published in 1935, with three further impressions in each of the three following years. Russell taught for thirty-four years in Tullygrawley Public Elementary School, a small school in a rural setting outside Ballymena in Northern Ireland. The book is a delightful account based on his own experience of how the poetic and artistic development of children can best be nurtured. Its one hundred and sixty pages are enlivened by the inclusion of over thirty lino-cuts and wood-cuts and about one hundred poems, all of which were produced in Russell's classroom by his pupils. (Russell, 1992:93)

*Woodcut by Andy Cochrane,
age 12, of Cock Teal*

(Russell, 1992:93)

Russell was in the habit of reading classic novels and poems to his classes and it was while reading 'Hiawatha' that he apparently chanced on a technique which turned out to be very rewarding. He asked the pupils to supply a word to complete the line: 'As he bore the red deer –'. The suggestions he received were 'proudly' and 'dripping'; the word used in the original is 'homeward.' This was fun! As the reading continued, the pupils enthusiastically suggested half-lines, lines, alternative words or phrases in keeping with Longfellow's tale. The genius of this approach is twofold: the selected word or words have to fit the meaning and fit the rhythm. I think of myself as an English teacher pleading with the poem-writing class: 'It doesn't have to rhyme!' Russell's approach diverted the pupils completely from rhyme. In 'Hiawatha' it is the dominance of the rhythm – trochaic tetrameter – that holds the lines together, with an additional bonus in the feminine ending of each line which further deflects attention from rhyme or the lack of it. Russell went on to paraphrase in prose a passage from 'Hiawatha' and then worked together with the class on expressing the same meaning in the correct metre. Or, when reading, he would sometimes change some words so as deliberately to spoil the rhythm. Or he would invite the pupils to insert a couple of lines into a passage. He gave them practice in changing around the order of the words in a line. Now his pupils were ready to write their own poems: 'The first essentials of verse-writing once grasped by my pupils, I proceeded to the further difficulties of rhyme and stanza-form, and found them no longer difficulties' (1992:33).

The initial focus was the disciplined making of meaning. Only then did they progress to the 'difficulties' of rhyme: 'The making of rhymes was preceded ... by plentiful reading of rhymed poetry to attune the pupil's ear to the pleasures of rhyme as an added beauty' (*ibid*). What poem would be enjoyable to read while providing a focus for attending to rhyme? 'The Pied Piper of Hamelin.' What would be the simplest form of rhyme in which to begin to write? Rhyming couplets. The approach was always through the ear, with imitation actively encouraged. Through this process, Russell's young writers gradually increased their confidence and expertise in experimenting with rhyme schemes and rhythms. Rural life was their natural theme and the subject-matter of their poems is almost invariably the seasons, the weather, trees and flowers, farm animals and birds. Only a few years later, twenty or thirty miles down the road, the young Seamus Heaney gathered blackberries and watched frogs. The children's precise observation of the rural landscape and their avoidance of cliché are striking. With their trained ear and confidence in manipulating metre, it is impressive how accomplished these pupils became. Here is a 13 year old boy writing in the 'Hiawatha' rhythm:

> Soon the rose-bush will be laden
> With its velvet, bowing blossoms.
> Then the clumsy bee will wander
> O'er its fleshy, clustering petals,
> Then like someone deep in study,
> Staring at the same old grass-blade,
> With its head to groundward drooping,
> Thinking as with heart of sorrow. (Russell, 1992:31)

A 14 year old boy composed a perfectly worked Petrarchan sonnet. Experimentation with rhythm can be seen in this poem titled 'Winter' by an 11 year old, Sammie Forgrave:

> Now the sleety winds do blow
> Bringing snow.
> As it comes without a sound
> To the ground.
> Soon we'll see it cover over
> Every field where singing larks did hover
> Above the clover.
>
> See the hedges black and bare
> In the air,
> As they quiver to and fro
> Through the snow,
> As it comes so softly down
> To the bare and naked frosty ground,
> Falling all around. (*ibid*:145-46)

Despite some triteness, Sammie displays close observation, effective selection of words, metrical interest and a sense of control. Russell never suggests that writing poetry is simply a matter of learning a technique or of acquiring competence in a set of skills. He would have agreed with Wordsworth that true poetry arises out of the emotions, the individual personality, even the moral sense, and is crafted by the application of cognitive and aesthetic faculties. It is the habit of voicing and hearing poems that has empowered these young people to express themselves poetically so impressively.

To conclude, I want to indicate the relevance of this excursion back to the past for 21st century teachers. Walter J Ong has traced the history of the 'technologising of the word' (the sub-title of his classic study, *Orality and Literacy* (Ong, 1982). Primary oral cultures operate with the spoken word only. Ong draws attention to what he calls the 'secondary orality' (Ong, 1982:11) of literary cultures such as our own, which have been rendered significantly oral and aural once again, after the comparative silence of print, by the appearance of dominant new electronic communication media. 'Affordance' is a word coined in the 1970s and associated with the digital revolution, referring to the potential for action latent in the ICT environment. I have shown how orality was powerfully and fruitfully harnessed through reading aloud, in the oral tale of Hiawatha and in Russell's poetry-teaching methodology. We should be encouraged that the affordances of our secondarily oral age will open up new ways in the classroom to hear, voice, experience and make poetry. Of course, while core principles do not change, we cannot simply repeat outdated methodologies. In order to be relevant to the contemporary context, innovation and adaptation will be necessary – for example, by harnessing the possibilities of rap or of the Poetry Archive. At a time when there is somewhat less prescription in the school curriculum and more scope for creativity, the example from the past which I have discussed offers guidance and hope that children and teachers, together as readers, can continue also to come together fruitfully both with poems and as poets.

Acknowledgements

The woodcut from Russell's book is reproduced by kind permission of the Mid-Antrim Historical Group and the Cochrane family.

Works Cited

Alexander, J (1998) Does it have to have rhythm? *The Use of English* 49(2) p 97-106

Alexander, J (1999) RL Russell: teaching for pleasure – the celebration of an educator before his time. *Oideas* 46 p68-81

Blamires, H (1951) *English in Education*. London: Geoffrey Bles

Board of Education (1921) *The Teaching of English in England* (The Newbolt Report). London: HMSO

Board of Education (1924) *Some Suggestions for the Teaching of English in Secondary Schools*. London: HMSO

Board of Education (1927) *Handbook of Suggestions for the consideration of Teachers and others concerned in the work of Public Elementary Schools*. London: HMSO

Board of Education (1937) *Handbook of Suggestions for teachers*. London: HMSO

Board of Education (1938) *Report of the Consultative Committee on Secondary Education with special reference to grammar schools and technical high schools* (Spens Report). London: HMSO

De Sola Pinto, V (1946) *The Teaching of English in Schools*. London: Macmillan

Eliot, TS (1981) *The Use of Poetry and the Use of Fiction*. London: Faber and Faber

Hourd, ML (1949) *The Education of the Poetic Spirit: A study in children's expression in the English lesson*. London: Heinemann

IAAMSS, (1952) *The Teaching of English*. Cambridge: Cambridge University Press

Longfellow, HW (1965) *The Poetical Works of Longfellow*. London: Oxford University Press

Ong, WJ (1982) *Orality and Literacy: The Technologising of the Word*. London: Routledge

Russell, RL (1935) *The Child and his Pencil*. London: Allen and Unwin

Thompson, D, Reeves, J (eds) (1947) *The Quality of Education: Methods and Purposes in the Secondary Curriculum*. London: Frederick Muller

24

Exploring Poetry Teachers: Teachers Who Read and Readers Who Teach Poetry

Teresa Cremin

Drawing upon data from the United Kingdom Literacy Association (UKLA) project *Teachers as Readers: Building Communities of Readers: Phase II*, this chapter focuses on the synergies between teachers' and children's engagement in poetry at the primary phase. It highlights the importance of widening teachers' knowledge and pleasure in poetry and reveals the advantages that can accrue when teachers share a developing love of poetry with younger learners. This research confirms US studies which show that 'Reading Teachers; teachers who read and readers who teach' (Commeyras, Bisplinghoff and Olson, 2003:161) offer active and strategic support to child readers. It also reveals that teachers who read poetry for their own pleasure and who teach poetry – Poetry Teachers – can make a marked difference to children's knowledge, experience and delight in poetry and poetic language.

International evidence suggests that children in England read less independently and find less pleasure in reading than most of their peers in other countries (Twist *et al*, 2003; 2006). In relation to poetry, whilst small-scale interview data indicates that children enjoy poetry (Lambirth, 2007; Ofsted, 2007), in a large-scale survey of four to sixteen year olds in the UK, the majority chose not to respond to the question about poetry. Of those who did respond, most did not identify a favourite poet or book of poems, commenting that they did not have a favourite or did not read poetry (Maynard *et al*, 2007:60). This lack of enthusiasm may in part be a product of their teachers' knowledge and use of poetry. In a UKLA survey of 1200 primary phase professionals, *Teachers as Readers: Phase I* (2006-7), it was evident that many teachers had extremely weak subject knowledge in relation to poetry: 22 per cent did not name a single poet, 58 per cent named only two, one or no poets, and only 10 per cent named six (Cremin *et al*, 2008a,b). Very few women poets were mentioned and there was reliance upon the work of poets or named poems that the teachers knew from childhood. In relation to their own reading, whilst three-quarters of the sample had read a book in the last three months, less than 2 per cent had read any poetry over this period and only 1.5 per cent named poetry as their favourite childhood reading (Cremin *et al*, 2008b). Despite this paucity of knowledge, 85 per cent noted that they relied upon their own repertoire of children's texts to select literature for the classroom.

Ofsted (2007) also observe that teachers are arguably neither keen nor regular readers of poetry, suggesting that they may have a narrow definition of poetry and tend to lean upon a limited range of poets and poems in school, relying upon those presented in publishers' resources or known from their childhood. In the UKLA survey, the highest number of mentions was for Michael Rosen (452) with five others gaining over a hundred mentions, namely Allan Ahlberg (207), Roger McGough (197), Roald Dahl (165), Spike Milligan (159) and Benjamin Zephaniah (131). After these, only three poets were mentioned more than fifty times: Edward Lear (85), Ted Hughes (58) and AA Milne (57). In the Ofsted report, a not dissimilar *canon* of children's poetry was revealed in the list of the most well used *primary poems* – poems regularly studied in literacy lessons. This included popular works by Alfred Noyes, Spike Milligan, Lewis Carroll, Edward Lear, RL Stevenson, Walter de la Mare, Kit Wright, Roger McGough, Roald Dahl and Alan Ahlberg. Disproportionately utilised, it is possible that these poets and poems comprise the principal school diet for many primary children.

In relation to teaching poetry, in recent years an emphasis on the study of poems in response to prescribed literacy requirements (DfEE, 1998; DfES, 2006) has been in evidence. Research also suggests that examinations of poetic form and feature are prevalent and that leaning upon and imitating particular poems has significantly reduced opportunities for the young to compose free verse about subjects of their own choosing (Frater, 2000; Wilson, 2005; Grainger *et al*, 2005; Ofsted, 2007).

Arguably, the culture of accountability in schools has also constrained both teachers' and pupils' engagement in and response to poetry; in the UKLA survey fewer than 2 per cent of those teachers who had read aloud to their classes for pleasure in the preceding six months mentioned reading any poetry.

In the light of these concerns, Medway Local Authority, one of the five authorities and 43 teachers involved in the Phase II project (Cremin *et al*, 2009) chose to focus on poetry within the overall study's aims. In order to develop children's reading for pleasure, the study aimed to develop teachers'

- knowledge of children's literature
- confident use of literature in the classroom
- relationships with parents, carers, librarians and families
- as 'Reading Teachers': teachers who read and readers who teach.

The nine teachers involved in Medway – working with five to eleven year olds – were challenged and supported to read outside their comfort zone and to widen their working repertoires of adult and children's poetry. In local sessions, poetry was read extensively to the group who had access to a large lending library of poetry anthologies. The teachers also regularly shared their personal forays into the work of self-selected poets and were involved in responding to and re-presenting poetry through art, drama, dance and writing. Nationally, they were supported to develop a reading for pleasure pedagogy, encompassing significantly more reading aloud, time for free choice reading – in which poetry collections were available – read and response sessions, and a profile on the environment – poetry corners and displays. Medway also organised an end-of-year poetry festival for all the teachers and children involved.

Significantly, the co-participant teacher researchers were invited to document their learning journeys – both as readers of poetry and as teachers of poetry – and to explore the new opportunities which emerged as a result of either stance influencing the other. They also tracked the responses of three 'disaffected and reluctant' child readers to their changing pedagogic practice – Moss's (2000) category of 'can but don't' readers was employed for this purpose. In addition to meta-analysis of the teachers' portfolios, data about teachers' and children's attitudes and practices were gathered through initial and summative audits, semi-structured interviews and ongoing observations of classroom practice.

Across the period of the project, an increase was noted in the teachers' personal pleasure in and breadth of knowledge of poetry, alongside shifts in pedagogy and new relationships with children, particularly for those who adopted a Poetry Teacher's stance. It is to an examination of these themes which this chapter now turns, seeking to illuminate their impact upon the children's knowledge, experience and attitudes towards poetry.

At the outset of the project, the group's familiarity with children's poetry was very narrow; 'the teachers described themselves as 'clutching at straws' as they strove to name five poets' (Wells and Swain, 2008:7) and appeared to rely upon a very small range of poems to teach literacy. Only one teacher read poetry aloud each day. Further affirming the Phase I findings (Cremin *et al*, 2008a, b), several also noted that they had encountered little poetry during their teacher training. Only three recalled memories of poetry in school with pleasure; the rest recounted dull de-contextualised analytical experiences. The children in these teachers' classes also knew only a limited range; in response to a request to name an author, none of the 93 five to seven year old pupils named a poet and when asked to name some poets or poems, only listed nursery rhymes, suggesting that perhaps they were unaware of any other forms or actual poets. The 157 pupils aged eight to eleven collectively named only twelve poets.

Notwithstanding this challenging start, across the year the teachers significantly widened their repertoires, deepened their knowledge of particular poets and expressed considerable surprise and delight at the satisfaction this afforded. It is possible that for some the opportunity, support and expectation to read children's poetry created what Britton (1993) described as a potent legacy of past satisfactions. As one observed, 'I've got more depth and experience of poetry now. I've really enjoyed reading more myself, I love Valerie Bloom's work and Jackie Kay's too'. Their reading was influenced by self-set reading challenges, local sessions and suggestions by peers and children, many of whom, experiencing more poetry in school and increasingly aware of their teachers' newfound interest, began to share their favourites.

Whilst the nine teachers' enthusiasm for children's poetry grew, it should be acknowledged that most of the group did not develop the same depth of interest in adult poetry. However, three did describe shifting dispositions. One said: 'I don't find poems such hard work now ... Recently I had to search for a poem for a funeral service and I felt I approached the task more positively than before.' These readers found different ways in: one enjoyed listening to the Poetry Archive, one re-acquainted herself with childhood favourites and another started by reading verse written by 'poets from my homeland – that was when I got really hooked'.

Finding satisfaction in children's verse, the Medway teachers, like others in the project, began to seek ways to share their new knowledge and emerging passion in school. Prior to this, their poetry teaching had centred on literacy units which profiled comprehension, mining the poem's meaning and/or structure, noticing literary features and writing imitative verse. These practices were not displaced or abandoned, but were extensively enriched by almost all the teachers, who actively sought to foreground pleasure in poetry, particularly through increased oral practices. By the end of the project, five teachers were reading poetry aloud daily, the remaining four more than once a week. In addition there were more informal reading and response sessions, dedicated poetry displays and opportunities for children to read poetry, both privately and with friends, in the newly instituted free-choice recreational reading time. Prompted by their reflections upon reading poetry, teachers also wove more drama, dance, art and free choice writing into their units of work to help children inhabit, explore and perform poetry. As one typically observed:

> I often find myself re-reading poems several times – to hear the music again I guess or kind of unravel it. I think children need to do this too and bring them to life like we're doing together, to get poems off the page so to speak. Before I think my teaching of poetry was too studious if you know what I mean, there wasn't enough active investigation, it was like a quiz with me asking the questions! Now it's different, they own the poems more and choose which ones they want to work with.

There was evidence that the teachers' increased knowledge, pleasure and use of poetry widened the children's repertoires and experience of poetry, positively influencing their understanding and attitudes. As the year progressed children were observed poring over anthologies, reading aloud to one another, choosing to perform poetry in *golden time*, writing poetry from choice and swapping collections. In the post-project questionnaire, when asked to name their favourite author, 50 per cent of the five and six year olds named a poet and 85 per cent of the six and seven year olds named a poem that was not a nursery rhyme. The older children's knowledge of poetry expanded considerably and 41 poets were named, alongside a much wider range of poems, the majority of which had *not* been introduced by their teachers. This suggests that the children had engaged with poetry for themselves and were reading it personally for pleasure. The observational and interview data confirms this: many previously reluctant readers talked about poetry with enthusiasm and detail. In a final interview three such seven year olds, whose teacher had made her love of poetry very explicit, offered a list of their favourites which included poems, not all well-known, by John Agard, Richard Edwards, Eleanor Farjeon, Edward Lear, Wes Magee, Tony Mitton, Gareth Owen, Gervase Phinn, Christina Rossetti, Robert Louis Stevenson and others.

First lines were frequently provided alongside titles and, in an interview packed with evidence of their pleasure in language-play and poetry, this trio of once disaffected readers spontaneously recited extended extracts and three complete poems. Whilst their teacher had read several of those listed aloud, and two had recently been performed by the class, the children had found others for themselves. What is significant is that the list is almost entirely comprised of texts in common – texts they shared, could all quote from and had begun to know well; texts which in some cases had been unconsciously committed in their entirety to memory.

During the final interviews there were multiple occasions when, quite unprompted, a case-study child would offer a first line of a poem and one or both of their peers, recognising the textual reference would join in, voicing the poem or part of it in delighted unison. Afterwards, they would often talk about it in a fluid and motivated manner, referring perhaps to when they first heard it, other poems by the same poet, the friend who had read it to them, whether their teacher liked it or the way it was written. This informal child-initiated *inside text talk* was noted across the project, particularly in classes where the teachers regularly and explicitly shared their own reading preferences and interests and positioned themselves as Reading/Poetry Teachers – readers who teach and teachers who read poetry. The children's perception of their teachers as fellow readers shifted considerably over the year in several of the classes. In the autumn, none of the children were able to offer information about their teachers' reading habits or preferences, but as teachers shared their reading lives and growing interest in the sense, sounds and savour in children's poetry, reciprocal child-teacher recommendations developed and their teachers' motivated and informed stance was mirrored by the children. In these classes, animated talk about poetic texts, based on repertoires in common, demonstrated that the children knew each other and their teachers as readers and offered evidence of engaged communities of poetry readers.

This study highlights the crucial role in reading poetry for pleasure of, not just subject and pedagogical content knowledge, but also personal passion and teachers' positioning. Poetry was afforded a high profile in all the Medway classrooms, but in those where the teachers adopted the stance of Poetry

Teachers and explicitly shared their delight in children's poetry in diverse ways, greater continuity developed between teachers and children as keen readers of poetry. The stance of these teachers strongly influenced the children's knowledge about and pleasure in poetry, which, it has been argued for the project overall, contributed to the children's development as motivated, engaged and able readers (Cremin *et al*, 2009). It is clear not only that 'the will influences the skill' (OECD, 2002), but that teachers, positioned as fellow readers, have the confidence to teach both effectively and affectively and draw in reluctant readers. As Martin observes, 'the best teachers of literature are those for whom reading is important in their own lives, and who read more than the texts they teach' (2003:16). Children deserve such teachers to expand and enrich their knowledge and pleasure in poetry.

Acknowledgements

The author wishes to acknowledge the funders: the Esmée Fairbairn Foundation and UKLA; Ruth Wells, the Medway co-coordinator; the research team – Marilyn Mottram, Fiona Collins, Sacha Powell and Kimberley Safford; and the teachers and children involved.

Works Cited

Britton, J (1993) *Literature in its Place*. Portsmouth: Boynton /Cook/ Heinemann

Commeyras, M, Bisplinghoff, B and Olson, J (2003) *Teachers as Readers: Perspectives on the Importance of Reading in Teachers' Classrooms and Lives*. Newark: International Reading Association

Cremin, T, Bearne, E, Mottram, M, and Goodwin, P (2008a) Primary Teachers as Readers. *English in Education* 42 (1) p1-16

Cremin, T, Bearne, E, Mottram, M and Goodwin, P (2008b) Exploring Teachers' knowledge of children's literature. *Cambridge Journal of Education* 38 (4) p449-464

Cremin, T, Mottram, M, Collins, F, Powell, S and Safford, K (2009) Teachers as Readers: Building Communities of Readers. *Literacy* 43 (1) p11-19

DfEE (1998) *The National Literacy Strategy Framework for Teaching*. London: DfEE

DfES (2006) *Primary National Strategy: Primary Framework for Literacy and Mathematics*. Nottingham: DfES

Frater, G (2000) Observed in Practice: English in the NLS – Some Reflections, *Reading*, 34(3) p107-12

Grainger, T, Gouch, K and Lambirth, A (2005) *Creativity and Writing: Developing Voice and Verve in the Vlassroom*. London: Routledge

Lambirth, A (2007) Poetry under Control: Social reproduction strategies and children's literature. *English in Education* 41(3) p94-107

Maynard, S, Mackay, S, Smyth, F and Reynolds, K (2007) *Young People's Reading in 2005: the second study of young people's reading habits*. Loughborough, USU, Roehampton, NCRCL

Moss, G (2000) Raising boys' attainment in reading: some principles for intervention. *Reading* 34(3) p101-106

Organisation for Economic Cooperation and Development (2002) *Reading for Change: Performance and Engagement across Countries: Results from PISA 2002*. New York: OECD

Ofsted (2007) *Poetry in Schools: A Survey of Practice, 2006/7*. London: Ofsted

Wells, R, and Swain, C (2008) *Teachers as Readers: Pick a Poem*. Project Report for Medway Local Authority

Wilson, A (2005) The Best Forms in the Best Order? Current Poetry Writing Pedagogy at KS2. *English in Education*, 39(3) p19-31

Twist, L, Sainsbury, M, Woodthorpe, A and Whetton, C (2003) *Reading all over the World: The Progress in International Reading Literacy Study*. Slough: NFER

Twist, L, Schagen, I and Hodgson, C (2006) *Readers and Reading: the National Report for England*. PIRLS, Slough: NFER

AFTERWORDS

25

Playing with Words: Two Children's Encounters with Poetry from Birth

Virginia Lowe

I kept a record, in 6000 handwritten pages, of my two children's responses to literature from birth until adolescence during the years 1971-1994. (Rebecca is three years and three months older than her brother Ralph). I took notes verbatim rather than use a tape recorder, partly because of its intrusiveness and partly because I was aiming to record *all* book-references in play and conversation as well as in reading sessions. I later plundered this material for my doctoral thesis.

Poetry was an important part of my children's lives. Playing with words is what infants do; babbling is all about rhyme and alliteration and my children's first encounter with poetry predictably begins with rhyme. Rebecca and Ralph recognised favourite nursery rhymes – especially 'Baa baa black sheep' – at six months or earlier, demonstrating their enthusiasm with excited physical responses. By 1-1[1], Rebecca objected strenuously to nursery rhyme repetitions sung on a long car trip: three repetitions in a row were allowed, then she insisted on new ones! At 1-6 she would demand 'more-ee' *before* the end of each rhyme, and fill in some of the rhyming words herself. By two, both Rebecca and Ralph could sing about ten nursery rhymes with the words and tunes more or less correct. At 1-11, Rebecca often added made-up words when she couldn't remember the actual ones, and then remarked 'funny song'; at 2-7 she described one of her own versions as 'a nonsense poem'.

Quotations from nursery rhymes served various purposes. At first the children would chime in with the reader, then they used the words as a label for the rhyme to request it or name it on the page. At 1-1, Rebecca used 'awfawdow' [all fall down] as a request for a singing session. 'Nut tree. Mummy sing' was one of Rebecca's longest utterances at 1-10. Eventually these phrases became part of their lexicon and were used appropriately with the activity at hand, such as 'I'm sure I don't know' ('London Bridge') or singing 'Jack and Jill' when pretending to fall off a lap. At 2-8, asking for help in climbing a fence Ralph beseeched me with, 'But my heart will break if you don't!' Rebecca at 3-6 still occasionally used her baby term for 'pick me up', so plaintively: 'Uff uff me, or my heart will break' ('There was a lady loved a swine').

AA Milne's poems were quoted more often than any other author's. Rebecca at 2-3 would often ask: 'Where are we going this nice fine day?' ('Puppy and I'). She could recite several of Milne's short poems at 2-1 when given the opening words. It was noticeable that the poetry learned by heart by both children, right up to adolescence, was always rhyming and usually humorous – 'Jabberwocky' and verse by Ogden Nash and Doug McLeod, for instance. At 10 Rebecca told me that 'Poems are meant to be funny, or there's no point to them'. She enjoyed listening to serious poems, but she never chose to learn them.

Rebecca, learning to speak, enjoyed 'literary' words that were not in the family lexicon, the meaning less important than the sound. Delicious items of vocabulary from Beatrix Potter were 'soporific', 'fortnight' and 'tippet', while 'mackintosh' and 'tasty' came from Milne. She enjoyed saying 'marmalade is tasty if it's very thickly spread' at 2-1 and a missing boot was 'lost, stolen or strayed' at 2-4. A reference to 'The King's Breakfast' – 'Butter eh – And bounced out of bed', was frequently recited and acted out during meals at 3-4. Ralph, almost at his fourth birthday, remarked, 'When I was three I was hardly me' ('The End'). Rebecca at 3-5 used Eliot's *Old Possum's Book of Practical Cats* to tempt our new kitten to stay in a house of cardboard cartons she had built for him: 'If I put you in a house, then you want to have a flat/if I put you in a flat then you want to have a house.'

There were rhyming picturebook texts as well. Dr Seuss's *Green Eggs and Ham* was a favourite: 'Would you like it in a box?' (Rebecca), 'I no like it in a box' (Ralph) and so on at 5-8 and 2-5 respectively. After hearing *Fox in Sox* only a couple of times at 3-2, Rebecca remarked, 'Fox and box rhyme because they've both got an X'. Nursery rhymes often employ unusual grammatical constructions. Ralph noticed at 3-4 that the Robin Hood song ('An outlaw bold was he') 'is like Old King Cole, because they both say, 'was he.''

Filling in rhyming words was always popular. At 1-8 Rebecca shouted 'hop', 'stop', 'tail' and 'flew' in the right places in 'Once I saw a little bird'. The imperative of rhyme also inspired the youngest deliberate joke from either of them. It was Ralph who at 2-3 chimed in, as so often, to a book of rhyming verse: the verse goes 'Here's a shy kitten/soft and sweet/and here's a white lamb/with four little black ... ' 'WHEELS!' – he shouted.

Here is Rebecca perched in a tree at 4-9 composing her own poem on the pattern of Russell Hoban's *Birthday for Frances* – 'Happy Chompo to me, is how it ought to be':

> Living in a tree
> Is how I ought to be
> Can't you see
> Living in a tree
> How I ought to be
> It's just like I have to be
> Doing what I have to do
> Living in a tree is all that I can do ...

When Rebecca was turning two, I decided it was time for something different, so for her birthday I gave her *In a Spring Garden* – a book of haiku by famous Japanese poets with delightful illustrations by Ezra Jack Keats, this one by Ryôta:

> The moon in the water
> turned a somersault
> and floated away.

'Decca [Rebecca] somersault!' she cried, with much delighted laughter. She also wanted many repeats of Issa's:

> The puppy asleep
> biting
> the willow tree.

One morning when she was 2-4, I was reading Rebecca animal haiku from an adult collection. After hearing many of these she suddenly announced: 'A frog jumps up in a willow'. After that she made up many short 'haiku' of her own, which she insisted we write down. They showed that she had understood the essence of this poetic form. For example: 'Frog goes in the water and croaks in the grass' and 'A hibiscus hides in a tree and wiggles his head, head, head.'

Strong feelings are inspired by poetry. We were in our first intense passion for Jansson's *Moomintrolls* when Ralph, at 4-3, asked me whether the threatening Groke was always awake. Then he went off to find the book, chanting to re-assure himself:

> We don't know and we don't know
> 'cause we've never seen one
> and there's nothing real about them.

The children encountered death in nursery rhymes. 'Who killed Cock Robin?' fascinated Ralph. When the title of a picturebook version was read at 2-9, he replied: 'A bird – a sparrow with an arrow – see?' However some months later he was still musing on it as Rebecca was singing the rhyme: 'What made him killed, Becca?' Anxiety was not the only emotion; there was also consolation. Rebecca at 3-10 quoted gently to a disturbed baby Ralph: 'Come little cub, don't look so sad' from Aileen Fisher's *Do Bears Have Mothers Too?* A year later she comforted him with a lullaby of her own based on 'All the pretty little horses':

> When you wake up in the morning
> you'll find a lamb in your cot.
> You'll find a mouse.
> A sheep, a mouse and a horse in your cot.
> The horse is a toy one,
> but the lamb and the mouse are real.
> Baa baa, squeak squeak, neigh!
> Little baby, go back to sleep now
> I've sung to you.

At 11-9 she wrote a poem on the drought in seven stanzas. Here are the first and fifth:

> I am happy,
> I lie back in the dewy grass
> I watch the river as it gleams in the sun
> the cockatoos screeching high in the trees.
> The river and I: we are one.
>
> The old gum
> see him
> happy like me
> in every limb.

Although many scholars maintain that metaphor/simile is not available to young children, I recorded many examples of their use by my children. 'They're as green as emeralds' said Rebecca of peas at 2-7, and, at 4-11: 'I've got a pail of water – I'm going to Jack and Jill it on Ralph!' Ralph at 7-7, talking about the problems of changing schools, came up with this telling analogy: 'It's as if you're climbing up a big mountain and you know what the landscape is like when you go down, but there's been an avalanche, and it's all different.' A couple of years later he was still struggling with school in metaphorical language. Having tried all week to win the class medal and being bitterly disappointed, he observed: 'It's as if you'd killed a lion and then got killed by a mosquito!'

This is just a brief indication of the part that poetry played in the lives of two young children who were not exceptional except for the amount of contact with verse. The poetic language they heard and read gave richness to their expression, different ways of perceiving the world and aided their understanding of other people. Amazing what something as simple as playing with words can do!

Note
1 I have used 1-6 to indicate that the child was 18 months old, 5-2 to show 5 years 2 months old etc.

Virginia Lowe's fascinating book which documents her children's responses to childhood reading is entitled, *Stories, Pictures and Reality: Two Children Tell* (Routledge, 2007).

26

Writing Alongside at the Poetry and Childhood conference

Philip Gross

Alongside the listening to papers and poetry, amongst the discussing and connecting and campaigning, some twenty of us spent an hour in a small room, doing the thing itself – writing poetry. Apart from being a pleasure in itself, this was a declaration of conviction and intent. We were practising what we would wish all teachers – and all adults helping children come to poetry – to experience: writing as curious listening and confident play. Our method was as important as the work produced: collaboration – not the kind that subsumes the individual, but one that gives each back a piece of her or his individuality, enlivened and subtly changed. Alongsideness was part of the point.

The writing we did was not specifically for children ... though the exercise has worked for every age group I have tried it with. The vital ingredient sometimes lost in transmitting poetry is not a *technique* for producing poems from young people; it is that relationship between teacher and students, between facilitator and participants, that even the best lesson plan cannot impart if the teacher has not felt it for herself. Children imbibe poetry from people who bring to it some ease and passion, and who see themselves as writers alongside the children ... and vice versa: the children as writers alongside them. The more teachers who can gain that feeling, the better the life of poetry in our schools.

Behind this lies the observation that, whatever most publishers think, young people *can* be bold readers of rich and demanding poetry – and writers of it too – when they come to it as participants, rather than as passive consumers, fingers on the remote, always ready to be bored. It takes some nerve to trust that. One of the jobs of good writers in schools is to remind us, adult and child alike, that:

- *poets* are not different from *people*
- p*eople-in-print* face the same choices as learning writers
- *writers* are not different people from r*eaders/listeners*
- *adults* writing – and especially teachers – are as worried, often, as the children ...
- ... and can/should be as playful

Gratifying as it is to be an entertainer and a small celebrity, the best poets-in-schools leave pupils and teachers with a sense of alongsideness, too.

To be writers together, we can start anywhere. The dullest classroom will do:

> I looked round the room. It was empty.
> Null. Nothing. Nobody at home –
> like a wet afternoon
> or a song with no tune,
> like a shrivelled balloon
> or a week on the moon.
> And yet ... no, I wasn't alone.
>
> It may be the way things were standing,
> how the floor creaked its one wonky board,
> or the curious feeling
> that up on the ceiling
> I heard a small voice
> from the paint that was peeling
> say *Nothing likes being ignored.*
>
> It said *Everything wants to be something.*
> The bracket that once held a shelf –
> just one of it,
> blatantly one of a pair,
> now useless and loose
> but mysteriously there -
> whispered: *Thanks, I can speak for myself.*
> (Philip Gross, from 'The Living Room')

That is the opening of a poem that invites us to give voice to those unremarked things. Everybody was asked to scan the room until something caught their attention – a thing that, just possibly, *no one had ever noticed*. We kept looking. Once everyone had noticed three such things, we talked in pairs: each told their partner their three things; that person told theirs back. The listener's job was to watch – which of the three things made their partner's eyes sparkle when they spoke about it? – and listen – which thing made their voice come most alive? In other words, not to judge but to observe and to reflect back those things that inspired the speaker ... even if that person did not know it yet. 'Tell me more,' said the listener, and then: 'Write that one.' And then everybody wrote.

We had less than an hour – no time to share all of the writing at the end. Small groups of three or four listened to each other's drafts, so nothing was left un-heard. Then each group chose one, again not passing judgement on the piece itself, but answering the question: 'Which of these poems would I most like to read out loud?' What we were listening for was voice – the mysterious trans-mission by which the 'voice' of the thing became the voice the listeners heard behind the writer's voice – the voice of the poem – which in turn made one reader want to lend it their own voice, out loud.

Maybe that was what made for the ease of the occasion: the game was about those wandering voices, not about ourselves. Some of the people might have known each other, most not. But the speed at which everyone worked, the sharing of partly-formed ideas and the *trust* was impressive. The poems below were written using the resonances from their groups. Sometimes the words seem to grow not so much from the people as the space between:

'The Green Man (over the fire exit)'

Look at me I am special.
And, if you were in any doubt
I flicker faintly, nudging that nerve
in your eye to notice me.
I am in your vision I am in your brain
You'll never not notice me again!

I am more than mere green.
I am two-tone and have a detachable shadow.
I am athletic I strut and I stride
I will be noticed, I will not hide.

I am in your vision I am in your brain
You'll never not notice me again!
(Mick Gowar, Steve Lott and Anthony Wilson)

'Four green neon lights'

I lie on the edge of two borders between two worlds,
four green neon letters that can change a man's life
if he enters or leaves the room,
for I am the caretaker of those inside.

I illuminate the passage,
the gateway to freedom,
a breath of fresh air
from the stifling heat inside the room.

But, beware! Once you leave you cannot turn back,
for your thoughts will become your memories
and closing the doors behind you will read my name:
four green neon lights: EXIT.
(Lorraine Kerslake)

'KEEP LOCKED SHUT'

What?

You heard.
That's how I'm scarred
And you, you're barred.

What form of torture lurks beneath
My perfect print, my plane-worn face?
Vacancy? Oblivion?
Unending tears of pain? Or death?

(Such enigmatic words conceal
A darker truth than even these.
Some minion in the library
Secured the locks
Then lost the keys.)
(Debbie Pullinger)

'A tasty morsel'

I lie abandoned
Discarded in the dirt
A lone crisp, waiting.
At first she held me firm
But as the intensity between them grew
She became distracted
Drawn in by his eyes, his words, his breath.
Their hot hormones mingled
Her fingers parted and
I descended to the dirt
No longer needed.
A lone crisp, waiting.
(Teresa Cremin)

'Screen Being'

I am shadows and change.
I live on a screen ...
I dance as light shifts
and forms move near me.
I exist in time and space
and the moment is my painter.

Some shapes exist only once
by chance.
Basic patterns – like habits –
return again and again.

In darkness I sleep.
In light I wait.

I am patient, though, and know
my quiet form will
dance again.
(Eliza Hopkins)

'Water of Life / Uisge Beatha'

When the Celts first distilled whisky, they gave it the Gaelic name 'water of life' (uisge beatha).

I am the water in a glass
I have my eye
On the firmament of the ceiling
The Shadowland of the screen
The world of betwixt and between
In my element, I have class.

In one form or another
I've been on this cranky planet
Since its conception
I am the rainbow's sperm
Seas' resurrection

Opaque as fish scales
I disappear a treat
Like the woman announcing
A terrorist intervention
As the bomb explodes at her feet

I'm water. My impact's Titanic
Try cutting me out of your life
I dare you. I double dare you.
The result's Satanic.
(Sheena Blackhall)

'Fire Exit'

This is where I must exit
where I must follow the rules
notice the signs
leave my coat on the hanger
fill the high white spaces with heat.

This is where I must exit
after flickering in through a vent
reaching out to sweep my warm fingers
over the flip chart
char and curl its pages
send the twisted words
spiralling up towards the pregnant ceiling.

This is where I must exit
the ragged raging me
leaving my smoke trail
leaving crackling fragments
locked shut
always locked shut
behind a slim wooden door.

This is where I must exit safely
following a sprightly green man
flinging open brass-handled doors
smouldering, snaking, sparking
blazing myself
out into the corridor
towards all that air.
(Sue Dymoke)

List of Contributors

Joy Alexander was a secondary school English teacher for many years and is now a lecturer in the School of Education at Queen's University, Belfast, N. Ireland. Her publications are on aspects of English teaching, while children's literature is a source both of professional interest and of personal enjoyment.

Karen Coats is Professor of English at Illinois State University. She is the author of *Looking Glasses and Neverlands: Lacan, Desire, and Subjectivity in Children's Literature*, and co-editor of *The Gothic in Children's Literature: Haunting the Borders* and *The Handbook of Research on Children's and Young Adult Literature*.

Peter Cook is a Senior Lecturer in the Faculty of Education at Anglia Ruskin University. He has published work on children's literature of the nineteenth and twentieth centuries, on the iconography of childhood, and on Romantic poetry.

Teresa Cremin is a Professor of Education (Literacy) at the Open University. She is involved in research and consultancy on creative English teaching, teachers' identities as language artists and the voice, verse and imagination of young literacy learners. Her forthcoming book (co-written with Debra Myhill) is *Writing Voices: Thinking Critically about Writing*.

Telma Franco Diniz is an English-Portuguese translator specialising in literary translation. She is studying for an MA in Translation with an emphasis on poetry and is editorial assistant to the literary translation journal *Cadernos de Literatura em Tradução*, published at the University of São Paulo, Brazil.

John Gordon is a Lecturer in Education and Tutor for Secondary English Teacher Education at the School of Education and Lifelong Learning, University of East Anglia. He is co-editor of the book, *Preparing to Teach: Learning from Experience*, and has published papers on poetry in schools in *The Curriculum Journal, English and Education* and *Changing English*.

Philip Gross's *The Water Table* won the TS Eliot Prize 2009 and *I Spy Pinhole Eye* is shortlisted for the Wales Book of the Year 2010. A new children's collection, *Off Road to Everywhere*, is a Children's Poetry Bookshelf choice. He is Professor of Creative Writing at Glamorgan University.

Shaun Holland completed an MEd in Children's Literature at the University of Cambridge in 2005. He has taught English for over fifteen years in schools in Suffolk and Essex.

Olga Holownia holds a PhD from the University of Iceland and Warsaw University. Her research areas include contemporary poetry in English, Icelandic literature and culture, children's literature, nonsense and elves.

Peter Hunt is Professor Emeritus in Children's Literature at Cardiff University, and Visiting Professor at Newcastle University. He has published 23 books and over 130 articles on the subject; his latest books are editions of *Alice's Adventures in Wonderland* and *The Wind in the Willows* for OUP World's Classics.

Michael Joseph is the Rare Book Librarian at Rutgers University and the author of several books, including *The True History of Puss in Boots*, Teaching Guide to the *Norton Anthology of Children's Literature*, and a collection of poems, *Intercourse Without Mirrors*.

Louise Joy is a Lecturer in English at Homerton College, Cambridge. Her research interests include eighteenth- and early nineteenth-century literature as well as children's literature. Her current work explores the representation of narrative voices in writing for children.

Lorraine Kerslake teaches English Literature and Language at Alicante University, Spain. Her research interests and work include ELT, Translation, Children's Literature and Ecocriticism. She has translated and published articles on art and literary criticism as well as poetry; her life-long passion and interest has always been children's literature.

Virginia Lowe has lectured, been a librarian, and now runs the manuscript assessment agency, Create a Kid's Book. *Stories, Pictures and Reality* is based on a parent-observer diary of her son's and daughter's responses to books from birth to eight. She is an Adjunct Research Associate of Monash University.

Stephen Miles is a Senior Lecturer at Bath Spa University and has been involved in English teaching for most of his life. He is working on a study of fiction and play in the 'Golden Age'.

Lissa Paul is a Professor in the Faculty of Education at Brock University in Canada. She publishes internationally on children's literature, is a former editor of *The Lion* *and the Unicorn*, and is an Associate General Editor of *The Norton Anthology of Children's Literature* (Norton, 2005). Her new book, *The Children's Book Business: Lessons from the Long Eighteenth Century*, will be published in 2011.

Pat Pinsent is a Senior Research Fellow at Roehampton University. She specialises in Children's Literature, the subject-matter of most of her twelve books, and supervises MA Children's Literature and PhD students. She researches the diverse ways in which children's literature is currently developing, and the relationship between it and spirituality/religion. She also edits three journals.

Debbie Pullinger worked for many years in educational publishing, then as a freelance writer and editor. Returning to academia in 2008, she wrote her Master's thesis on the poetry of Charles Causley, and is now researching for an ESRC-funded PhD on children's poetry.

Michael Rosen, writer, performer and broadcaster, was born in 1946. He took his first degree at Oxford University, his MA at Reading University and his Ph.D. at the University of North London. He is now Visiting Professor of Children's Literature, Birkbeck, University of London, where he is co-director of the MA in Children's Literature.

David Rudd is Professor of Children's Literature at the University of Bolton, where he runs an MA in Children's Literature and Culture. He has written some 100 articles, several books, including the recent *Routledge Companion to Children's Literature* (2010), and edits the journal *Children's Literature in Education*.

Angela Sorby is Associate Professor of English at Marquette University in Milwaukee, Wisconsin, USA. Her books include *Bird Skin Coat: Poems* (2009); *Schoolroom Poets: Childhood, Performance, and the Place of American Poetry, 1865-1917* (2005); and *Distance Learning: Poems* (1998).

Morag Styles is a Reader in Children's Literature at Cambridge Faculty of Education. She is the author of many books and articles on children's poetry and has compiled 20 anthologies of poetry for young readers. She has co-edited two other books for Trentham: *Acts of Reading: Teachers, Texts and Childhood* (with Evelyn Arizpe) and *Art, Narrative and Childhood* (with Eve Bearne). This volume is the outcome of an international conference and exhibition at the British Library.

C.W. Sullivan III is Distinguished Professor of Arts and Sciences at East Carolina University and a Full Member of the Welsh Academy. His books and articles on medieval Welsh Celtic myth and legend, folklore, fantasy, and science fiction have appeared from various publishers and in a range of journals.

Laura Tosi is Associate Professor in English Literature at the University Ca' Foscari in Venice. Her research spans the areas of Elizabethan and Jacobean drama, women's studies, postmodernist fiction and children's literature. Her latest book, La *Fiaba Letteraria Inglese* (2007), is on the literary fairy tale in England.

Victor Watson has co-edited several critical works on children's literature, including *The Cambridge Guide to Children's Books in English*. He also wrote *Reading Series Fiction*, and, with Margaret Meek, *Coming of Age in Children's Literature*. In September 2009 he published his first novel for children, *Paradise Barn*. The second is to be published in 2011.

Jean Webb is a Professor of International Children's Literature at the University of Worcester. She has given papers and keynotes across the world. Her publications include: Thacker, Cogan and Webb, *Introducing Children's Literature: Romanticism to Postmodernism* (2002) and as editor, '*A Noble Unrest': Contemporary Essays on the Work of George MacDonald* (2007).

David Whitley teaches in the Education Faculty at Cambridge University. His research engages with poetry, film, children's literature and environmental education. He is particularly interested in the way the arts explore human identity in relation to the natural world; his book, *The Idea of Nature in Disney Animation*, was published in 2008.

Index

INDEX